THE FLOW OF POWER

This book was published with the help
of the Charles Phelps Taft Memorial Fund,
University of Cincinnati.

THE FLOW OF POWER ≋

ANCIENT WATER SYSTEMS AND LANDSCAPES

≋ VERNON L. SCARBOROUGH

For Jared
and the pleasure
of meeting you
All N best,
Vern

A School of American Research Resident Scholar Book

SAR Press ≋ Santa Fe, New Mexico

SCHOOL OF AMERICAN RESEARCH
Post Office Box 2188
Santa Fe, New Mexico 87504-2188

Director: James F. Brooks
Executive Editor: Catherine Cocks
Copy Editor: Kate Talbot
Design and Production: Cynthia Welch
Indexer: Catherine Fox
Printer: Maple-Vail Book Manufacturing Group

Library of Congress Cataloging-in-Publication Data
Scarborough, Vernon L., 1950-
   Flow of power : ancient water systems and landscapes / Vernon L.
Scarborough.
      p. cm.
   "A School of American Research resident scholar book."
   ISBN 1-930618-32-8 (pbk. : alk. paper)
1. Irrigation engineering, Prehistoric. 2. Irrigation engineering—History. 3. Water-supply,
Agricultural—History—Cross-cultural studies. 4. Water rights—History—Cross-cultural studies.
5. Water resources development–History—Cross-cultural studies. 6. Civilization, Ancient.
7. Civilization, Classical. I. Title.
GN799.E4 S33 2003
333.91'3'09–dc21
                                              2003011176

Cover illustrations: Top: Oasis, El Fasher, Darfur, Sudan © Vernon L. Scarborough;
Bottom (l-r): Rice terraces near Sebatu, Bali, Indonesia © Vernon L. Scarborough; Shalimar Gardens,
Lahore, Pakistan © Vernon L. Scarborough; Structure 5C, Cerros, Belize © Vernon L. Scarborough.

Dedication ≋

To Pat Mora and Barry Isaac
for their patience, intelligence, and support

Contents ≋≋≋

List of Illustrations

Color Plates (following page 78)

Acknowledgments

This book draws from the wealth of the many individuals who have listened to me, advised me, or established the corpus of literature on which it is built. Of fundamental importance was my year as a Weatherhead Fellow at the School of American Research (SAR), 1995–96, followed by a summer residency there. SAR's past president, Doug Schwartz, and his hardworking, thoughtful staff made the fellowship an unforgettable experience. Doug has set a standard in anthropological excellence—intellectually and in style and grace—most conducive to broadly creative thought.

My time in New Mexico cultivated not only an intellectual engagement with water studies but also an emotional one. One morning, over *huevos rancheros* at the Mesa Vista Café in Ojo Caliente, several miles north of Santa Fe, my best friend, my wife, Pat Mora, and I listened to a heated debate that brought home the importance of water management. In the adjoining booth could be heard vociferous concerns about the apportionment of a nearby canalized water source: Should allotment be based on acreage cultivated or on timed water release irrespective of plot size? The conversation was in Spanish, but it could have been in Arabic or Chinese. Water issues are fundamentally similar everywhere.

I shared the SAR with five other resident scholars, to whom I am grateful for feedback. Gil Stein was the only other archaeologist in the mix. At the far end of the grounds, we occupied marvelous neighboring offices—complete with kiva fireplaces and a shared coffee room. Gil and I tried to keep our enthusiasm for the Southwest in check, investing long solitary hours in our books but enjoying the landscape and sunsets from our respective windows. André Gingrich is a social anthropologist, recently appointed director of the Institute for Social Anthropology of Austria in Vienna. André's knowledge, wit, and cultivated manner would brighten any exchange. Marisol de la Cadena, a social anthropologist now at the University of North Carolina, provided a focused, intellectual intensity and depth that helped me think more clearly about my topic. Jill Furst and I were closest by way of our shared Mesoamerican experiences, although Jill was most interested in Aztec religion, a topic she helped me better understand. Chris Steiner inspired me with his flashes of brilliance in examining an aspect of anthropology—transnationalism—on which I had seldom reflected.

SAR's entire staff was marvelous. I can single out only a few here. Cecil Stein, the immediate coordinator of the scholars and the fellowship program, made the experience logistically smooth. Without her watchful eye, a lot would have gone undone. Jane Gillentine was extremely helpful as the principal librarian. During my tenure as a resident scholar and again during my sabbatical year in Santa Fe, Jane obtained books and articles truly difficult to find. Duane Anderson, former SAR vice president and now director of the Museum of Indian Arts and Culture, also in Santa Fe, was supportive of my work on several occasions and kindly included me in his Cultural Heritage advanced seminar. Richard Leventhal, recently selected SAR president, has enthusiastically championed the publication of this volume.

Joan O'Donnell, then editor in chief of the SAR Press, encouraged me to consider the SAR Press early in my residency. Her interest and competence in anthropological inquiry further drew me in that direction. Her staff members were bright, cheerful, and helpful. James Brooks, Joan's successor, provided the necessary support to reach publication closure. Catherine Cocks, editor at SAR Press, was especially helpful and, with copy editor Kate Talbot, improved the accessibility of the text.

I composed portions of this book during my sabbatical leave from the University of Cincinnati, 1996–1997. With a Competitive Faculty Sabbatical Leave grant from the Taft Memorial Fund, I was able to devote an entire academic year to water management issues, and to the writing of this book. The Taft Fund also provided me a term of released time to work on the book at its inception in the fall of 1993. This book was subvented, in part, by a grant from the Taft Publication Committee.

I collected much of the field material for this volume firsthand in the Maya Lowlands (principally Belize and Guatemala), the U.S. Southwest, Pakistan, Sudan, and, most recently, Greece and Bali. In each case, support was provided by several funding sources: the National Science Foundation (Belize), National Geographic Society (Guatemala), Wenner-Gren Foundation (Bali), and Fulbright Research Support (Pakistan), as well as Southern Methodist University (Sudan, U.S. Southwest, and Belize), University of Cincinnati and its Charles P. Taft Fund (Greece and Belize), and the U.S. Corps of Engineers of Fort Bliss, Texas (U.S. Southwest). In addition, many generous colleagues have made opportunities available to me over the years by inviting me to participate in their respective field projects. They include David Freidel, Anthony Marks, Anne Woosely, Richard E.W. Adams, Gisela Walberg, Fred Valdez, and Steve Lansing. I also have benefited greatly from sometimes lengthy exchanges with Wendy Ashmore, Garth Bawden, Tim Beach, Peter Bellwood, Glenn Conroy, Dora Crouch, Carole Crumley, Pat Culbert, Bill Doolittle, Nick Dunning, Clark Erickson, Barbara and Bill Fash, Suzy Fish, Willie Folan, Dick Ford, Joe Foster, Joel Gunn, Jim Hagen, Tom Hakansson, Rhoda Halperin, Norman Hammond, Peter Harrison, Andy Hofling, Bob Hunt, Barry Isaac, Grant Jones, John Jones, Frank Korom, Eleanor King, Laura Kosakowsky, Laura Levi, Brandon Lewis, Lisa Lucero, Sheryl Luzzadder-Beach, Andrew Manning, Joyce Marcus, Ray Matheny, Bill Mitchell, Kathy Morrison, Jim Neely, David Pendergast, Sylvia Rodriguez, Bill Sanders, Robert Santley, John Schoenfelder, Leslie Shaw, Sam Sherrill, Alf Siemens, Mike Smyth, Barbara Stark, Wilson Tabor, Gair Tourtellot, Jim Uber, Kent Vickery, Glenn Vivian, Chip Wills, Henry Wright, and Norm Yoffee—among others. I extend my special thanks to Bill Sanders, Bob Hunt, and Jane Kepp, each, for carefully examining my initial manuscript submission and offering very useful suggestions.

My closest intellectual colleague remains Barry Isaac at the University of Cincinnati, who has read almost everything I have written in the past decade and has offered incisive critiques—saving me significant professional embarrassment, I am sure. Those scholars who have been published under his editorial direction know just how generous he is with his time, knowledge, and literary skills. Barry performed several thorough editorial passes through this volume, including substantial copyediting. A second close colleague who has strongly influenced the direction of this book is Rhoda Halperin, also at the University of Cincinnati. Her efforts at making Karl Polanyi's contributions more accessible are reflected in my own work.

I also thank the many students who have helped refine my water work over the years: Jeff Baker, Matt Becher, Bob Connolly, Pat Farrel, Danica Fernand, Laura Ferries, Kirk French, Gary Gallopin, Jennifer Gerwe, Ned Graham, Jon Hageman, Brett Harper, Gary Harris, Rick Hedrick, Jason Herrmann, Beth Hoag, Brett Houk, Paul Hughbanks, Rick Hutchinson, Julie Kunen, Jon Lohse, Steve McDougal, Nicole Osswald, Claudia Paxton-O'Neal, Steve Ross, Kerry Sagabiel, Justine Shaw, Thea Smith, Sarah Stoutamire, Lauren Sullivan, Chris TenWolde, Skye Wagner, Holly Winwood, and others. Nicole Osswald has been especially helpful in preparing the manuscript for publication.

More than anyone, however, my wife, Pat Mora, has made the greatest contribution to my successes. All aspects of this volume have benefited from her critical reading and literary skills. In addition, she has maintained a positive view of the project, encouraging me from the outset. Her emotional and intellectual support have made this work possible.

ONE ≋

Water, the Fundamental Resource

*This is not a technological issue. The technology is easily available. It is a political
and organizational issue. Water is a social good.*

—Peter Gleick, in Marq de Villiers (2000:17)

This book represents the first systematic, worldwide study of water management in
antiquity. It surpasses previous surveys (Downing and Gibson, eds. 1974; Stewart, ed.
1955; Scarborough and Isaac, eds. 1993) by providing greater breadth. It also proposes fresh concepts and models for understanding water management from ancient
times to the present day. These ideas are exemplified in six case studies—three in the
Eastern Hemisphere and three in the Western Hemisphere—of early states or statelike developments. Although my bias as an archaeologist is clearly evident, I have also
drawn liberally upon ethnographic (anthropological) studies of living peoples to
enrich my knowledge of water management in general and to illuminate the prehistoric and protohistoric materials.

As was true in the past, water is the most precious natural resource we can manipulate and control. For organic matter, humans included, the presence of water means
life itself. Humans require a minimum of 2 to 3 liters of water a day in a settled environment under normal living conditions (White et al. 1972:252). Obviously, this
amount varies with work activity level, body type, and environmental conditions. In
the dry sands of the Negev Desert, the settled Nabataeans of the first century AD
made some of the earliest successful adaptations to severe aridity (Eadie and Oleson
1986; Oleson 1988). There, a present-day nomadic family (six people, two camels,
one donkey, two dogs, and ten sheep) survives on 18 m^3 of water per year (Evenari et
al. 1971:150). Compare this with the consumption habits of the average U.S. citizen,
who uses more than 225 liters (0.225 m^3) of water daily, or more than 82 m^3 per year
(White et al. 1972:table D).

Because water access and use resemble food, sex, and shelter—basic needs always
satisfied within culturally prescribed rules—an anthropological approach to this subject is important. These cultural rules, broadly defined, direct the flow of this book.

By illuminating the social origins and maintenance activities associated with the development of complex water systems, we see how humans have engaged fundamental aspects of their economy, political organization, and power relationships. In fact, throughout time a deeply enduring set of factors have affected water allocation and use.

The Importance of Studying Water Management

Water management is—or should be—a pressing contemporary concern as both natural and artificial water resources become severely stressed. For instance, the recent damming of the Euphrates' upstream margins will strengthen an expanding Turkish economy, but the resulting downstream water deficit to Syria and Iraq will surely inflame regional hostility. Interestingly, this very region gave birth to one of history's earliest recorded treaties (second millennium BC), an agreement between the city-states of Umma and Lagash that settled water claims along this same Euphrates drainage.

Developed economies, most dramatically typified in the western United States, have altered their most rugged terrain to drain vast regions in directing and concentrating water to other, more arid zones much smaller than the watersheds of origin. The technology and physical effort required for these massive, earthmoving enterprises have cost billions of dollars. Rivers such as the Colorado have been so heavily dammed and diverted that scarcely a trickle of their once raging waters now reaches the sea. Throughout the United States, thousands of miles of concrete canal length complement monumental dam construction. The environmental cost has been heavy. The most recent catastrophe caused by decades of damming and flood control comes not from the semiarid western reaches of the Colorado or Columbia, however, but from the largest river in North America. The engineering history of containing the Mississippi's margins has enabled the building of homes and businesses on the ancient waterway's floodplain. The cost of this reclaimed land will always be high because at unpredictable intervals the generationally recurrent floods will push beyond and rise above the most fortified retaining walls.

Only now, and only in a few affluent Western democracies, the conventional wisdom permitting the highly centralized state to control water systems is giving way. For example, the recent flushing of a short segment of the Colorado River by removing one of its smaller dams is an initial attempt to restore that river's environmental health. This effort acknowledges the severe threat to these great natural watersheds, a perception not yet accepted by much of the developing world.

China's highly publicized Three Gorges Dam, soon to straddle the Yangtze, typifies the current, global water management crisis. Despite the West's widely circulated cautionary tales, the Chinese government insists on constructing this dam of dams, the world's largest hydraulic monument, across one of the great, seasonally inundating rivers of Asia. This technology will contain the "River of Sorrows," aptly named because of its annually destructive swollen force. Most Western civil and hydraulic engineers would argue strongly against the dam's construction. Of major concern is its location in an area of seismic faulting. Also, the dam will eventually retain tremendous amounts of agriculturally rich sediment, preventing distribution to needy farming communities along the Yangtze's lower reaches. Most frightening, however, is the possible structural weakness from the weight of accumulating sediment against the dam's interior surface, in association with even a mild seismic tremor. Like much of the developing world, though, China regards the West as suspect at best, believing that we do not want to share our wealth and most certainly not our technological advancement. To China, our objection is simply a predictable ideological reaction to its recently acquired technological prowess. China's stance is not necessarily unwarranted, but it places yet another area of the planet in peril.

Many developing-world governments view massive hydraulic installations not only as a significant way to increase food production but also as monumental political symbols challenging the legacy of dependency. Unfortunately, major environmental planning errors may occur in this nationalistic scramble to establish political and economic sovereignty over territorial resources. All too frequently, these errors translate into economic and political turmoil.

A case in point is the Aswan Dam, Egypt's material and symbolic statement against the legacies of British colonialism. The High Dam did help tame the Nile and did generate much-needed electricity. However, it also trapped the rich Ethiopian sediment load that alluviated a ribbon of Egyptian desert for millennia, making possible the food production that supported the world's second-oldest state. Not only has this negatively affected cropping cycles, but also the Nile Delta is eroding because of Mediterranean current action against it—a force formerly neutralized by the prograding deltaic sediments deposited from the river's heavy silt load. Furthermore, the impossibility of effectively dredging the dam means that it will eventually hold much less water as an abundance of fertile but unrealized planting soils displaces its volume.

The Aral Sea is another case. In the last generation before the total meltdown of the Soviet economy, water from this freshwater sea was pumped and diverted for commercial cotton production many kilometers away. A substantial region now depends on this crop and the water it requires. Unfortunately, the sea has a very slow recharge rate, so sea level has dropped dramatically. Salinization is an increasing concern for both the faraway cotton fields and the expanding shoreline. The fishing industry has failed, and its fleets now rest on dry land.

Fortunately, conflict and disruption constitute just one aspect of water system organization. More frequently, water management and the allocation systems developed from the interplay between the physical and cultural environments accentuate cooperative organization. These result in the equitable sharing of water through a consensus often sanctioned by formality and law. As in religious systems, the more flexible and encompassing the rules of access and usage are, the more lasting and resilient the water management system. Stated differently, the systems with the best chance for uninterrupted longevity have slowly evolved on the highly variable landscapes from which people make a living. Even under appreciable stress, water management systems tend to persevere because of their adaptability. This aspect of water management receives less attention because it is less spectacular than the origin or collapse of a system. Nevertheless, societal maintenance and sustainability deserve greater scrutiny in our rapidly changing world.

The Study of Ancient Water Management

This book treats water management in the early state as an economic and political force—an aspect of the production mode, the social relations organizing culture—to identify basic variables for assessing the adaptational effectiveness of cultural organization. Doing so entailed examining the everyday tasks and routines that influence decision making in the management of water resources. For this, I drew upon the ethnographic record to define the range and organization of mundane activities sustaining adequate water access and use in varied environments and sociocultural milieu. I then applied this knowledge to the material remains of the earliest civilizations (states) as an aid to understanding their water systems, economic scale, and political organization. I have attempted to show how water management affected ancient social structures and organization and how feedback from a highly engineered physical environment (transformed by the culture) influenced subsequent decision making as economic and political complexity increased.

Considerable variation exists among early states and the environments in which they evolved. Accordingly, I have very carefully selected six case studies that demonstrate the social and environmental conditions leading to sociocultural complexity (see figure 1.1). Cultural anthropologists may ask why I did not simply assess six contemporary groups from dissimilar environments and look for the kinds of underlying organizational themes I identify from the less nuanced archaeological record. Without putting too fine an edge on it, my rationale is that an examination of the earliest states exposes environments less abused and influenced by previous occupants, who were simple hunter-gatherers in some cases. Because archaeologists invest considerable energy in getting to know the natural environments of the ancient groups we study, we can address degrees of sustainability on the landscape through time. Thus, when archaeology—the study of the material remains, the unevenly preserved remnants, of an ancient past—is informed by the ethnographic record, its longitudinal time depth provides a better view of landscape and cultural sustainability than any other data set.

By examining six very different early state developments in widely varied environments, I present a broad range of cultural manifestations and the interplay of landscape and culture. Beneath their variability, we can discern certain fundamental, underlying economic relationships that react in broadly predictable ways when stimulated by similar environmental and cultural conditions. Divergent cultural paths, on the other hand, are attributable to the complexity of the variables confronted and the multiplicity of histories woven into past cultural patterns. This book attempts to elucidate the character of the economic variables present in complex societies. Although

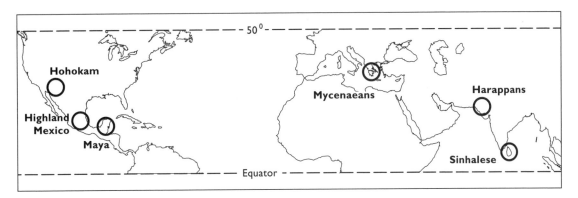

Figure 1.1 Location of the six regional case studies, prepared by Sarah Stoutamire.

I concentrate on the early state, many forces and social relations that gave rise to past sociocultural complexity are also relevant to today's world—despite huge quantitative differences in technology and qualitative differences in modes of production, means of distribution, and patterns of consumption.

My rationale for selecting certain early states or areas of the world and not others involved the following:

1. The scale and complexity of the groups involved
2. The climatic and geomorphological conditions affecting water management decision making
3. The quality and availability of information
4. My firsthand knowledge of certain archaeological data sets

The case selection enables such contrasts as those between the canal and lake/reservoir systems of highland Mexico and the human-made microwatersheds of the Maya Lowlands (Scarborough 1993a, 1994a, 1998; Scarborough and Gallopin 1991). In South Asia, early Harappan society tethered to the fertility of the lower Indus is juxtaposed with the huge tank systems of the ancient Sinhalese. These juxtapositions show that the organization of labor for constructing and maintaining watershed and reservoir sources differs markedly from purely distributary canal systems. Grounded in ecology and economy, such comparisons permit meaningful cross-cultural linkages.

Within their respective hemispheres, the New World (highland Mexico and the Maya Lowlands) and the Old World (the Indus Valley and north-central Sri Lanka) cases are in relative proximity and may have cross-fertilized each other's development. At the same time, though, each hemisphere allows the study of an arid setting and a humid setting. In addition, the book includes two secondary zones influenced by neighboring primary civilizations: the prehistoric, canalized U.S. Southwest and Late Bronze Age Greece (Mycenaeans). Inclusion of the Mycenaeans adds an example of spring-dependent hydraulic systems to the book's technical range. From these case studies, I make a formal division between still-water schemes (reservoirs, lakes, and spring containment) and flow-water schemes (canal organizations). This distinction permits a broad-based comparison of hydraulic adaptations among early states.

The selection of these examples reflects my contention that environment is a necessary variable in any discussion of water manipulation and the development of early archaic states. Accordingly, to make meaningful interhemispheric comparisons, similarity of environmental settings had to be a factor in my selection of prehistoric cases—three examples from the Old World juxtaposed with three from the New World. Additionally, the Maya Lowlands, the Basin of Mexico, and the Sonoran Desert of the U.S. Southwest form a logical comparative set within the New World, given their diverse environments and relative proximity. Their south-to-north latitudinal progression provides a degree of environmental control while spanning a semitropical rain forest setting, an elevated and topographically complex basin, and an arid surround interrupted by an important but diminutive set of drainages.

Two New World areas that gave rise to important early states—the Valley of Oaxaca and Peru—were not chosen, for the following reasons. The archaeology of the Valley of Oaxaca is not as well known with regard to water management, although I do refer to it on several occasions. Furthermore, I selected cases to provide contrasts, and Oaxaca is a diminutive version of what is better reported in the Basin of Mexico. I do not use Peru as a case study because I have not worked in the area and because the highland example I chose for the New World is the Basin of Mexico. However, this book does not ignore Peru's sizable corpus of water management data, much of it well documented and creatively interpreted. I present Peruvian data sets frequently throughout the book, especially in chapters 4, 5, and 6.

In the Old World, selection was more difficult because of the highly diverse set of cultures occupying the landscape through time. My selection of Harappan systems reflects, in part, my long-term fascination with that cultural area. Furthermore, by including it, I could juxtapose Old World environments in a manner similar to the New World comparisons. Using either Mesopotamia or Egypt as a principal case study would have prevented the highlighting of linkages between an arid, riverine setting (the Indus) and a semitropical setting (Ceylon) for the early archaic state. I occasionally discuss ancient Mesopotamia and Egypt, however, and present considerable Mesopotamian ethnographic material in various sections. Because the semiarid environments of the great riverine civilizations along the Nile, the Tigris and Euphrates, and the Indus have much in common, I decided to include only one of them (the Indus). By including Late Bronze Age Greece (Mycenae), I could examine a more topographically rugged water system associated with the early archaic state. It might be best contrasted with the Basin of Mexico. Again, what I strived to attain was a similar south-to-north comparative package of culture areas in the Old World and the New.

Much explanation is necessary, however, before using the six archaeological case studies to build an adequate anthropological framework for the study of water management. For two reasons, I begin with prominent ideas of past students of water management. First, we must not needlessly reinvent the good ideas of our predecessors or pretend that their ideas are our own inventions. Second, we must dissect their work if we are to overcome some false starts that are inherent in the literature and impede further understanding. Chapters 2 and 3 accomplish these tasks. Chapters 4 and 5 carry out the next step, namely, explicating the physical properties of water that affect its management by humans, as well as the means of such cultural management in both Old and New Worlds. Because neither subject (water or water management) is self-evident or even familiar in useful detail to the average reader, chapters 4 and 5 provide a necessary prelude to the case studies. The economic outlays and political risks of water management, discussed in chapter 6, also require detailed discussion. The archaeological case studies follow in chapter 7 (New World) and chapter 8 (Old World). Chapter 9 readdresses the book's main themes and places them in the comparative context of the case studies. It also returns to the theme of centralization and addresses the significance of control and power.

T W O ≈≈≈

The Organizing Concepts of Water Work

Natural phenomena are converted into resources through culture, and here multiple
cultures coexist. Each culture defines the natural resources it will exploit, the form
in which it will obtain and transform them, and their final use and meaning.

—Guillermo Bonfil Batalla (1996:158)

Ancient water management, as an economic and political force, shaped the mode or relations of production in archaic states. The goal of this book is to demonstrate how water management empowered ancient complex societies by providing labor and technology options that restructured the political economy. In other words, how did these societies employ *power relationships*—those established and sustained by a coercive elite—to organize water use? I focus on complex societies because they were the first to alter (and potentially degrade) their environment significantly. Because water is essential, controllable, and primarily responsible for configuring both natural and built landscapes, complex interrelationships evolved between people and their environment. An analysis of early states—ecologically invasive social orders—reveals fundamental organizational aspects shared with present-day societies. By identifying the economic and political variables influencing the early, less complex states, we can more clearly assess the causal stimuli of social change today.

Water was a principal resource, perhaps the most important one, even when population densities and consumption needs were slight. Ethnographic data from Australia to South Africa illustrate that water holes across a desertscape guided the seasonal movements of the technologically least complex foragers. Even in tropical ecosystems occupied by mobile hunters and horticulturalists, water availability is woven tightly into the fabric of everyday life. For instance, the rise and fall of the great Amazonian river system strongly affects Amazonian riverine peoples. Flood-force inundations carrying the renewing organics for the next year's harvest necessitate seasonal relocation from the riverbank fields.

A principal theme of this book is that human-developed landscape offers the best insight into how a culture understands and adapts to its ecology. Furthermore, the built environment reveals many deep structures that configure social organization by providing the rationale and underpinnings for economic and political decisions. Over the long term, decisions stemming from the history and use of the landscape keep land, labor, and water in a complicated check and balance. By focusing on the rate and process of landscape transformation, we can achieve a fresh view of social complexity.

The study of water management has clear implications for anthropology, most significantly, land use and related aspects of economy and human ecology. Of all resources and natural agents, water plays the most fundamental role in shaping the natural and cultural landscapes. Together with temperature fluctuations and wind erosion, water sculpts the earth's surface—from the abrasive expansion of a sluggish glacier to the scouring action of a swollen waterway. As early as 1830, Charles Lyell's *Principles of Geology* copiously detailed the *uniformitarian view* of geologic history, that the physical world has been altered by the same forces existing today. The tectonic uplifting of the earth's surface creates a mountain, but water is principally what wears it down. Of course, this book is less concerned with the physical properties of water in shaping the natural setting than with the economic and political decisions made by societies in arriving at the environment they culturally choose to occupy.

Early complex societies constructed striking monuments—pyramids, palaces, temples—that modified early urban space, but their long-term manipulation of the greater landscape, away from concentrations of urban life, transformed the environment most dramatically. Full sedentism and complex agrarian adaptations depended on predictable water allotments. With growing populations, greater social complexity, and attention to circumscribed territorial boundaries, agricultural plots became fixed and definable. The earliest fields did little to change the environment, being positioned in naturally elevated water table settings or on the flanks of well-drained, rainfall-dependent slopes. Later, experiments in irrigation and watershed alteration brought creative and extensive modifications of the hinterlands. Initially, the need to manage water stimulated most human-induced changes to the landscape—before, during, and after urbanism.

Because landscapes maintained populations even after the demise of adjacent towns and cities, rural alterations continued. Labor intensity and coordination corresponded to the scale and influence of the urban quarter, the political nerve center. However, even a small, less conspicuous, sustaining rural population would continue to crop and reinvent the landscape following the city's collapse. In highly engineered landscapes with elaborate hill slope terracing or carefully reclaimed wetlands, marked reduction in the politically coordinated labor force responsible for construction and maintenance resulted in a severely unkempt, negatively altered terrain. Subsequent occupants frequently made very different economic decisions than their predecessors because of these degrading modifications.

The consequences of cutting away a forest or digging drainage ditches through a swamp disclose a more diagnostic landscape signature of a culture and its socioeconomic organization than all the pyramids of the Valley of the Kings or the ziggurats in Uruk and Ur. Marx's (1967) notion that history is made by altering the urban landscape remains an important concept but must be broadened to encompass the subtle role of the countryside. Water—as a broadly defined unit of analysis and the most fundamental resource in constraining social and environmental relationships—determines the process by which land and history are transformed and the rate of this process.

Heterarchy versus Hierarchy

Of special importance to this book is the role of centralization and power in the early state. *Centralization* is a process by which resources and labor are economically concentrated, frequently influencing the degree of political and ideological control within and among constituent groups. *Power* is the exercise of political control by individuals or subgroups within a community or society. Power is not an all-or-nothing phenomenon; it would be a mistake to interpret power as either present or absent in any complex social order, especially the archaic state. My definition extends beyond strength sanctioned by weapons of violence. I view power as a dynamic process accessible in degrees. Critical resources legitimate political control and societal organization. Here, I discuss power as the way a complex society coordinates and schedules focused control over labor, information, and goods. Power frequently constitutes a unique, organizational aspect of the archaic state, but one incapable of longevity at heightened levels. Nevertheless, power does manifest itself in the archaeological record in every example of the ancient state, to varying degrees and in various ways over the life span of each state.

Water management requires cooperation among people who might otherwise be in conflict, because it always entails a set of prescribed relationships rooted in a notion of smallholder inequality (Netting 1993:12). The long-standing inequality within most village economies (even where stratification does not become visible within the village) and the necessary coordination of access to water lead to some degree of centralized decision making. Although any village will employ social mechanisms to stimulate a sense of solidarity and identity, the everyday routines associated with adequate water access schedule workloads in ways that communitywide feasting and kinship, for example, do not (Gray 1963:171; Leach 1961:234). This daily coordination of labor makes water management the social, political, and economic force that it is.

Most archaic state models stress hierarchical economic and political organization, assuming *power relationships* (established and sustained by a coercive elite) between vertical levels of society. Although regularly dismissed today, Wittfogel's (1957) *hydraulic society theory,* viewing water management as the primary vehicle for the evolution of societal control, still exercises a significant, supportive influence on this notion of power relationships. *Hierarchical models* propose a highly centralized set of economic and political linkages leading to the exploitation and control of resources by a limited number of powerful individuals at the upper tier of society. These models entail an exaggerated degree of resource concentration within urban centers.

An alternative interpretation of centralization in archaic states suggests that resources did not need to be as highly concentrated and controlled as in models assuming a single, coercive elite. Instead, many linkages between social groups or nodes within the state were horizontal instead of vertical. Such a *segmental state*—not to be confused with the segmentary state defined by others (Southall 1956, 1988; Fox 1977)—was characterized by a highly diverse set of hinterland activities revolving around principal exchange nodes, or cities. Compared with the nucleated concentrations of people and resources assumed by the hierarchical model, the nodes of the segmental state were typically more sparsely occupied. Nevertheless, a comparable or larger population occupied the greater region.

Heterarchy (Crumley 1987, 1995) is a good term for the kinds of network relationships I have in mind. Unlike models emphasizing hierarchical relationships and urban-focused centralization, the *heterarchy model* sees the groups within a densely settled hinterland as interacting largely among themselves, using the city as their exchange and communication node. The result is a highly flexible, yet specialized, set of exchanges through time and space. Communities in the countryside are resource-specialized and organized economically to produce a few things well (Scarborough and Valdez, in press). A set of interdependencies evolves across a region, connecting communities in a web of exchanges. Although degrees of hierarchical relations occur between larger or more successful centers, their force is tempered by the web of horizontal economic and political linkages within and among the smaller, resource-specialized communities.

A fundamental difference between my segmental, heterarchical state and the segmentary state envisaged by many archaeologists is that the latter homogenizes the countryside, suggesting the replication of village form and function across a region. Even though the segmental, heterarchical state has numerous, widespread resource-specialized communities, it also contains communities of the type characterizing the hinterland in the hierarchical models—relatively isolated, more risk-averse, not resource-specialized, poor. Nevertheless, the hinterland, resource-specialized community and its limited number of specific resources or products supply the key to my definition of the segmental state. Whereas traditional notions of hierarchy have emphasized conflictual power relationships within the densely urban context, heterarchy entails cooperation and resiliency within a densely occupied hinterland.

These two models of the archaic state are the poles of a continuum on which no actual state occupies the extremes. Furthermore, the term *heterarchy* does not imply that centralization and coerced order are absent within a state. It simply emphasizes the role of interdependency within and among communities of variable size and production/consumption needs. Heterarchy can encompass periods of centralized activity at a specific site, as well as periods of resource concentration at a limited number of communities within a regional system. The concept suggests, however, that such focused activity at only a few sites is a relatively unstable organizational adaptation, a fleeting one in the history of statecraft. I return to this topic in the final chapters.

Accretional versus Expansionist Development

To assess water management's role in the early development of agriculturally based, complex societies, I propose a temporal approach involving two possible paths for civilizations: accretional and expansionist. These paths are implicit in the overarching models just introduced. The *accretional approach* is a slow, stable development of the agrarian resource, modifying the landscape with fewer risks than the more rapid, expansionist approach. If food and water are not abundant, slow agricultural growth is possible with measured population growth and by steadily improving the long-term productivity of water sources and soil. Accretionally organized systems tend to produce complicated interdependencies between groups and their environment. In short, their organization is highly heterarchical.

The expansionist approach radically and rapidly exploits resources necessary for certain kinds of statecraft. Many management risks are taken, even without plentiful or varied resources. Innovative technology, harnessing new varieties of edible plants, or more effectively distributing an old crop can significantly alter the course of an agricultural system (Scarborough 1991a). Rapid agrarian growth usually accompanies major population increases, which can place the society at risk if the population exceeds the resource base (Culbert 1977; Renfrew 1978). Rapid decline, even catastrophe, is a possible consequence of the expansionist approach. Nevertheless, during periods of extreme resource stress, an adaptive realignment of the sociopolitical system may result if social collapse can be averted. Groups employing the exploitative approach to resource acquisition and consumption are highly hierarchical in their organization.

Economic Logics

The accretional and expansionist approaches are poles on a continuum of the process by which resources are managed and consumed and the rate at which this occurs. To study process well requires another level of analysis: culturally distinct economic orientation, or logic, shaping natural environments and intersocietal relations. I distinguish three—*labortasking, technotasking,* and *multitasking*—to explain the kinds and degrees of land alteration and water management practices adopted by archaic states.

Some cultures, principally in ancient and present-day East Asia (Bray 1986), invest in highly efficient divisions of labor for constructing and maintaining grandly engineered landscapes. These *labortasking* societies assign specific tasks to the members of an extended family or more broadly defined kin group, creating a very differentiated, highly skilled labor force. With enough laborers trained in the specific tasks necessary to transform and sustain a productive landscape, extremely complex and intricate land and water systems evolve. Judging from the East Asian cases, such societies develop when skilled labor is abundant, farmland is limited, and laborsaving technological devices associated with economies of scale are undeveloped or not employed.

Other cultures focus on technological buffers in producing economies of scale where land is abundant but not labor. They employ a *technotasking* logic (cf. Bray 1986:115). Found notably in European contexts, societies organized by this logic readily incorporate novel, laborsaving technologies and can rapidly alter terrain. Because each new technological input requires new skills and even structural adjustments in production, however, the labor force cannot routinize tasks intergenerationally. The result is a less sustainable, anthropogenic environment. Predictably, these societies may experience considerable social unrest.

With the third kind of logic, *multitasking,* people diversify the tasks necessary for survival, but in a less measured routine and without a great demand for technology. Such an economic adaptation emphasizes the variety of tasks individuals can accomplish using a generalized knowledge of their environment. A society adopts multitasking logic when survival depends on greater flexibility. Less effort is invested in specific, task-oriented knowledge because its future success is unpredictable (see figure 2.1). For example, the ethnographer Annis (1987) suggests that some indigenous Maya communities of highland Guatemala employ a highly practical economic adaptation to ensure their local subsistence while coping with capitalism and the global market. Here, a marginalized, politically and economically subordinated group resists the lure of investing its subsistence energies in producing only the few crops that profit on international markets. By maintaining diverse crops on their swidden plots, they avoid the risk of losing everything to a bad market year and secure an immediate food source under any economic condition. Although different forces and relationships have driven this multitasking orientation in the ancient past, the foregoing example captures the wisdom of remaining open and responsive to rapid changes in the natural and cultural environments.

It remains to link the three economic logics—labortasking, technotasking, and multitasking—to the accretional and expansionist models (refer to figure 2.1). At the outset, an accretional approach to the built environment appears best associated with labortasking. Here, the slow, cumulative investment in carefully altering a landscape can result in a highly sustainable, stable, anthropogenic setting as long as individuals can pass on their refined skills generationally without major disruption. The altered, present-day landscapes associated with rice terracing in portions of Southeast Asia exhibit the most elaborate adaptation of this (Scarborough et al. 1999).

The expansionist model (as a function of rate) may best fit with technotasking (as a function of process). The sociocultural effects of technological breakthroughs, whether indigenous inventions or externally introduced discoveries, are well known (R. McC. Adams 1996; Clark 1992; Diamond 1999). Societies never accept a new technology automatically, but some seem more receptive than others to novel tool use and manufacture. Under conditions of rapid technological change, the landscape and its use are altered to accommodate each successive technological system, and maintaining long-term or predictable stability across such landscapes is difficult. For example, the North American Plains experienced changes, from nomadic peoples employing buffalo jumps and hunting blinds, to rifle-wielding horsemen vastly

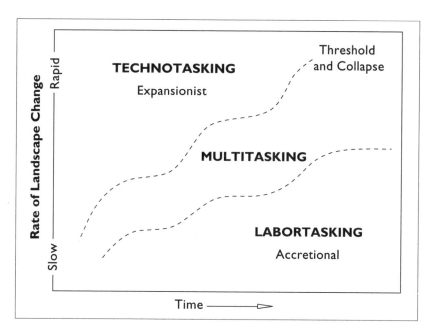

Figure 2.1 Rate and process of landscape change in accretional and exploitative models, prepared by Sarah Stoutamire.

altering animal and plant populations, to windmills and animal-traction agriculture, to riverine urban growth, and, finally, to the advent of the railroad, automobiles, and agribusiness—all within less than 200 years.

The expansionist model is also compatible with multitasking logic, which may be followed by peasants or other subordinated groups struggling to sustain a predictable economic base outside a rapidly changing, dominant, technotasking economy. In short, these two logics may coexist, each predominating in a different subset of a state (archaic or present-day) that fits the expansionist model.

Multitasking can also be an independent, freestanding approach to the economy, without any immediate linkage to technotasking or its associated expansionist approach. Multitasking may develop where population is small and land abundant, a condition prevailing widely in sub-Saharan Africa. Long-term alterations to the environs are less necessary with a low population density and a natural ecological setting that provides adequate resources. These circumstances permit the establishment of stable social organization. Such populations tend to develop opportunistic tasking adaptations, sometimes investing in accretional production and consumption rates and other times investing in more exploitative practices. Rates of resource use vary among groups practicing multitasking, because these groups are strongly affected by the condition of their landscape, which generally depends on how long the group has drawn resources from a delimited territory. Even a small, dispersed population can overuse a region's initially abundant resources if resources cannot renew themselves naturally. Generally, multitasking entails greater community mobility to prevent overexploitation of the environs.

Juxtaposing the rate of landscape change and the logic underlying societal organization suggests several possible organizational pathways leading to social complexity. As mentioned, the adaptations of a subordinate group practicing a multitasking logic—partly in reaction to the more formal coordination of activities by a dominant technotasking sector—are identifiable along the accretional-to-expansionist continuum (refer to figure 2.1). Nevertheless, groups generally gravitate toward either the accretional or expansionist approach and maintain that organizational profile through time.

THREE

Contemporary Thought and Recent Intellectual History

Yet, if the kings did not control irrigation, who did?

J. Stephen Lansing (1991:4)

This chapter features many contemporary thinkers who are directing research on water management from a decidedly anthropological perspective. Beginning with a brief history of water management studies, it discusses old and new views of Balinese water systems and how these studies significantly affect questions of centralization, statecraft, and water management. The chapter then turns to two cross-cultural examinations of the economic logics presented in chapter 2.

I have elected to abbreviate the historical backdrop because several others have already covered this extensively (Anderson 1974; Isaac 1993; O'Leary 1989), especially the influences of Karl Marx, Karl Wittfogel, Julian Steward, and Robert McC. Adams. Marx's notion of the Asiatic Mode of Production and his embedded view of history assumed only slight alterations to the "oriental" landscape. For several reasons, not the least being Eurocentrism, Marx saw Asia as lacking significant history, befitting his view of its less consequential investment in architecture even within high-density urban settings. The Asiatic Mode of Production precluded social change because of Asia's supposedly stagnant history, which, in Marx's view, ultimately allowed the despotic quality of Asian states.

Karl Wittfogel was the first scholar to devote a career to the study of water management. Although heavily influenced by Marx and Weber, he politically distanced himself as far as possible from the former. In his well-known tome *Oriental Despotism* (1957), Wittfogel expressed a deterministic view of the role of irrigation in stimulating statecraft and "total power." The hydraulic society controlled by a despot and his evolving bureaucracy could develop in a region that was

1. "Above the level of an extractive subsistence economy"
2. "Beyond the influence of strong centers of rainfall agriculture"

3. "Below the level of a property-based industrial civilization" (Wittfogel 1957:12)

Although Wittfogel overstated his case, state centralization and resource management became a testable hypothesis using irrigation data. The "hydraulic hypothesis" was challenged and eventually dismissed, in part because it generalized beyond what was reasonable. The limited archaeological and ethnographic data of Wittfogel's day, coupled with his exclusion of the myriad water management techniques that did not incorporate classic irrigation schemes, prevented a more nuanced view of the subject.

Julian Steward can be credited with developing the study of "man-land" relationships and significantly refining the methodological and theoretical underpinnings of cultural ecology. His explicit concern with the environment continues to influence archaeologists. The hydraulic hypothesis attracted Steward because it incorporated his expectations about the significance of base-level subsistence traits—water and associated technology—in defining cultural "cores." Also, it afforded a true opportunity to test for cultural regularities through time and space (Steward 1955a). Through Steward's influence, Wittfogel's hydraulic hypothesis was championed to a broad anthropological readership, beginning with Steward's *Irrigation Civilization: A Comparative Study* (1955b).

Robert McC. Adams was one of the pioneers who attempted to test Wittfogel's argument that irrigation and its complex bureaucratic order gave rise to early state complexity. However, Adams (1966) viewed irrigation as only one component in a complicated web of factors that stimulated the rise of civilization. Indeed, he thought that irrigation was not a major condition for centralizing and controlling resources or managers. What Adams (1978) saw in the archaeological and ethnographic record was a continually shifting association between pastoralism and agriculturally based sedentism before the archaic state. Formal irrigation seldom triggered social complexity, let alone Wittfogel's "total power" and the centralization of resources.

An early dissenter to Adams's interpretive conclusion derived from the ancient Middle East was William Sanders (Sanders and Price 1968), who argued that irrigation was a critical variable in the emergence of the Mesoamerican archaic state. Because irrigation required centralized authority, complementary demographic vectors leading toward urbanism combined to produce a highly complex social system (Sanders et al. 1979). Unfortunately for this argument, irrigation canals at the critical periods in prehistory for triggering urbanism in Mesoamerica have not been documented (see chapter 7). Nevertheless, Sanders has influenced the course of Mesoamerican archaeology more than any other researcher. Two generations of students have engaged in one long dialog with him as their mentor, taking the cultural ecological approach.

A substantial body of ethnographic and archaeological work reexamines Wittfogel's hydraulic hypothesis. Indeed, that ground is so well trod that it hardly requires another review. Suffice it to say that the two most damaging arguments are that

1. Cities and associated indicators of complexity and scale often predate canal systems of consequence (R. McC. Adams 1966, 1981).
2. Many ethnographically observed non-state groups have developed sophisticated water management schemes (Millon 1971).

Although frequently in the shadows of any discussion concerning water management, *Oriental Despotism* (Wittfogel 1957) has been generally abandoned by the social sciences (contra Sidky 1996).

Contemporary thought on water management and landscape modification is varied and complex. Less time is devoted to debunking Wittfogel's hydraulic hypothesis, and more energy is directed toward understanding the economic underpinnings of water use. Current thinking also places more emphasis on clearly defining terminology. Furthermore, we have come to recognize that water management systems are much more complex and textured than previously thought. Bali—with water systems displaying a complex interdependency of social units across the landscape—once seemed an oddity but is now regarded as a type case. Indeed, water management studies show that communities and the states they compose are influenced by different kinds (heterarchy and hierarchy) and degrees of centralization affected by access to water.

The Balinese Problem

For decades, the small Indonesian island of Bali has been the center of considerable anthropological debate. The island's extensive, beautiful rice-paddy terracing, coupled with its inhabitants' ritualized public devotion, attracts study by humanists and social scientists alike. The complexity of a small society capable of engineering its landscape while investing heavily in ritual performance captures the interplay between human ecology and the social relations underpinning this ecology. How water is managed in microcosm on Bali has much to say about social complexity, centralization, and aspects of power.

The For-or-Against Syndrome

Wittfogel's (1957) model of the hydraulic society with hegemonic control over resources drew strong reaction but little interest in altering his grand theory to accommodate local variability and conditions. Scholars were either for or against the hydraulic society as an explanation for early statecraft. One of the most contentious arenas for debating the theory's applicability was the Basin of Mexico, although some of these first researchers drew from cross-cultural, comparative studies to deny any correlation between irrigation and the rise of statecraft. At present, the small Indonesian island of Bali has become the principal ethnographic source for this evolving debate.

In contrast to Sanders's supportive views of Wittfogel's theory (Sanders and Price 1968), René Millon—the archaeologist most responsible for the Teotihuacan Mapping Project (Millon 1973) within the Basin of Mexico—argued that little existing evidence supported a central authority model of water management. In an influential article drawing on an ethnographic survey of seven small-scale, irrigation-dependent societies, Millon (1971) presented Bali as a decentralized system and likened it to Japan (Beardsley et al. 1959), an erroneous assessment of the clearly hierarchical, centralized Japanese case. Drawing on Geertz's (1959) early work, Millon stated that the Balinese *subak*, the corporate unit responsible for a bounded irrigation system, was not isomorphic with a village or a group of hamlets. To Millon, this lack of geographical concordance was incontrovertible evidence of decentralization, therefore justifying the rejection of Wittfogel's grand theory. The argument did not incorporate the subtleties and complexities of Balinese centralization and heterarchy. Thus, even though Millon refuted aspects of the hydraulic hypothesis, especially the notion that the archaic state always developed from irrigation efforts, ultimately he was unable to argue convincingly against a centralizing role for water management.

The Autonomous Water Users

Clifford Geertz brought Bali to the attention of a broad audience of anthropologists with his book *Negara: The Theatre State in Nineteenth-Century Bali* (1980). Even before that, though, his ethnographic account of Bali (Geertz 1959; Geertz and Geertz 1975) had attracted much attention from scholars interested in the hydraulic hypothesis proposed by Wittfogel (1957), Steward (1955b), and others. These scholars used Geertz's Balinese material as the single best case against the necessary correlation of centralization and irrigation.

As early as 1959, Geertz argued that the Balinese village was not a corporate territorial unit, but that Balinese village structure was constituted by a series of "organizational themes" or "planes" underlying shared temple obligations, as well as ownership and maintenance of rice paddies. Unlike the closed-corporate peasant communities modeled by Eric Wolf (1957, 1966), Balinese villages differed in structure from one community to the next, depending on the mix of structural components or which components were emphasized. Geertz (1959:993) argued that "religious and political units are not coordinate but instead crosscut one another." He (ibid.:995) continued:

> Unlike peasant societies in most parts of the world, there is in Bali almost no connection between the ownership and management of cultivable land, on the one hand, and local political (i.e., hamlet) organization, on the other. The irrigation society, or *subak*, regulates all matters having to do with the cultivation of wet rice, and it is a wholly separate organization from the *bandjar* [basic territorial political unit, the hamlet].
>
> *Subak* are organized according to the water system: all individuals owning land which is irrigated from a single water source—a single dam and canal

running from dam to field—belong to a single *subak*. *Subak* whose direct water sources are branches of a common larger dam and canal form larger and less tightly knit units, and finally the entire watershed of one river system forms an overall, but even looser, integrative unit. As Balinese land ownership is quite fragmented, a man's holding typically consisting of two or three quarter- or half-acre plots scattered about the countryside, often at some distance from his home, the members of one *subak* almost never hail from a single hamlet, but from ten or fifteen different ones; while from the point of view of the hamlet, members of a single *bandjar* will commonly own land in a large number of *subak*. Thus, as the spatial distribution of temples sets the boundaries on Balinese religious organization, and the nucleated settlement pattern forms the physical framework for political organization, so the concrete outline of the Balinese irrigation system of simple stone and clay dams, mud-lined canals and tunnels, and bamboo water dividers provides the context within which Balinese agriculture activities are organized.

In short, Geertz argued that Balinese agriculture and the economy in which it is embedded are disassociated from most aspects of political and, to a lesser degree, religious organization operative within and among villages. Nevertheless, his account reveals the considerable importance of an intervillage network in the construction and maintenance of water management features, water allocation decisions, and conflict resolution. In his subsequent book-length treatment of Bali, Geertz (1980:85) suggests that a system of ritual activity and ceremony, instead of immediate political authority, coordinates the *subak* organization, as well as other structural components in society. Indeed, he argues that kings had little involvement in the organization of irrigation (ibid.:69). Implicitly foreshadowed by the careful work of Thomas Glick (1970), Geertz identified the same "consensual authority" that Glick attributed to the irrigation systems of medieval Valencia (Spain). For both authors, *consensual authority* is the idea that organization and control of a water management system develop from a diffuse, collective societal consciousness or understanding. The data in Glick's book would seem to show, however, that Valencian authority was more hierarchical and politically centralized than he—or Geertz, in the Balinese case—would have us believe (Hunt and Hunt 1976).

The Subtleties of the Engineered Landscape

"Yet, if the kings did not control irrigation, who did?" With these words, Stephen Lansing (1991:4) counters Geertz's structuralism with historical materialism and a processual explanation of the *subak*. Lansing's book *Priests and Programmers: Technologies of Power in the Engineered Landscape of Bali* (1991) acknowledges much of Geertz's argument but more thoroughly explores the Balinese approach to land and water. Lansing shows that precolonial Bali was probably not organized in a politically centralized manner like feudal European states, a model imposed on Bali by the Dutch imperialists. Bali was not an example of Oriental despotism, either, as both Marx (Marx 1959, 1967) and Wittfogel (1957) had suggested. Furthermore, and contrary to both Wittfogel (1957) and Geertz (1959; Geertz and Geertz 1975), the *subak* was neither autonomous nor isolated—conditions necessary, surprisingly enough, to both those authors' very divergent arguments. Implicit in Geertz's argument and overtly explicit in Wittfogel's position is the presence of hierarchical modes of production. Although Geertz sees little evidence of a coordinating, centralizing set of economic forces in Bali, he does identify a controlling ritual elite with political authority, influence, and degrees of power. According to Lansing, however, Balinese economy is not directed by top-down, hierarchical modes of production.

Lansing proposes, instead, that the Balinese irrigation system is highly organized and is centered around a regionwide heterarchy of water temples, removing much fuzziness from Geertz's "consensual authority." A nested order of temples and associated priests geographically placed at principal nodes—water control points such as weirs or dams—along the irrigation and water source system provides a network for decision making (see plates 3.1 and 3.2, and figure 3.3).

> Temples and shrines are situated…to exert influence over each of the major physical components of the terrace ecosystems, including lakes, springs, rivers, weirs, major canals, blocks of irrigated terraces, *subaks* and individual fields. The temples link these physical features of the landscape to social units according to a logic of production: the congregation of each temple consists of the farmers who obtain water from the irrigation component controlled by the temple's god. (Lansing 1991:53)

Lansing contends that priests at water temples, strategically placed relative to the water system, coordinate ritual and also schedule the planting and harvesting cycles within and between watersheds.

> Hydrological interdependency is built in to the very engineering structure of the irrigation systems, with long and fragile systems of weirs, tunnels, canals, and aqueducts threading their way down the mountainsides. Thus, the physical constraints of Balinese irrigation require a system of control extending well beyond the *subak* level, connecting weir to weir and watershed to watershed. (Lansing 1991:48)

The stringent requirements for wet rice production, including precise timing in flooding the terraces and diverting excess water at other times, make the entire regional irrigation system interdependent. Additionally, the water temples and priests play a key role in controlling pests during the annual agricultural cycle.

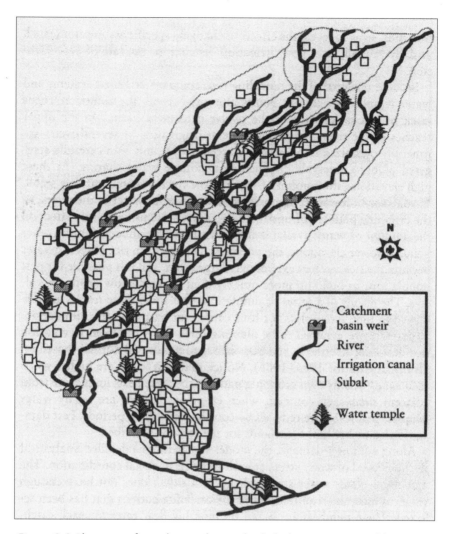

Figure 3.3 Plan map of canals, temples, and subak divisions, reprinted by permission of Princeton University Press from J.S. Lansing (1991).

Consulting with individual farmers, the temple priests prepare a complex set of calendrical manipulations to coordinate planting and harvesting schedules. In addition to controlling water distribution, the calendar minimizes pest damage by synchronizing an area's fallow periods so that weevils cannot easily spread from infested fallow land to planted fields. The temples are the repositories of agricultural information, ancient and current, and rapidly disseminate cropping schedules in a manner acceptable to Balinese tradition and social relations—a situation quite different from the regimen of the current, ill-fated foreign aid programs (Lansing 1987, 1991; Lansing et al. 2001).

Many rhythms drive Balinese society, but the water temple priests set the central tempo by regulating and scheduling water for each *subak*. Lansing shows that water amounts are finite, and allocation at each diversion dam depends on a complicated variety of information made most intelligible within the water temple. I suggest that the *subak* system structure, with farmers coming from several *bandjars* (hamlets), spreads agricultural risks and allows irrigation of geographically dispersed paddies (Scarborough et al. 1999).

Centralization and Taxation

Lansing's work on Balinese social relations of production provides the clearest perspective yet on the question of centralization and irrigation. Bali is not an anomaly but rather a very complex system revealing forces of production shared with many other irrigation systems described ethnographically. Its irrigation system is not presently embedded in, or concordant with, the state. Centralization in that sense occurs only occasionally, in Bali and globally. Nevertheless, irrigation systems are highly coordinated and structured by a decision-making hierarchy embedded in an overarching heterarchy. In Bali, the water temples form a bureaucracy (based on my interpretation of Lansing's data and my personal observations in Bali in 1997). Other "organizational planes" (Geertz 1959) influence and crosscut the individual *subak* and villages, but water practices and use are ultimately answerable to the high priest of the Temple of the Crater Lake—the geographical summit of central Bali and the understood source of irrigation waters. In his occasional conflicts with the state (or, in past times, with the "princelings"), the high priest does not claim superior power, but his control does extend over the sovereign boundaries of several political districts or past kingdoms. One of the clearest indications of power is his ability to call down police-enforced sanctions. These appear to be at the high priest's disposal through the state apparatus itself, although Lansing's presentation is vague on this point (ibid.:80).

More apparent in the control of the greater Balinese water system is taxation. Although the overlay of Dutch colonial bureaucracy clouds the allocation structure of the precolonial water system, water taxation was an independent revenue source extracted from water users, separate from other taxes paid to the state.

Like the Dutch, but for different reasons, the Balinese also attached great symbolic value to the *soewinih* [water tax]. Lacking the means and, perhaps, the desire to coerce *soewinih* contributions, the Temple of the Crater Lake nonetheless received a steady flow of *soewinih* from the *subaks*. (Lansing 1991:104)

> From a purely metaphysical point of view, the Temple of the Crater Lake is a place of interchange between the visible and invisible worlds. But it is also a major redistributive center. Tons of *soewinih* offerings are brought to the temple each year, providing the raw materials for the grand rituals and feasts that validate the temple's cosmological role. (Lansing 1991:106)

The use of sanctions and taxation by those coordinating the Balinese water system reveals the group's economic underpinnings. Heterarchical organization does not imply the absence of centralizing forces or a lack of power.

Centralization and "Centering"

The authority of the high priest and the water temples in the operation of a "centered" water hierarchy in Bali is clear (Valeri 1991). Valeri coins the term *centering* in opposition to a rigidly hierarchical interpretation of centralization. He emphasizes the coordination of the many societal units and associated activities within society—the kind of interdependency among societal units that typifies heterarchy (see chapter 2). In traditional Bali, farmers grounded their social relationships on various organizational planes, that is, on the nested interrelationships of the rice economy, kinship, and political affiliation. Nevertheless, within the "humanized nature" (after Marx) that the farmers created, there existed an uneasy tension between the *subaks* and the state—both the precolonial princelings and the colonial Dutch. Both had authority, even power, over village farmers but depended on the farmers' labor and loyalty for success.

Competition to be the most effective channel for *soewinih* offerings seems to have flourished among both temples and princes. Proof of the efficacy of *soewinih* offerings was always to be found in next year's harvests. Bad harvests might demand more offerings next time, but they might also mean that the wrong channels were being used for the offerings. A temple or a prince who could not amass the material and labor needed to perform the necessary rituals on an impressive scale was in danger of losing the mandate of heaven. (Lansing 1991:109)

> Indeed, so similar were their functions that princes sometimes competed with
> water temples for the right to collect *soewinih* offerings. (Lansing 1991:131)

Lansing's study illustrates the difficulty in isolating irrigation districts and their degrees of political and economic centralization. Highly focused centralization is usually associated with a hegemonic state organization, and except for Wittfogel and Steward, few scholars view irrigation schemes as absolutely fundamental to a state's functioning. Nevertheless, irrigation systems do influence state-level decision making and are usually cooperatively organized in a hierarchical fashion within a heterarchical system. Lansing's study of Bali shows just how autonomous the irrigation hierarchical structure can appear, while still interacting with the many facets of an early, often heterarchical state. His Balinese ethnography reveals the overarching heterarchy of control (see chapter 2) regulated by the water temples operating at the regional level. This organization refutes both Millon's (1971) and Geertz's (Geertz and Geertz 1975) views of a decentralized irrigation system. Lansing (1991) demonstrates that the analysis of irrigation systems must extend beyond the confines of closed, socially drawn boundaries—in this case, the *subak*—and into the greater physical watershed from which the water emanates. I will return to this point in chapter 6.

It is true, then, that conventionally defined hydraulic centralization—the embeddedness of an irrigation system within a state's territorial boundaries—may occur. This was suggested by Eva and Robert Hunt (1974, 1976) for the political economy of Cuicatec, Mexico, but the intensity of concordance varies considerably. Commonly, a water management system's congruity with the state reflects not so much the state's centralized formal control of an irrigation district as the superimposition of the water hierarchy organizational plane upon the state's physical jurisdiction. When these two planes (state jurisdiction and water control) are geographically concordant, sharing the same landscape, a dependency relationship exists. I suspect that it is more usually a mutualism than commensalism (after Odum 1971).

In most ethnographic cases (and very clearly in Lansing's Bali), the irrigation system operates in complementary fashion with the state, not independently of it. As in the Japanese case (Beardsley et al. 1959; cf. Kelly 1982), the state does not really want to exercise its power over the irrigation district, even when such power exists de jure, because the state's tax base is the same landscape and labor pool. To meddle in the agricultural affairs of a rural, sustaining population is to cultivate distrust. This may lead to the disruption of the production cycle, potentially affecting the availability of tribute and taxes.

The cooperative element of irrigation is one of the strongest mechanisms pulling a group together on a shared landscape. This unity can be further expanded by the incorporation of large-scale hydraulic installations or can be fragmented by the encroachment of other state agendas or other organizational planes.

Struggles for Terminological Rigor

The 1980s and 1990s introduced a more applied anthropological view of water and society to the water debate. This change was fueled by large foreign aid packages from the United States to areas of the world suffering from water mismanagement, a partial consequence of earlier, less well-conceived foreign assistance. To justify these aid programs, significant interest developed in defining the terms employed in water management proposals (cf. Mabry, ed. 1996).

Explicit Definitions

William Kelly set the tone for future research in water studies with a report titled "Concepts in the Anthropological Study of Irrigation" (1983), which followed the influential articles by Mitchell (1973) and Hunt and Hunt (1976) reassessing and rewording the hydraulic hypothesis. The Hunts' piece was especially significant to Kelly's thinking because it reexamined the linkages between power and the tasks associated with irrigation. To the Hunts, labor input was more than allocation of the resource; it was also construction, maintenance, conflict resolution, and the organization of ritual.

Kelly discusses the scope of the irrigation question and then facets of thought less immediately related to state origins and centralization but fundamental to understanding the cultural effect of water manipulation. Nevertheless, he reviews power and the social relationships of production in terms of centralization. One of Kelly's most significant contributions in this article is that he explicitly defines and elucidates terminology for subsequent use by water management scholars.

> [I]rrigation is more than an act of hydraulic engineering. It requires insti-
> tutional arrangements for the construction and maintenance of physical facil-
> ities and procedures for the movement and distribution of water. Irrigation is
> economically important as the disposition of a critical input of agricultural
> production; it is politically significant as a source of power and leverage in
> local, regional, and national political arenas; and it is of considerable social
> consequence because it defines patterns of cooperation and conflict in irrigat-
> ed agricultural regions. (Kelly 1983:880)

Kelly presents four overlapping methodological concerns that point in the direction
water studies are taking:

1. The widely used concept of an "irrigation system" typically conflates
    three distinct dimensions of agricultural water use: natural water flow
    patterns, physical networks of facilities and environmental modifica-
    tions, and organizational configurations of irrigation roles.

2. In identifying patterns of irrigation organization, there is a tendency to
    focus exclusively on water delivery roles, overlooking roles dealing with
    three other, often equally complex phases of agricultural water use:
    water source control, application to crops, and drainage.

3. "Centralization," a key concept for those concerned with the relationship
    of irrigation to political power, is often used loosely to refer both to the
    internal configuration of authority among the various irrigation roles
    and to the external articulation of irrigation roles to general state
    authority.

4. Finally, forms of irrigation organization are all too frequently attributed
    directly to "natural facts of water" like aridity and flow stochasticity
    and/or to the scale of the physical network rather than to the variable
    cultural meanings of those natural and technical "facts" for the social
    actors in a given setting. (Kelly 1983:88–81)

Kelly successfully dichotomizes centralization, as it relates to water organization,
into *internal* (local) and *external* (overarching state-to-local) relationships. He further
subdivides internal water organizations into *hierarchically based* (with or without elite
water managers) and *decentralized* (lacking well-defined authority and functionally
fragmented). External organizational relationships separate into those water systems
that are autonomous and outside the state's political authority and those that articulate closely with the state through local elites. Although Kelly carefully defines the
terminology now so widely incorporated into the water debate, he does not include
the notion of heterarchy—a necessary concept for explicating the Balinese case and
many others.

Additional Aspects of Centrality

Robert Hunt (1988) further elucidates Kelly's treatment of centralization by examining the degree to which an irrigation district is either articulated with a state political apparatus or autonomous. He identifies three kinds of administrative control that define the range of authority and hierarchical structures in societies dependent on water management systems: the national government, the irrigation community, and private enterprise systems. This last is exemplified by entrepreneurial investments such as haciendas or foreign capital placed in sugar mills or related agribusinesses (Hunt 1988:342).

Hunt (1988) states that in only a very few societies is there no constituted authority over water decision making. In the three cases Hunt discusses in which the ethnographic record suggests the absence of hydraulic authority—the Swiss Alps (Netting 1974), Hawaii (Earle 1978), and a small system in the Philippines (de los Reyes 1980)—the scale of the irrigated area is less than 20 ha and involves a limited number of families. Despite the diminutive scale of these three cases, Hunt questions the robustness of the data sets, given the decision-making challenges associated with even an extremely small irrigation system, especially during periods of limited water availability.

> Several universally found work tasks have been identified in canal irrigation systems, including construction of the physical system, capture of water from the environment, allocation of water once captured, maintenance of the physical system, conflict resolution, and accounting. Drainage and ritual tasks are also sometimes found. If an authority structure is responsible for these tasks, then administrative roles must exist to perform them. Systems with constituted authority are headed by a chief executive officer, defined as that officer responsible for allocation at the facility where the system takes water from nature. (Hunt 1988:341)

Hunt's article, like Kelly's before it, is a methodological contribution that attempts to define indices of authority and scalar complexity in irrigation studies. Hunt questions how we define the dimensions of an irrigation system. He proposes that the number of canal gates may be a valuable index because it indicates the number of allocation decisions made and reflects "administrative density" (Hunt 1988:344). Canal length is also posed as a potentially useful measure of administrative structure, but the precise correlation of the two variables remains unclear. He recounts the difficulty of retrieving such information, but his approach to assessing scalar complexity does warrant additional thought, especially by archaeologists. For example, can aerial photographic coverage reveal *diversion loci,* that is, locations where canals divide or markedly change their dimensions? Can these nodes be treated as indexes of scalar complexity and hydraulic decision making in the same way as canal gates? Furthermore, Hunt indicates that irrigation scheme size (in hectares watered) is a poor index of the kind of authority operative within a irrigation district, although an area of less than 50 ha is more likely to be acephalous than one associated with larger tracts.

To conclude, centralization is a complex phenomenon involving local authority structures and supralocal or state power relationships. Most ethnographic case studies examining community-based systems demonstrate varying, though significant, degrees of hierarchical organization in the management of water.[1] Frequently, elite managers influence the decision-making process quite disproportionately to their numbers. How and why local systems articulate with the overarching state and its bureaucracy may be best explained in the Bali case, as deconstructed first by Geertz (1959, 1980) but most successfully by Lansing (1987, 1991) with his regional approach.

Organizational Planes

Water decision-making systems are a key aspect of the economic organizational plane. Restated in Karl Polanyi's (1957) terms and William Kelly's (1983), water systems are a principal facet of a society's overall institutional arrangements, which order or structure it.

The water management organizational plane (after Geertz 1959) differs fundamentally from such planes as kinship or religion. This is so for two reasons. First, the physical constraints of water—its natural properties and availability—limit the range of adaptations water users can make. Second, at some point, planes such as kinship or religion must bend to adjust to the economic underpinnings of the water and land resources (see figure 3.4). Paraphrasing Ingold (1993:171), one can say that organizational planes do not simply "cover over" the landscape; they are the landscape. Their definition and interrelationship chart the future and reflect the past.

All early states depend on the water supply and its local manipulation for sustaining an adequate supply of food. States tend not to control the water resource despotically, however, and if they do, never over the system's entirety. Too many decisions must be made within the local arena for there to be state agents at every turn. Moreover, as Beardsley et al. (1959) note, the state needs the tax base and political support from a successful agrarian population to further its own agendas. Thus, it is unlikely to force its will on the local community unless regionwide considerations require this. Only sometimes, then, is the water system organizational plane concordant with the state's boundaries or even the state's forceful authority and power. Nevertheless, the state's political plane and the community's water plane move across each other through time and may even become superimposed for a period, much like two overlapping and projecting transparencies. The integration of these two or more planes remains limited, though, unless they rest concordant for an extended period. This is not to say that irrigation systems do not occasionally influence state hierarchies and their exercise of power. They do. It is when the state political plane overlaps or aligns with the economic water plane that significant change in both

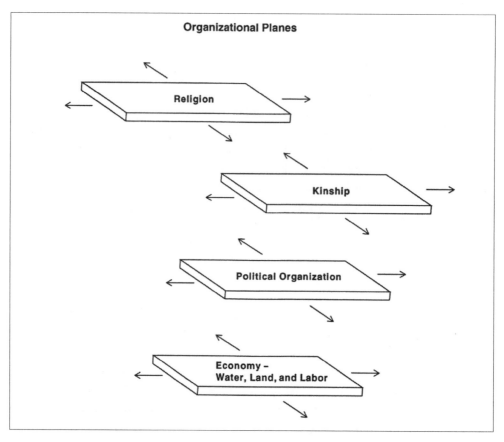

Figure 3.4 Organizational planes, prepared by Sarah Stoutamire.

organizations occurs, especially the first time such superposition takes place. Early states were strongly affected by such alignments, which sometimes forced them into more complicated organizational structures. Nevertheless, this was probably an infrequent occurrence lasting for only a short period (see figure 3.5). Usually, local water planes expanded within the state system, only to degrade into disrepair after the two planes drifted out of overlapping focus. At this juncture, local elite or autonomous water system organizations again reasserted themselves and became less dependent on the state. Unless state water policies greatly damaged and disrupted the *water facts*— the natural and artificial storage, distribution, and consumption of the water—the local water system likely continued. The local water system is the more resilient force, given its immediate, fundamental economic base and importance.

Initial Conditions and Common Property

Although Lansing's work, especially *Priests and Programmers* (1991), captures the direction of water studies into the 1990s, another recent approach (Park 1992; Park, ed. 1993) draws upon the notion of chaos theory as applied to the social sciences.[2] The theory originally evolved from weather and climate simulations and the so-called *Butterfly Effect.* This is a metaphor for complex causal relationships initiated by seem-

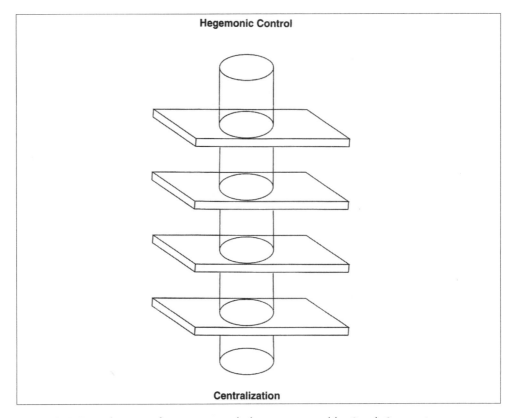

Figure 3.5 Centralization of organizational planes, prepared by Sarah Stoutamire.

ingly inconsequential agents. For example, the fluttering of a butterfly's wings beating the air in Beijing Park precipitates a series of incremental weather changes resulting ultimately in a storm system over New York City the following month. Worster (1990:15) and others refer to this set of events as "sensitive dependence on initial conditions" (cf. Horgan 1995:104–09). Our inability to predict a region's weather and associated rainfall—even today, with satellite technology—indicates that most past societies depended heavily on short-term adaptive strategies with various levels of risk for coping with the environment.

Drawing upon chaos theory, Thomas Park (1992; Park, ed. 1993) proposes that the erratic levels and duration of flooding along the floodplain margins of the Senegal River basin result in a flood recession variety of agriculture that promotes social hierarchy within the context of common property ownership. Park's argument emphasizes the role of stratification in complex pre-state societies based on flood recession farming and its chaotic timing and extent. He demonstrates that a well-defined hierarchy of land ownership and inequality can exist within communities organized around a system of common property. His position challenges the "tragedy-of-the-commons" scenario (Hardin 1968), in which common property inevitably succumbs to overuse and abandonment. He further illustrates the hierarchical potential of water and land-use management in small-scale, local water systems, even those functionally based on less traditional irrigation technology. As argued earlier, the idea of a consensual authority organizing local, decentralized, or acephalous water systems seems ever less tenable. In fact, the very existence of extensive, decentralized, local water systems is questionable, except during periods of socioeconomic collapse.

Park uses a variation on Fredrick Barth's (1973; cf. Barth 1961) model, initially incorporated by R. McC. Adams (1978). Park explains the "sloughing off" of excess agricultural populations during nearly random periods of land and water scarcity and the addition of labor to the common property pool at times of adequate or even abundant farmland and water. Barth based his model on the priorities of pastoralists, the forced acceptance of a sedentary agrarian lifestyle by poor pastoralists during times of stress and their reentry to nomadism in periods of pastoral abundance. Park's model, unlike Barth's, emphasizes the role of common property ownership of land and the hierarchy of control based on land tenure longevity: the deeper one's ancestral roots on the landscape, the stronger one's claim to the best available farmland. Park's argument emphasizes the primacy of the land and water organizational plane and how the availability of water and the allocation of land significantly influence both kinship and political organization. Too, as Edmund Leach (1961:234) noted for Pul Eliya, Ceylon, "the recognition of kinship is constantly being adjusted to fit the ground," an idea reenforced by Park's data (also see Gray 1963).[3]

> From an ecological perspective, reallocating land from common property on an annual basis is an adaptation to risk. An individual will, each year, receive a proportion of the common lands suitable for agriculture rather than run the risk of owning a specific parcel that is simply not suitable for cultivation in a given year. At the group level, reallocation also maintains the hierarchical status quo. Common ownership of a portfolio of lands distributed around the floodplain carries this process one step further by increasing the likelihood that the corporate group has suitable lands despite the unpredictable flood. In the Senegal River Basin, stratification involves both ownership of land and a system of tithes and obligations. (Park 1992:95)

Park's model of chaotic riverine flooding also applies to the lower Nile. He suggests that social stratification and, ultimately, early states arose under these conditions.

Park's approach employs Ester Boserup's (1965) theory that populations invest in the land that provides the highest return for the labor expended, a position grounded in the earlier cultural ecology school. When there is no scarcity of land or related resources, no incentive exists to intensify the agricultural base or modify the landscape. If the population increases, however, land scarcity eventually occurs, and technological adjustments may be developed to enhance productivity. Nevertheless, productivity per unit of labor on the landscape may drop. In Park's use of Boserup's model, adjusting to obtain greater productivity means developing a hierarchical organization dependent on a surplus labor pool, not a technological advance leading to intensification. The less rigid, shallow hierarchy Park describes is readily identifiable as heterarchical organization (see chapter 2). Here, the judicious deployment of a structurally flexible, somewhat limited labor pool enables the most expeditious use of an unpredictable water source.

The Process of Economic Change

Chapter 2 introduces the three economic logics—processes—modeling this book. At this juncture, however, I present a more explicit ethnographic focus to show the applicability of these logics for contemporary water and land use cross-culturally and to place the material presented in this chapter in an intellectually holistic context.

Asia and Europe

Francesca Bray's *The Rice Economies* (1986) implicitly suggests that the model proposed by Boserup (and, by extension, Park) may be simplistic. Bray's approach permits a more flexible and globally meaningful interpretation of landscape modification and water systems. She illustrates the complexity of adaptations made by societies with respect to land, water, and labor. Population remains a key variable but does not determine human adaptations to the same extent as in Boserup's and Park's models.

Bray discusses the social relations embedded in agricultural economies, based on two orientations. Her concept of "mechanical" economies (my technotasking logic) draws upon a European model in which labor productivity is increased by substituting animals and, later, machines for humans. When human labor is scarce or more attractive, nonfarming employment is abundant, and technology is advanced to increase the agrarian labor force's productivity. Economies of scale evolve from this strategy. However, when land is scarce and labor abundant, productivity is increased by enhancing the land base and intensifying the exploitation of resources at a much reduced spatial scale. This mode of production emphasizes the household, the immediate community, and their association with the small, intensively cropped plot. Bray presents this scenario as an Asian model, characterizing it as "skill-oriented" (my labortasking logic) and dependent on sophisticated local agricultural knowledge. The household or village makes the decisions about land, and the intensity of the tasks performed necessitates the exchange of skilled agricultural labor among households. Bray's dichotomy of mechanical and skill-oriented economies emphasizes the unique requirements of Southeast Asian wet rice compared with those of wheat, barley, oats, and rye in early Middle East and subsequent European agricultural adaptations (Harlan 1992). Bray (1986:48) admonishes us "to remember that in wet-rice agriculture a simple tool such as the hand-hoe may well represent a more advanced technical stage than the more complex animal-drawn plough and harrow."

The idea that a skill-oriented (here, labortasking) economy based on abundant labor and limited land and water resources leads predictably to agricultural involution (cf. Geertz 1963) simply reflects a European bias, according to Bray. She contends that the same Eurocentric prejudice underlying the Asiatic Mode of Production theory has affected our interpretations of the forces and relations of production in non-European societies that harvest the landscape by drawing upon limited capital, wet-rice technologies, and a different labor organization (see figure 3.6).

> A significant difference between the technical development of Western grain-farming and Asian rice cultivation, which has important implications for socio-economic change, is that while wet-rice agriculture has enormous potential for increasing land productivity, most improvements are either scale-neutral and relatively cheap, or else they involve increasing not capital inputs but inputs of manual labour. It has often been assumed that this implies a corresponding reduction in the productivity of labour, but this is not necessarily true. Where a transition from broadcast sowing to transplanting, or from single- to double-cropping is made, the increases in yield will certainly outstrip concomitant rises in labour inputs. The additional labour requirements are spread out over the year, and for most tasks household labour suffices to run a wet-rice smallholding. (Bray 1986:5)

The important point is that an increasing population does not necessarily lead to overexploitation of landscape or the labor force. That can occur, though, if a labor-tasking mode of production is employed indefinitely. Regardless of the mode of production, it may occur if population rises higher than the social relations parameters can tolerate, that is, if the accommodating social structure destructs because of an inability to employ or direct the labor force. Nevertheless, simple population pressure interpretations of economic forces and relations of production are just that, simple (cf. Cohen 1977).

Bray's presentation emphasizes the fundamental adaptive role of culture. "Often organisational improvements or a more careful carrying out of operations can make important contributions to increasing output without requiring any increase in capital outlay at all" (Bray 1986:115). The manner in which a landscape is utilized and water is manipulated forms a "package" of routine behavior and accepted relationships. Bray implies that readjustment to significant change in the economic order and lasting transformations to the landscape may be more difficult for what I call a *labortasking* economy than for a *technotasking* economy (see chapter 2). In the labortasking rice economies of Asia, for instance, the highly focused transformation of land and water sources

> ...requires years of hard work, in return for decades if not centuries of stable yields. It is not surprising, then, that rice-farmers often prefer to work existing fields more intensively rather than opening up of new fields which, at least for the first few years, will produce less than long-established ones.... Perhaps "build" is a more appropriate term than "open up," when one con-

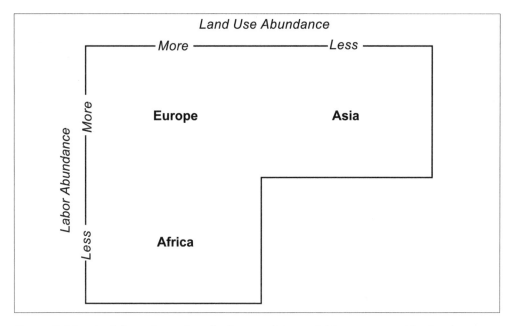

Figure 3.6 Land-to-labor relationships for Europe, Asia, and Africa, prepared by Sarah Stoutamire.

siders the engineering skills which are often required. Rice-fields come in an astonishing and ingenious variety, from dizzying flights of terraces perched high up on mountainsides, to dyked fields reclaimed from marshes or the shores of the sea. (Bray 1986:29)

In summary, Bray's book shows that the rate of culture change is a function of a society's economic underpinnings and its organizational decision-making strategies. No single principle guides all the rates of change in cultures. Rather, an adaptational continuum stretches from an accelerated to a slower, more measured rate (refer to figure 2.1).

Africa

All continents display variability in economic adaptation, even where one type of orientation has predominated over time. In much of Africa, a variety of multitasking economic adjustments are evident, as outlined in chapter 2. Like Europe and Asia, Africa shows considerable variation in land and water use, as well as in labor organization. Nevertheless, Africanists indicate that underpopulation in many regions has been a chronic problem for land-use development since the inception of settled life and that it has constrained the types of economic orientation manifest there. Paul Richards (1983) explains the multifaceted nature of the demographic situation in Africa, arguing that both political agendas (precolonial and postcolonial) and biological concerns (human diseases and plant and animal pests) have affected the availability of labor. After identifying the significance of Africa's limited labor pool when compared with Europe's or, more dramatically, with Asia's, Richards assesses the complexity of ecological and economic adaptations made in Africa, given the environmental constraints from region to region (Isaac 1998). Like Bray, he (1983:6) suggests that Boserup's model may be Eurocentric.

> Underpopulation has been Africa's lot.... According to arguments of Boserup and followers, lack of population pressure is held to account for technological backwardness, including limited capacity to control tropical disease. This vicious circle—disease/underpopulation/low level of technological develop-ment/disease—has remained unbroken until recent times. (Richards 1983:14)

Richards also indicates, though, that much of this "backwardness" is a consequence of the colonial embrace. Exploitation, dislocation, and externally reintroduced and spread diseases culminated in severe underpopulation in many areas.

Nevertheless, underpopulation is a relative concept, and Richards convincingly argues that the landscape and the domesticates utilized were in a loose balance with the human population in some regions of Africa, perhaps in much of the continent, before European colonialism. In discussing the geographic and climatic intermediate zone—a set of challenging agricultural environments south of the Sahara—Richards (1983:25) states that

> A long and varied agricultural season allows much scope for "riding with the system." Highly diversified, and therefore risk-spreading, sets of manage-ment strategies which copy rather than override a number of the natural ecosystem's key characteristics are possible. This might help explain the rela-tive lack of gross capital-intensive modifications of the natural environment for agricultural purposes in this zone.

Richards characterizes traditional rural Africa as having economies based on small-scale producers dependent in part on nonkin labor groups. He views African labor groups as highly adaptive to the constraints of climate, disease, and soil limitations. He suggests that dense or highly compacted populations may seldom have existed among agriculturalists in Africa (cf. Linares 1981). Although using a different termi-nology, Richards states that a version of the labortasking economic orientation may have driven agrarian adaptations in Africa, characterized by highly evolved, indigenous knowledge about soil conservation and intercropping. "Intercropping, then, is one of the great glories of African science. It's to African agriculture as polyrhythmic drum-ming is to African music and carving to African art" (Richards 1983:27). As in the Asian example, Richards's African labortasking economies are not necessarily enhanced by laborsaving technologies, because labor organization drives these economies.

> African peasant farmers are right, then, to concentrate a great deal of their attention on management of soil physical properties. As argued previously,

mulching, ridging, heaping, and the like are as plausible evidence of intensification as the use of manure. Were such criteria to be used, many systems of
shifting cultivation would have to be considered intensive. Conversely, in
some circumstances, it might be anticipated that the introduction of the
plough and wheeled machinery, two among Goody's (1976) favored indices of
agricultural progress, would lead to little apart from intensification of the rate
of erosion. (Richards 1983:26)

The African case offers a different kind of labortasking orientation to the landscape, however, than does the Asian case. Compared with Asia, Africa is severely
labor-deficient, but small-scale African labor groups coordinate intensively to avoid
scheduling bottlenecks, as in Bray's skill-oriented adaptation (my labortasking economy). The principal difference rests in the significant degree to which the landscape
has been altered in the Asian rice economies, compared with agrarian Africa.
Although many kinds of land and water adaptations have been made, Park's (1992;
Park, ed. 1993) model of flood recession farming in the Senegal River basin may best
characterize the farmers' creative, risk-minimizing strategies on much of the African
landscape. Under the conditions outlined, many portions of Africa operate within a
multitasking economic logic, as outlined in chapter 2 (refer to figure. 2.1). The
evolved risk-reduction adaptations argued by Park are a developed and formalized
version of multitasking, an independent economic orientation based on low population densities and the availability of land and water resources (refer to figure 3.6).

Although complicated water management schemes—formal irrigation works and
polder construction to reclaim wetlands by means of dikes and weirs—have existed in
West Africa for some time (Linares 1981), water systems in much of Africa attempt to
utilize the natural flow of water with as little alteration of the topography as possible.[4]

> These are, in effect, natural irrigation systems. There is no need to invest in
> complex water control schemes if the annual hydrological cycle will do the
> work unaided. The trick in the African case is to understand the complexities
> of this cycle, and to have a relevant range of crops and institutions for labor
> mobilization capable of responding to these opportunities. (Richards 1983:29)

Arguing from a specific African case study (Diola of Senegal), in contrast to
Richards's more global approach, Linares (1981) examines the social and ideological
differences between intensive wet-rice, tidal-swamp dwellers and more extensive
farmers of the inland valley:

> It may well be that traditional swamp cultivation everywhere promotes
> highly individuated rights in productive land, contributing to the organiza-
> tion of the family into small nuclear units of production and reproduction.
> Where the unit of production is the conjugal family, it is free to recruit extra

labour on an impermanent and intermittent basis, and also to engage in all sorts of land transactions [labortasking]. The reverse hypothesis [is] that shifting rice cultivation is associated with larger households, more formally recruited work groups and, for historical reasons, with more hierarchical and Islamised societies [multitasking].... (Linares 1981:578–79)

Netting (1993:58–101) reached the same conclusion more globally. In addition to opening Park's stratification thesis to another perspective, Linares has succinctly captured the dichotomy between Asian rice economies and the more typical African extensive use of water and land. Her work reveals the variability that occurs across any landform as vast as a continent and demonstrates that even within a single river basin, labortasking and multitasking orientations may occur simultaneously.

For Linares, the small-scale household practicing a domestic mode of production (Sahlins 1972) undergirds the population of the more densely occupied tidal swamps of Senegal—the same forces at work in the Southeast Asian rice paddy systems. These populations maintain degrees of autonomy at the household and village levels but skillfully and energetically transform the environment (labortasking). Neighboring populations manipulate kinship and land-use strategies differently. The larger work groups associated with larger, Islamised households (sometimes drawing on corvée laborers, probably former slaves) are more dispersed and show a dependency on shifting millet or rice cultivation reflective of a less landscape-altering adaptation (multitasking). This latter adaptation is precisely the organizational track taken along the Senegal River basin, as outlined by Park (1992; Park, ed. 1993).

Rates, Process, and Economy

From the preceding examination of current thinking about landscape alteration and water management, it is apparent that Wittfogel's (1957) hydraulic hypothesis continues to wield influence. Researchers castigate the theory, but few have truly escaped its theoretical reach. The reason for this is not that Wittfogel presented a highly convincing argument about the origins of the state or definitions of power but that his theory concerned the role played by a fundamental resource that is everywhere potentially controllable and certainly capable of being manipulated. Wittfogel's theory continues to elicit extremely strong reactions in the social sciences, with two recent, empirically based case studies taking diametrically opposed positions (Kirch 1994, Sidky 1996). In these examples and others, the integration of water management into a meaningful social science framework has been inhibited, in part, by its overwhelming focus on ecological relationships. Clearly, the social relations underpinnings of the economy direct the course of decision making. At this level of analysis, the cooperative and conflictual dynamics of water management affect culture change and stability. The ecological laws of water systems do not cause centralization or decentralization. Rather, the organizational planes within a culture regulate the rates of cultural change and influence the processes or overall organizational outlooks of a group.

Engineering the Landscape for Water Management

The Zuni claim to have here practiced a curious method of water storage. They say that whenever there was snow on the ground the villagers would turn out in force and roll up huge snowballs, which were finally collected into these basins; the gradually melting snow furnished a considerable quantity of water.

—Victor Mindeleff (1891:91)

This chapter and the next two assess the physical and social aspects of water management. Here, the focus is on the functions of the specific facilities ancient humans have built on the landscape to direct and control water systems. Chapters 5 and 6 examine the immediate material (economic and political) ends to which water is directed and its varied social and symbolic uses.

Functionally, *water management* is society's interruption and redirection of the natural movement or collection of water. Dams, reservoirs, canals, and wells enable us to evaluate a group's land-use practices, even without the aid of living consultants or historic texts. The scale and complexity of these features provide archaeologists, ethnographers, and geographers a powerful database for examining economic behavior.

Characteristics of Water

Water has several unusual properties, but two are particularly important for any discussion of settled community life: fluidity and gravity flow. *Fluidity* permits ease of transport. Water does not usually require beasts of burden or wheeled vehicles for its immediate relocation. Thus, its cost to the consumer is intrinsically low. *Gravity flow* denotes water's characteristic movement from higher to lower elevations via a path of least resistance. Gravity flow is both the cardinal principle in manipulating water within a canal scheme and the primary obstacle to controlling water in rugged areas.

In turn, fluidity and gravity flow are responsible for two characteristics imposed by humans. The first involves the many mechanical problems associated with lifting water vertically. Its bulk and unwieldiness require sealed containers for this movement. Before the widespread use of hand pumps, siphon tubes, and the Archimedes'

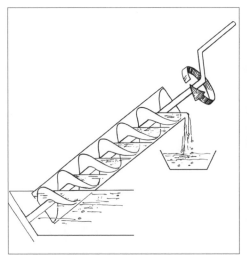

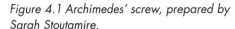

Figure 4.1 Archimedes' screw, prepared by   Figure 4.2 Shaduf, reprinted from
Sarah Stoutamire.   A.B. Edwards (1888).

screw (see figure 4.1), standing water was pulled upward by hand or by using a simple manual device called a *shaduf,* or well sweep (see figure 4.2). Used widely today in the Middle East, as it was in pharaonic Egypt, the shaduf consists of a counterweighted lever or pole with a dipping line and bucket attached at the far end. In China, one of the earliest water-raising inventions, known by the second century AD, was the dragon-backbone machine (see figure 4.3), a square-pallet chain pump powered by human or animal labor (Bray 1986:54; Needham and Ling 1965:581–82). Another such invention is the *noria,* or current wheel, which originated in Persia before 300 BC (Glick 1970; cf. Hsu 1980:275) (see figure 4.4). Frequently animal-powered, this device lifts water with buckets attached to a rotating wheel. Early states used simple lifting techniques that were labor-costly.

The second human-imposed characteristic made possible by fluidity and gravity flow is the ease of diverting or abruptly cutting off water to a consumer. Diversion dams and conventional reservoirs with sluice gates enable individuals or small groups of users to treat water as a commodity. Water allocation frequently involves localizing distribution points through sluice gates and related features. Under these conditions, water becomes a single-source medium, with the initial investment in controlling it particularly apparent in irrigation schemes.

Climate and Geomorphology

Water use is partially conditioned by the natural environment. Although most environments can be transformed into agricultural settings, given sufficient technological and labor investments in water manipulation (Ferdon 1959), regional differences in climate and geomorphology dictate the amount of work necessary. Tolerable climatic conditions for agriculture are based on precipitation rates and temperature, which translate to evaporation and transpiration rates. By scheduling around season-

Figure 4.3 Dragon-backbone machine, reprinted by permission of Cambridge University Press from C.A. Ronan and J. Needham (1995).

Figure 4.4 Noria (saqiya), reprinted by permission of Cambridge University Press from C.A. Ronan and J. Needham (1995).

al fluctuations in these variables, water can be manipulated to an agricultural end within an otherwise inhospitable natural setting. Geomorphology is more difficult to modify, and it poses the principal obstacle to water control in a climatically acceptable environment. The primary geomorphological variables conditioning water management are topography and soil permeability (the latter being measured by rates of seepage). Complicated geomorphological structure is sometimes the impetus for hydraulic innovation when population demands reach a critical threshold.

A dichotomy exists in the natural environments within which early complex societies emerged. Complicated experiments in water management occurred in both arid regions (with rugged and low reliefs) and humid regions (with gentle, topographic contours).

Arid Regions

In the New World, the most celebrated early centers of complicated, regionwide water management appeared in coastal Peru (and later in highland Peru, Ecuador, and northern Bolivia), highland Mexico, and the U.S. Southwest (Donkin 1979; Price

1971). In the first two areas, the topography is precipitous, with relatively small, less consequential natural drainages, especially compared with Old World civilization areas. In Peru and to a degree in highland Mexico, water management systems utilized the topography as an advantage in tapping water moving rapidly over steep gradients. Although terraces, dams, aqueducts, and canal networks functioned within valley-limited drainages, their construction and maintenance were sometimes performed by groups knit together by empires.

The seats of primary state development in the Old World were Egypt (Butzer 1976), Iraq (R. McC. Adams 1981), southern Pakistan and western India (Allchin and Allchin 1982), and west-central China (Hsu 1980). A major river meandered through each of these arid territories, sometimes reaching unanticipated flood levels. These rivers were not only permanent sources but also abundant stores of water. The topographic relief associated with them in proximity to the early states is gentle, particularly compared with New World examples. In most Old World cases, this condition allowed extensive canalization, restricted only by the breadth of the floodplains in these old, slow-moving drainages. Although elaborate diversion dams were clearly perfected, conventional dams with reservoirs or sophisticated terracing systems (characteristic of the Peruvians) were little deployed (except in the Tigris-Euphrates drainage). These great rivers, in part, charted the course of civilization.

Humid Regions

The Maya Lowlands is the principal humid region in the New World where complex water systems evolved. In a zone of limited relief and abundant though sharply seasonal rainfall, the Maya pioneered intensive swamp agriculture and terrace systems (R. E. W. Adams 1980; R. E. W. Adams et al. 1981; Dunning and Beach 1994; Healy et al. 1984; Pohl, ed. 1990; Scarborough 1983a, 1983b, 1993a, 1994a; Turner 1974; Turner and Harrison 1981). Well-designed dams for the deliberate entrapment of water within naturally low-lying areas permitted the drainage of excess water during the wet season and its judicious distribution during the dry. Secondary societies adopting potentially similar techniques may have included the Woodland and Mississippian chiefdoms of the southeastern United States (Sears 1982; cf. B. Smith 1978) and the chiefdoms of northern South America (Denevan 1970, 2001; Roosevelt 1991; Steward and Faron 1959). Unlike the Maya, generally, these secondary developments took advantage of major riverine settings.

In the Old World, early tropical, intensive water systems are poorly reported from sub-Saharan Africa, although West Africa may yield some evidence of intensive water manipulation (McIntosh and McIntosh 1983; Wolf 1982) (see chapter 3). The best evidence comes from South and Southeast Asia, principally from Sri Lanka, Cambodia, and Java. Here, rainfall rates compare with those recorded in the Maya Lowlands, and the topography is similar. A clear comparative study by Bronson (1978) examines the ecological underpinnings of these early states in both Southeast Asia and the Maya Lowlands. He shows that none commanded a major riverine arterial.

Landscape Alterations

Four principal landscaping features account for most water manipulations in early states: wells, reservoirs, dams, and canals. All four entail major earthmoving investments demanding significant labor, exact timing, and precision, in both construction and maintenance. Many hydraulic installations identified for archaic states are actually composites of these four features, adding to the range of ancient variability for archaic states and water management facilities.

Wells

Wells are vertical shafts excavated to a buried water table. Frequently, an aquifer is tapped and made available by means of a well. Numerous variations exist, depending on the local geomorphology and technology. Simple wells exist in nearly every society and require limited resources to construct where the water table is elevated. With its fluctuations, they can be enlarged and deepened. In some settings, such as the Valley of Oaxaca in Mexico, shallow wells have provided abundant sources of water for agriculture since the prehispanic past. Today, *pot irrigation* entails watering individual plants from gallon jars close to the many wells there (Flannery et al. 1967). Also, shallow wells at the eighth-century Maya community of Quiriguá, Guatemala, were found to be lined ceramic shafts (Ashmore 1984), presumably to prevent the walls from collapsing.

More elaborate wells consist of large subterranean reservoirs permitting foot access to the source. A complex example of a *walk-in well* distant from the heartland of a civilization appears in thirteenth-century Casas Grandes, northern Mexico. DiPeso et al. (1974) indicate that a stepped entranceway descended 12 vertical meters from the surface before reaching water (see plate 4.5). On the Yucatán Peninsula, walk-in wells were enormous. Many deep, subterranean water channels and the naturally forming solution cavities *(cenotes)* that contacted them formed sizable caverns (Mercer 1975). The soft limestone was frequently carved to accommodate foot access to the underground source. Near Bolonchan, one well descends more than 100 m from the surface (Matheny 1978; Stephens 1843:96) (see figure 4.6).

In the Old World, walk-in wells were excavated during the Late Bronze Age (1500–1150 BC) at Mycenae, Tiryns, and Athens (T. Smith 1995). The carved rock tunnel at Mycenae descended 18 m by way of three flights of stairs and three landings (Mylonas 1966; Wace 1949) (see figure 4.7). The Athenian example extended 40 m below the surface along eight flights and numerous landings (Broneer 1939). The underground passageway associated with the Acropolis at Athens was less deliberately constructed than the Mycenae and Tiryns examples. This is partly because the natural karstic jointing (rock fracturing) and channel formations made extensive excavation less necessary.

By far, the most complex well systems are the *karez*, also *qanat* or *foggara* (see figure 4.8, and plates 4.9 and 4.10), reported chiefly in the Middle East but also

Figure 4.6 Bolonchan cenote, reprinted
from J. L. Stephens (1843).

Figure 4.7 Mycenae well, reprinted courtesy of
W. Rowbotham (2003).

along a narrow belt from south-central China to Mediterranean North Africa and
Spain (Cressey 1958). The *karez* is a horizontal well consisting of an underground
tunnel allowing the channeling of water from an elevated aquifer to a low-lying oasis.
Such aquifers are usually at the juncture of elevated bedrock associated with an
exposed mountain range and overlying alluvium and/or colluvial deposits. The
amount of water available to the *karez* system depends on the amount of precipitation
and the size of the rainfall catchment recharging the aquifer. A series of vertical shafts,
each separated by 30–50 m, provides access to the hand-dug tunnels. Shaft depth
depends on the depth of the *mother well* (the initial and most elevated shaft) and on
the surface contours under which the tunnel courses. The deepest mother well reported (at Gonabad in Iran, near the Afghan border) descends some 300 m below the surface, but most are excavated in the range of 20 to 100 m (English 1966). The tunnel's
gradient cannot be significantly altered, and for a short *karez*, the maximum slope can
be little greater than 1:1,500. Too steep a gradient may result in erosion that impedes
or blocks water flow. If the gradient is not steep enough, water will issue too far from
the village and fields it is intended to reach, accelerating evaporation and seepage loss.

The Persians probably spread the *karez* system (the word *karez* being Persian),
although Middle Eastern countries where the technique is still practiced use the
Arabic word *qanat*. The oldest evidence for a *qanat* system is a cuneiform clay tablet
of Sargon II of Assyria (722–705 BC) describing a *qanat* used for irrigation during an
invasion of Urartu, Armenia (Garbrect 1987:8). Sixth-century BC Persepolis also had

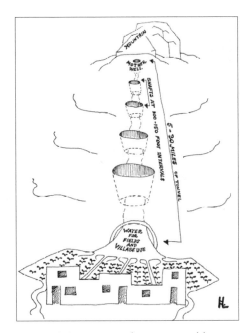

Figure 4.8 Karez in plan, reprinted by permission of the American Geographical Society from V.L. Scarborough (1988).

a clearly defined *karez* system (Cressey 1958; English 1966). In Jerusalem, subterranean springs associated with karstic jointing were tapped by at least 700 BC through excavation access to the springs of Gihon (Gill 1991) (see figure 4.11). Also at this time, Greek tunneling is indicated at Samos (Crouch 1993: fig. 4.1) (see figure 4.12), although karstic jointing and cavity formation associated with natural underground water movement may have strongly influenced the course of the passageways. The Moors introduced *karez* construction to Spain, and Spanish conquest appears to account for its later presence in Mexico, Peru, and northern Chile (Woodbury and Neely 1972; Barnes and Fleming 1991). However, recent findings suggest an independent and earlier aboriginal origin (Schreiber and Lancho Rojas 1995). In South America, the *karez* system is referred to as the *puquios*.

Springs and artesian wells occur naturally and involve little if any excavation. A surface catchment reservoir is sometimes constructed to permit the ready use of the discharge, and in arid regions, canal systems can issue from these more permanent water sources. Prehispanic spring and canal systems are found at Casas Grandes in northern Mexico (DiPeso et al. 1974), Creeping Dunes Spring in Colorado (Sharrock et al. 1961), and the Hopi Mesas in Arizona (Hack 1942). At Hierva de Agua in Oaxaca, Mexico, channeling of springwater dates to the very origins of canal construction in the New World, c. 300 BC (Flannery et al. 1967). In the Tehuacán Valley of central Mexico, Woodbury and Neely (1972; Neely 2001a) report the presence of *fossilized canals*—ancient canal beds encrusted with travertine, preserved and frequently pedestaled above the eroded surrounds—that once carried mineralized springwaters, dating as early as 200 BC (Doolittle 1990a:60).

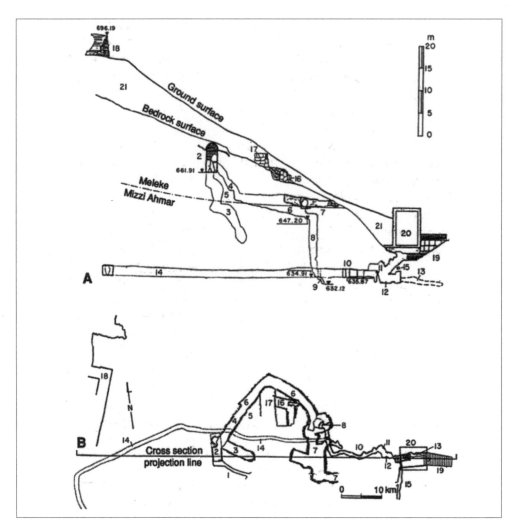

Figure 4.11 Plan of Jerusalem's system, copyright 1991, reprinted by permission of the American Association for the Advancement of Science from D. Gill, Science 254:1468.

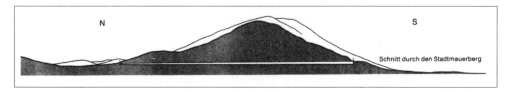

Figure 4.12 Tunnel at Samos, reprinted by permission of the Deutsches Archäologisches Institut, Berlin, from H.J. Kienast (1995).

The excavated field depressions, or sunken gardens, of Peru function like shallow wells (Parsons and Psuty 1975; R. Smith 1979; West 1979). Still employed today, these ancient fields were dug down nearly to the water table. Directly dependent on neither precipitation nor irrigation (although the seepage from widespread irrigation possibly raised the water table), these fields took advantage of an abundant water source to help feed such great cities as Chan Chan near the north coast (c. AD 1000).

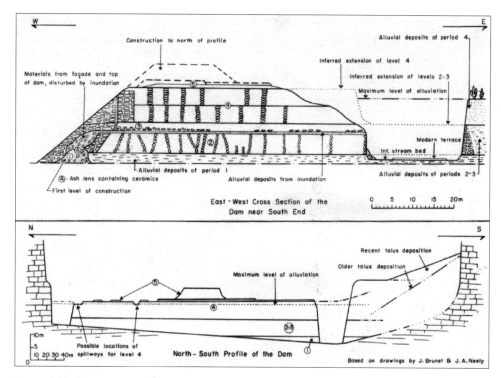

Figure 4.13 Cross section of Purron Dam, copyright 1972, reprinted by permission of the Robert S. Peabody Museum of Archaeology, Phillips Academy, Andover, Massachusetts, from R.B. Woodbury and J.A. Neely (1972).

Moseley (1983) has shown that tectonic activity, perhaps coupled with the overexploitation of the sunken field water table, forced the downward excavation of the garden plots over time. Near the core of the community, fields descended 5 to 7 m before they were abandoned (Parsons 1968). A conceptually comparable system of lesser scale and unknown origins, pit cultivation, occurs on certain Pacific atolls (Kirch 1994:5).

Reservoirs and Dams

Reservoirs are open catchment basins that hold intermittent surface runoff or water from formal canals or less formal channels. *Storage dams* are frequently associated with reservoirs; *diversion dams* (or *weirs*) are employed by canal users. Dams built at the egresses of reservoirs can slow the velocity of water coursing through them, especially during flash flooding. At other times, they can serve to raise reservoir water levels by slowing outflow into issuing canals. Generally, reservoirs and storage dams are constructed in regions without dependable riverine water sources. These features have an ancient past, and many small, deliberately constructed ponding areas have probably gone unnoticed as a consequence of rapid sedimentation following their disuse.

New World

In the New World, the earliest water system is thought to be that associated with the Olmec site of Teopantecuantlan in northern Guerrero, Mexico (Doolittle 1990a:

20–22). There, a small reservoir was formed behind a stone *gravity dam*—one that resists perpendicular flow because of its mass rather than its shape. A slab rock-lined canal segment issued from it. This small-scale system dates to 1200 BC and is temporally unique in its sophistication.

Dating to the Middle Formative period (700 BC) is the dam and reservoir system in central Mexico's Tehuacán Valley (Woodbury and Neely 1972). Although diminutive at this early moment, by the Early Classic period (AD 100–300) the Purron Dam—a gravity dam—was 100 m wide by 400 m in length and reached a height of 18 m (see figure 4.13). One of the most impressive hydraulic works in highland Mexico, the Purron Dam was located in an area relatively peripheral to centralized polities. It appears to have fallen into disrepair by AD 200–300, ironically, a period of accelerated political growth in the nearby Basin of Mexico. In addition to the major storage dam, the Purron reservoir contained a substantial *cofferdam*—a segregated, dammed reservoir nested within, but at the margins of, the main reservoir body. The cofferdam was probably constructed to entrap sediment (removing it before it could enter the main body of the reservoir) and to divert water during periods of reservoir dredging or dam maintenance. The precise function of the Purron Dam remains an enigma because there is no evidence of canalization issuing from it.

Perhaps the best studied, early storage reservoir associated with a canal system is located in the Xoxocotlán Piedmont immediately below Monte Albán, Oaxaca (O'Brien et al. 1982). Doolittle (1990a:30) indicates that the 10-m-high by 80-m-long dam "was V-shaped in plan with the apex pointing upstream." This made it an *arch dam*—one dependent on its curvature rather than its weight for strength (see figure 4.14). The dam's floodgate directed water into the 2-km-long main canal, a portion of which was carved into bedrock. The entire system dates to the Late Formative period, sometime between 550 and 150 BC, and was designed to irrigate as many as 50 ha.

Near Mitla, Oaxaca, the spring-fed irrigation system at Hierva el Agua left an intricately latticed network of basins and canals "fossilized" in travertine and covering an artificially terraced area of 50 ha (Neely et al. 1990) (see figure 4.15). The system is dated to c. 300 BC, coeval with the nearby reservoir-based irrigation system at Xoxocotlán. Some have argued that salt production was the primary aim of the Hierva el Agua system (Hewitt et al. 1987), but this idea seems less convincing today. Kirby (1973) and others indicate that water was hand-lifted from small circular pits *(pocitos)* dug into the courses of small branch canals flanking the outside margins of the terraced plots (see figure 4.16). These depressions would pond water and permit the hand watering of plants, a form of pot irrigation more commonly associated with shallow wells or an elevated aquifer closer to the valley bottom (Flannery et al. 1967).

Several reservoirs have also been identified in the Greater Southwest of the United States and in northern Mexico (Bayman and Fish 1992; Crown 1987a; Scarborough 1988a) (see figure 4.17). At Casas Grandes, northern Mexico, an elaborate reservoir system has been reported (DiPeso et al. 1974). Two centrally located reservoirs were identified, along with a large water-retention basin and a stone-lined settling tank

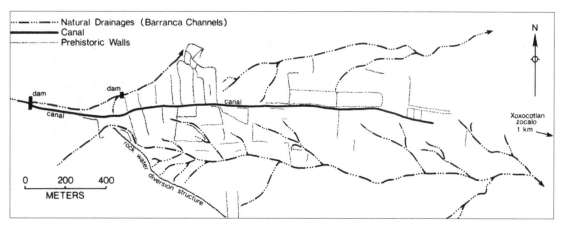

Figure 4.14 Xoxcotlán Piedmont Dam, reprinted by permission of the University of Texas Press from W.E. Doolittle (1990).

Figure 4.15 Hierva el Agua system, reprinted by permission of Museum of Anthropology Publications, University of Michigan, from J.A. Neely, S.C. Caran, and B.M. Winsborough (1990).

Figure 4.16 Pacitos of Hierva el Agua, reprinted by permission of Museum of Anthropology Publications, University of Michigan, from J.A. Neely, S.C. Caran, and B.M. Winsborough (1990).

(see figure 4.18). In the adjacent Hohokam area, reservoirs were canal-fed and sometimes dug to a depth of more than 4 m (Raab 1975). Farther north, at Mummy Lake, Mesa Verde is a masonry-lined reservoir with a silting tank (Rohn 1963) (see figure 4.19). In neither case is downstream canalization considered of principal importance. At Chaco Canyon during the Puebloan Period (AD 1020–1120), diversion dams at the base of side canyons directed seasonal runoff waters into *overflow reservoirs*—diminutive reservoirs that slowed the erosive effects of runoff while enabling subsequent water use—and into extensive gridded gardens. Water issuing from main canals, in turn, irrigated 400 ha of farmland and bordered gardens (Vivian 1990:309–10).

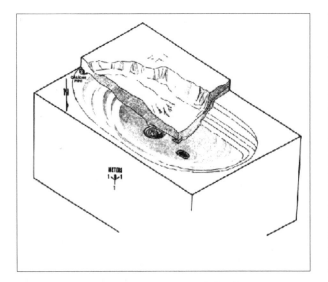

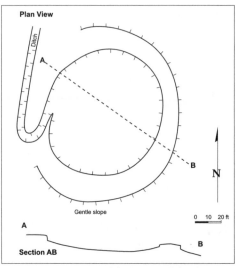

Figure 4.17 Hot Wells Reservoir, reprinted by permission of the Journal of Anthropological Research from V.L. Scarborough (1988).

Figure 4.19 Mummy Lake, prepared by Sarah Stoutamire after A.H. Rahn (1963), by permission of American Antiquity.

Reservoirs in the Maya area were of several varieties. The large, bell-shaped cisterns *(chultuns)* of the dry northern Yucatán Peninsula caught rainfall from a prepared platform surface (Brainerd 1958; McAnany 1990) (see figure 4.20)—in form and function like the cisterns described for the ancient Greek atria (see chapter 5). Also similar to the cisterns in Nabatea of the Negev Desert (Evenari et al. 1971), these containers had highly constricted orifices to curb evaporation. Open-surface reservoirs, in contrast, were the outcome of quarrying for monumental building, although natural drainage gradients were utilized. At the Late Preclassic community of Cerros, Belize (c. 200 BC–AD 150), the volume of construction fill used in the built structures compared to that removed from the extensively quarried canal and reservoir depressions. Through the manipulation of *sills*—horizontal blocks of stone extending into a tank or canal segment permitting access to the lower reaches of the water-holding basin—and dams, water was conserved in "basin canals" during the dry season, and the community's core area was drained during the wet season (Scarborough 1983a) (see figures 4.21 and 4.22). At the much larger, Late Preclassic site of Edzná, Campeche, the Maya used a system of linear canal reservoirs for potable water and transportation (Matheny 1976) (see figure 4.23). Elsewhere in the Maya Lowlands, large depressions *(aguadas)* were frequently modified from the naturally low-lying terrain (Matheny 1978). It is hypothesized that even the internally drained swamps *(bajos)* covering extensive tracts of the Maya area today were altered to establish predictable water levels for supporting raised-field agriculture (Harrison 1977).

At Classic period (AD 250–900) lowland Maya sites such as Tikal, La Milpa, and Kinal (Scarborough 1993a, 1994b; Scarborough and Gallopin 1991), runoff across the sculpted surface of a convex microwatershed permitted vastly greater control over

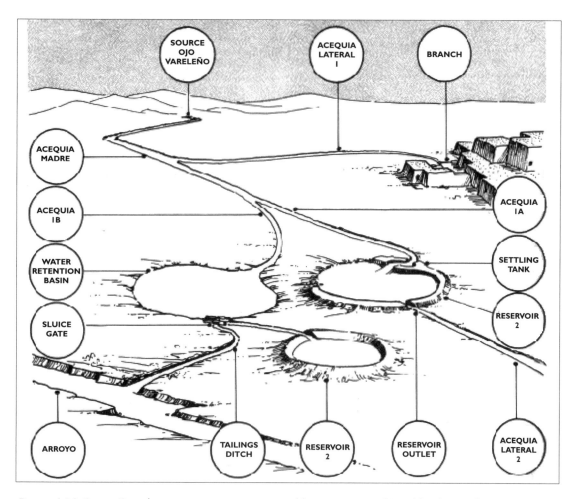

Figure 4.18 Casas Grandes reservoir system, reprinted by permission of Northland Press from C.C. Di Peso, J.B. Rinaldo, and G.J. Fenner (1974).

the resource than did the earlier lowland systems (see plate 4.24). The hillocks on which these sites rest, removed from permanent springs or streams, were heavily paved with plastered surfaces canted toward elevated reservoirs. The most elevated central precinct catchment at Tikal covered an area of 62 ha. Because the impervious plaza pavements and plastered monumental architecture limited seepage loss, this area alone could collect more than 900,000 m^3 of water (based on 1,500 mm of rainfall annually) (see figure 4.25). The runoff from this and adjacent catchment areas easily filled the associated reservoirs and natural depressions *(aguadas)* leading ultimately into the flanking swamps *(bajos)* (see plate 4.26).

The largest and most elevated reservoirs at these Classic Maya sites were associated with the central precinct, which occupied the gentle summit slopes of the hillocks. Collectively, the six central precinct reservoirs at Tikal contained 100,000–250,000 m^3 of water. The tiered character of its reservoir system allowed the controlled downhill release of water during the dry season. Causeways connected many portions of the

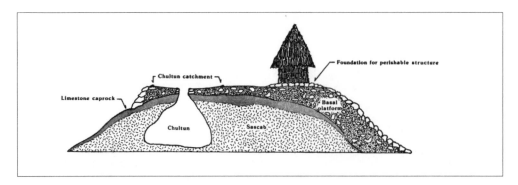

Figure 4.20 Chultun, reprinted by permission of the University of New Mexico Press from
P.A. McAnany (1990).

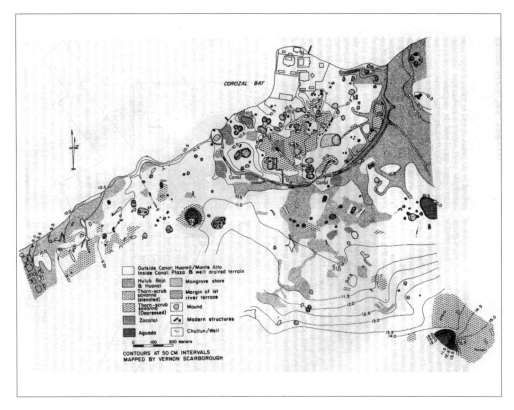

Figure 4.21 Cerros environment map, reprinted by permission of Southern Methodist
University Press from V.L. Scarborough (1991b).

site, but just as at Cerros perhaps 500 years earlier, these same features functioned to
retain water and define the reservoirs' outer margins. The causeways are believed to
have acted as dams (see figure 4.27).

In both the Maya area (Dahlin 1984; Matheny, ed. 1980) and the five-lakes region
of the Basin of Mexico (Armillas 1971; Palerm 1955; Sanders et al. 1979), causeways
maintained land transportation routes through swamp margins. Also functioning as

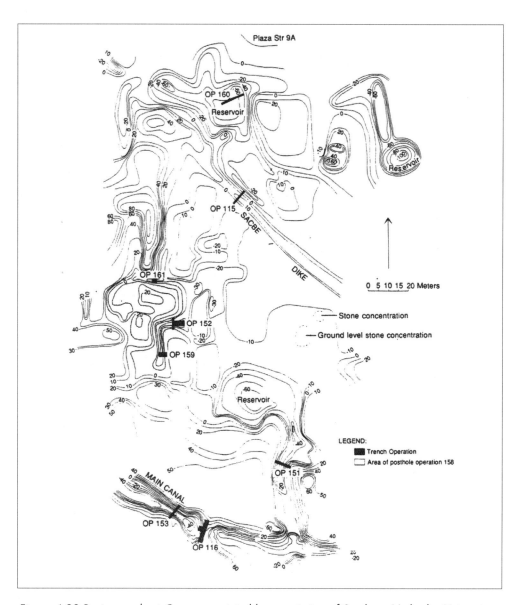

Figure 4.22 Basin canals at Cerros, reprinted by permission of Southern Methodist University Press from V.L. Scarborough (1991b).

dams, these features reduced the salinity of the water surrounding the island metropolis of Tenochtitlan during the Aztec period (AD 1150–1519). The bulk of Lake Texcoco received the highly mineralized runoff from the surrounding terrain, but the dike system enclosing Tenochtitlan allowed only sweet springwater to enter the city (see figure 4.28; see chapter 7).

The archaeological evidence for reservoirs in ancient Peru and Ecuador is sparse, but Fairley (2003) argues for "geologic water storage" in ancient Peru. He demonstrates that damlike walls were erected to contain deliberately deposited, porous, water-holding soils that would retain considerable amounts of water when saturated

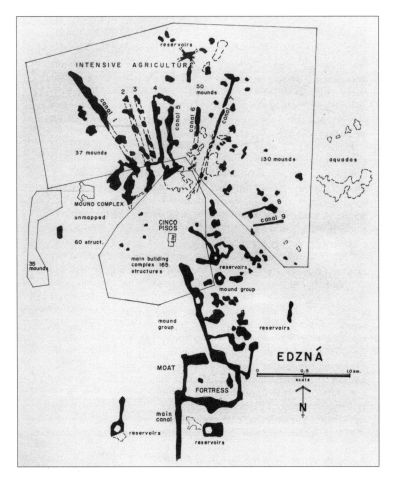

Figure 4.23 Edzná map, reprinted by permission of the University of New Mexico Press from R.T. Matheny (1978).

with infiltrating precipitation and runoff. Because the source was relatively filtered and protected from severe evaporation exposure, this water was cleaner and available for longer periods than was water in open-body reservoirs. These human-made aquifers were designed to seep through specially constructed wall openings.[1]

Old World

The earliest-reported Old World evidence for complex water management associated with a reservoir and canal system comes from the ancient city of Jawa, Jordan (Helms 1981:30, fig. 13, and 86, fig. 31) (see figures 4.29 and 4.30). By the late fourth millennium BC, the rapidly colonizing Jawaites built a planned water management system in highly precarious desert environs, requiring 15,000 tons of basalt in hydraulic construction fill alone. Ten reservoirs behind gravity dams built with downstream revetments (external stone buttresses), core walls for internal support, and stone waterfaces to reduce seepage were associated with sluice gates and spillways

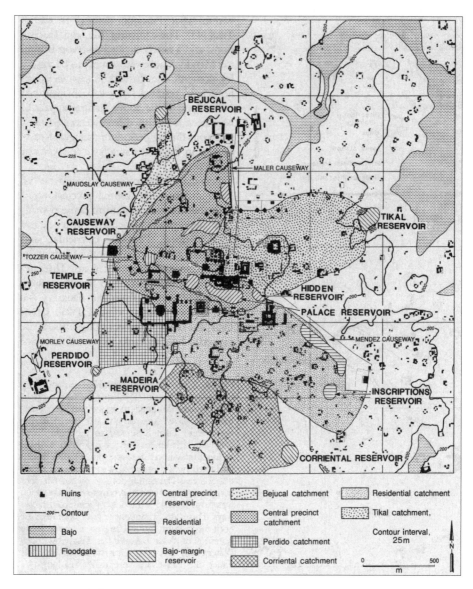

Figure 4.25 Tikal water catchment map, copyright 1991 and reprinted by permission of the American Association for the Advancement of Science from V.L. Scarborough and G.G. Gallopin, Science 251:659.

(ibid.:175, fig. 81) (see figure 4.31). One excavated section revealed a waterface apron indicative of seepage control and dam protection from wave action. This dam, which was 4–5 m high and 80 m long, served as a causeway in the same manner as in the ancient Maya and Aztec examples. Positioned in a small valley that received 2,000,000 m^3 of rapid floodwater annually, Jawa captured perhaps 70,000 m^3 of water during the final Phase 3 of occupation, sustaining 5,600 urbanites in an area with only 150 mm of annual rainfall (Helms 1981:210–11).

Helms (1981:167) indicates that Egypt's Sadd el-Kafara, or Dam of the Pagans, is

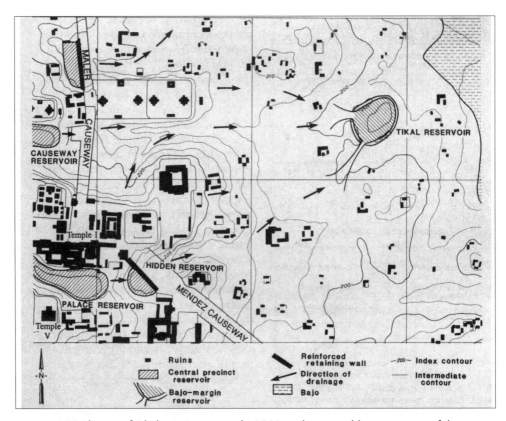

Figure 4.27 Blowup of Tikal system, copyright 1991 and reprinted by permission of the American Association for the Advancement of Science from V.L. Scarborough and G.G. Gallopin, Science 251:660.

the next-oldest known dam, dating to 2700 BC. Located near Helwan (south of Cairo), it consists of 60,000 tons of gravel and 40,000 tons of stone masonry laid across the wadi el-Garawi, a sizable reservoir. It was short-lived, however, and the breach in it is more than 40 m wide today (Shaw 1984:154). Helms (1981:167) mentions five other early dams for the Near East:

> However, the earliest record of a dam comes from a tablet of the time of Ur-Nammu, a ruler of the Third Dynasty of Ur (c. 2140–30 BC) which refers to a reed dam. Another dam is attributed to Marduk, a Babylonian god of about 20 years later. South of Samarra a dam dating from the second millennium, called Nimrod's Dam, was built to divert the River Tigris into a new course. The clearest structural and design parallel to Jawa's deflection system at DaI comes from Nineveh where King Sennacherib built two dams about 694 BC to supply his city with water from the nearby Khosr river.

Large reservoirs are also apparent in the Sahel of northern Sudan, East Africa. The *hafir,* or reservoir, system within the expansive Butana grassland appears to have per-

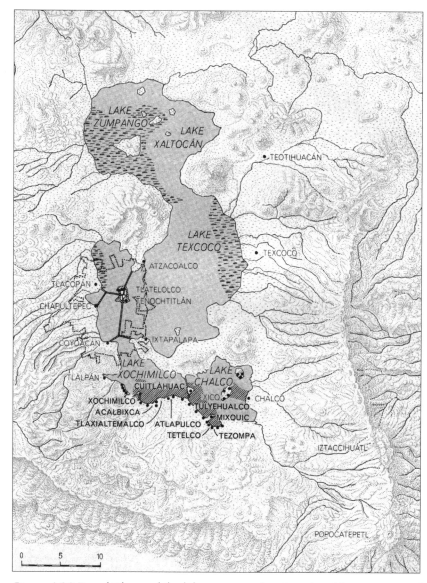

Figure 4.28 *Tenochtitlan and the lakes, prepared and reprinted by permission of the estate of Eric Mose from M.D. Coe (1964), courtesy of Scientific American.*

mitted this zone's long-term colonization (350 BC–AD 350) away from the Nile by large, well-organized Meroitic communities (Crowfoot and Griffith 1911; Shinnie 1967) (see figure 4.32). Canals have not been associated with these reservoirs. (Instead, this settled agricultural state made a pastoral symbiosis possible by the strategic placement of excavated *hafirs*.) In contrast, during a comparable period, the great Marib Dam (Sadd-el-Arim) of Yemen provided a canalized source of water for irrigation and drinking. Serving the city of Marib of the Sabeans, the dam began as an earthen embankment and was markedly expanded during 750 BC–AD 575 (Bowen and Albright 1958). With a height of 14 m and a length of 600 m, it was the largest

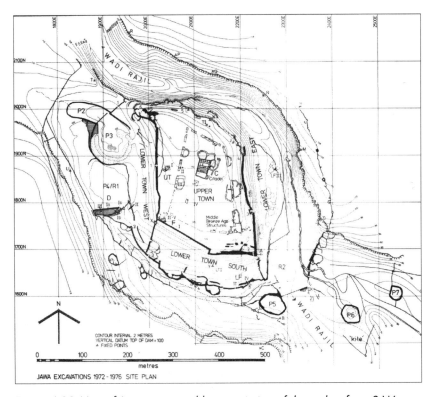

Figure 4.29 Map of Jawa, reprinted by permission of the author from S.W. Helms (1981).

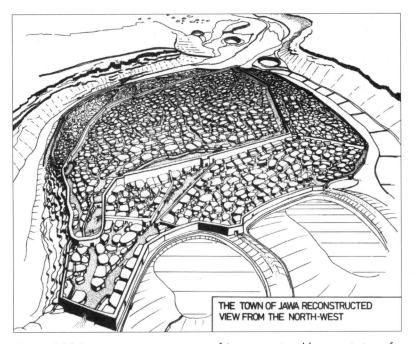

Figure 4.30 Perspective reconstruction of Jawa, reprinted by permission of the author from S.W. Helms (1981).

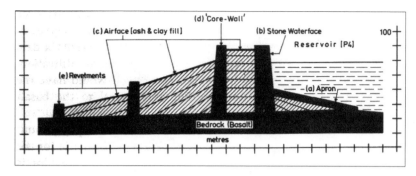

Figure 4.31 Cross section of dam at Jawa, reprinted by permission of the author from S.W. Helms (1981).

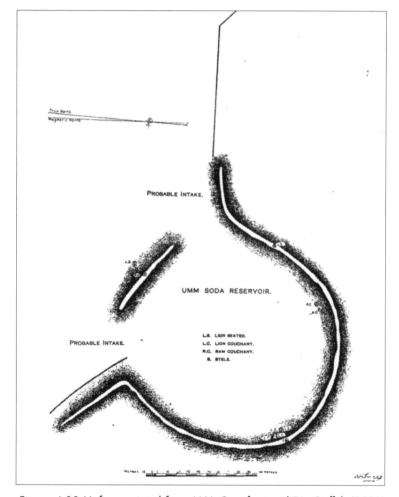

Figure 4.32 Hafir, reprinted from J.W. Crowfoot and F.L. Griffith (1911).

hydraulic installment for many kilometers. Nevertheless, eighty smaller dams ranging 1–5 m high by 100–200 m long, depending on the topography, are reported in the region of Yadib between Aden and Marib (Garbrecht 1987:9).

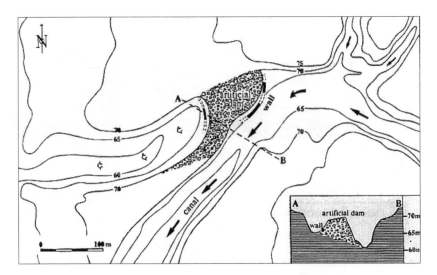

Figure 4.33 Tiryns Dam, reprinted by permission of the author and the
American Journal of Archaeology from E. Zangger (1994).

A dam dating to the early Roman occupation of the Maghrib was the largest of
the Tripolitanian wadi (arroyo or gully) dams. This feature was more than 900 m
long, constructed of a cut-stone veneer and a poured concrete and mortar core. Within
it may have existed an earlier but less consequential structure (Shaw 1984:152).
Other dams were built in the area, but this one across the Wadi Caam was the largest
in North Africa. However, Shaw (ibid.) argues that often this new fixed-dam technology, introduced from Rome, inadequately controlled the surging runoff waters in
the seasonal wadis of North Africa and portions of the Near East (cf. Kennedy 1995).
This water source differed significantly from that tapped predictably by the Romans
at northern Mediterranean spring or stream sources. The antiquity of dam construction on the European shore of the Mediterranean is probably no greater than the Late
Bronze Age date (1500–1150 BC) for the Tiryns Dam in the Argive Plain of southern
Greece (Zangger 1994) (see figure 4.33), a construction form subsequently modified
very little by the Romans.

Large shallow basins seasonally inundated along the ancient floodplain of the
lower Nile functioned as reservoirs and huge silt traps. Managed through a series of
short canals and well-designed embankments, these basins became the planting surfaces for pharaonic Egypt (Butzer 1976; Hamdan 1961). (An adaptation of this technique has been recently proposed along the Euphrates for the Old Babylonian period
[Hedrick 1997].) However, except for the regulation of lake levels with dams and
dikes within the Faiyum Depression by the Middle Kingdom (2040 BC), little evidence exists for centralized management of Nilotic floodwaters (Butzer 1976; contra
Helms 1981:171).

Reservoir construction in South Asia had few parallels elsewhere in the ancient
world. At the Harappan port city of Lothal in the state of Gujarat, India, a human-
made basin 219 by 37 m was constructed, with sunken sidewalls dropping 4.5 m

Figure 4.34 Lothal reservoir, reprinted by permission of authors from B. Allchin and R. Allchin (1982), courtesy of the Archaeological Survey of India.

Figure 4.35 Tank in Sri Lanka, reprinted by permission from R.A.E. Coningham (1999).

Figure 4.36 Cistern sluice, reprinted by permission of Cambridge University Press from E. Leach (1961).

below its surface (see figure 4.34). This feature dates to the late second millennium BC. Earlier interpretations suggest that it functioned as an elaborate docking facility connected by canals to the nearby estuary. More recent examinations indicate that the basin served to capture freshwater from an elevated watershed and isolate it from the brackish waters of the estuary (Allchin and Allchin 1982).

The celebrated tank systems of western and southern India and northern Sri Lanka are the largest known non-Western reservoirs. At Bhojpur near Bhopal, Madhya Pradesh, the king of Dhara built a huge tank in the mid-eleventh century. The embankment supporting it, breached in the fifteenth century by the Moguls, is estimated to have impounded more than 650 km^2 of water (Basham 1968:195). Similarly constructed, the grand temple tanks of Anuradhapura, Sri Lanka, covered

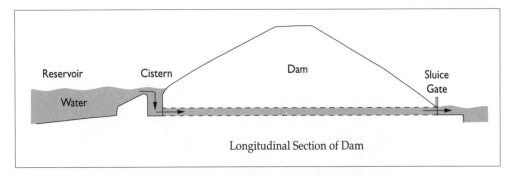

Figure 4.37 Cross section of cistern sluice, prepared by Sarah Stoutamire.

Figure 4.38 Angkor Wat plan, reprinted by permission of Cambridge
University Press from C. Higham (1989).

an area of 2,500 ha and controlled the movement of nearly 90,000,000 m³ of water
(Murphey 1957:185) by canal over a distance of 90 km (Leach 1959:9). Gunawardana
(1971, 1978) shows that reservoirs of the dimensions identified in Sri Lanka were not
possible until the appearance of the *bisokotuva,* or cistern sluice (see figures 4.35 and
4.36). Introduced by at least AD 200, this invention controlled the outflow from a
reservoir without damaging the catchment dam. The L-shaped, watertight conduit
within the reservoir was positioned with its vertical end slightly above the reservoir's
surface waters. The shaft descended through the reservoir into the tank's underlying
bed and then extended horizontally beneath the dam. Lowering or removing the vertical shaft's upper tier controlled the release of water, which poured down the shaft
and then laterally under the dam. This design prevented the explosive erosion or collapse of sluice gates from the pressure exerted by the large volume of water in reservoirs of this size (see figure 4.37).

Huge tanks and canalization efforts are also apparent in the Pagan dynasties of
Upper Burma, the kingdom of Majapahit in Java, and the Cambodian Khmer
Empire. In Pagan, Burma, one royal tank served 15,000 ha of irrigable land; other

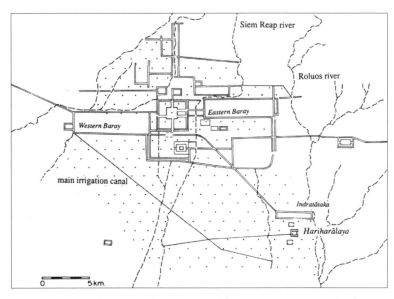

Figure 4.39 Angkor area plan, reprinted by permission of Cambridge University Press from C. Higham (1989).

reservoirs accommodated another 7,000–10,000 ha from the ninth to the thirteenth century (Bray 1986:72; Stargardt 1983:195). At its pinnacle of control, from the ninth to the twelfth century, the Khmer Empire exhibited perhaps the most impressive construction investment in water management in the nonindustrial world. The Khmer engineered landscape is represented best at the showcase Angkor Wat Complex (see figure 4.38)—a hydraulic city reestablished by King Indravarman, who reigned in AD 877–889. In the hinterlands, Khmer waterworks irrigated 167,000 ha on the northern plain of the Tonle Sap basin (Bray 1986:72; Groslier 1979:190; Higham 1989).

Within Angkor, rectangular-shaped, symmetrically positioned *barays*—enormous tanks—were excavated to retain the flow of a small Mekong tributary. King Indravarman's hydraulic construction included a *baray* covering 300 ha and containing more than 10,000,000 m^3 of water—a volume 150 times greater than anything built before (Bray 1986:73; Groslier 1974:100; Higham 1989:325) (see figure 4.39)—but his successors were responsible for the great Eastern and subsequent Western Barays. Perhaps as many as 800 smaller residential reservoirs were excavated along the axial avenues at Angkor (Briggs 1951), but the 60,000,000 m^3 of water in the Eastern Baray and the 70,000,000 m^3 in the Western Baray are what distinguish the city. The addition of the 195-ha outer moat excavated during the construction of the magnificent, gigantic temple-mausoleum of Angkor Wat (after which the hydraulic city is named), coupled with completion of the Northern Baray, provided another 15,000,000 m^3 of water, most of it used in irrigation (Higham 1989:325–27, 337, fig. 6.10). Angkor had the architectural grace and symmetry of fifth-century Sigiriya, Sri Lanka (an elaborate water park; see chapter 5), but with immense scale to allow significant agricultural usage.

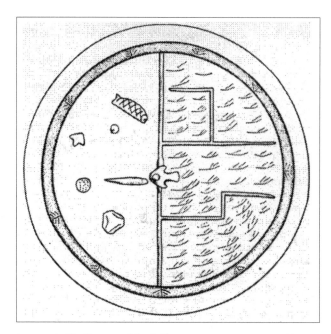

Figure 4.40 Clay model of Chinese system, reprinted by permission of the author from E. Bray (1986).

Chinese water storage consisted of many small ponds and reservoirs for rice culti-vation in the central and southern portions of the country, where rainfall was more predictable and abundant than elsewhere in Asia. Late Han grave offerings (AD 25–220) include clay models of irrigation ponds with adjacent rice fields separated by dikes or bunds (Bray 1986:78, fig. 3.3) (see figure 4.40).

> In Sichuan, the Yangzi region, Guangdong and Guizhou, as well as in the Tai kingdom of Yunnan, individual farmers dug small ponds which served to grow lotuses and water-chestnuts and to raise fish and turtles, as well as to irrigate the rice-fields (Bray 1984:110; Yangzi 1979:59). A text of slightly earlier date than the grave models, relating to the provinces just north of the Yangzi, refers to much larger ponds, in fact reservoirs, covering an area of one or more *qing* (i.e., well over 50 ha); these, it says would irrigate four times the area of the rice-fields. (Bray 1986:78–9)

Although relatively small tanks appear to have been the rule in China, as early as 600 BC the construction of the Peony Dam produced a great reservoir nearly 100 km in circumference (Ronan and Needham 1995:196). An expanse of water this great makes it the largest known area of deliberate inundation in the ancient world.

> Both Sima Qian and *The Book (of the Prince of) Huainan* of 120 BC make it clear that this had been built under the superintendence of the Sunshu Ao, minister to the Duke Zhuang of the Chu State between 608 and 586 BC. The

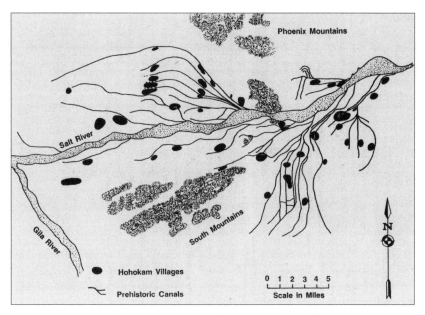

Figure 4.41 Hohokam Canals, reprinted by permission of the author and JAI Press from J.B. Howard (1993).

dam simply flooded a rather flat valley of no less than 24,000 square kilometers with water from the Yangtze, and was repeatedly repaired during the Han and Tang dynasties. (Ronan and Needham 1995:196)

Preindustrial water management in China was elaborate, sophisticated, and of scale.

Canals

After canals are established, their use and maintenance influence the distribution of settlement along their length, with *head-end* (upstream) communities having an advantage over their *tail-end* (downstream) counterparts, except, perhaps, during times of severe flooding. Two principal kinds of water sources feed canal systems: *unpredictable* (springs, reservoirs, or intermittent stream flow) or *predictable* (permanent streams). Here, *canals* are broadly defined as artificial waterways put to agricultural ends—including intermittent channel flows across terraced landscapes and aqueducts, piped systems, and conventional open linear basins. Sedentary agrarian communities frequently managed water for drainage or flood control, but even nomadic or pastoral groups flood-irrigated wild grasses for edible tubers (Steward 1933:247) or inundated meadow pasturage for fodder (Steensberg 1976).

New World

Most ancient New World canal systems were supplied by unpredictable water sources. In the extremely arid heartland of the U.S. Southwest, for example, Hohokam groups along the Gila-Salt drainage system constructed more than 500 km of major canals

Figure 4.42 Trincheras, reprinted by permission from J.A. Neely, S.C. Caran, and B.M. Winsborough (1990), courtesy of Museum of Anthropology Publications, University of Michigan.

Figure 4.43 Canal at Tehuacán, reprinted by permission of Robert S. Peabody Museum of Archaeology, Phillips Academy, Andover, Massachusetts, from R.B. Woodbury and J.A. Neely (1972).

and another 1,600 km of feeder canals (Masse 1981). Howard (1993) has demonstrated that many of these canals date to the eighth century and represent a degree of planning not previously reported in the Southwest for any period (see figure 4.41). Also, the antiquity of canalization was dramatically extended recently in the Tucson Basin of southern Arizona, with irrigation systems and associated pithouse villages dating to 1000 BC (Mabry, ed. 1998).

For the arid northern portions of Mexico, less is known about canalization. Nevertheless, the recent report by Hard and Roney (1998; also, Hard et al. 1999) identifying significant agricultural terracing in northern Chihuahua by 700 BC suggests the likelihood of water diversion techniques associated with crude water channeling. Well-documented *trincheras* (rock water spreaders), on low terraces and in the floodplains of arroyos, are reported by c. AD 1000 (Doolittle 1990a, 1990b) (see figure 4.42). Significantly more sophisticated, floodwater irrigation systems existed in the Mimbres Valley of southern New Mexico at a comparable time (Neely 1995, 2001b). The site area of Casas Grandes in Chihuahua, however, reveals the most complicated water management systems outside the Hohokam area by AD 1100 (DiPeso et al. 1974). In addition to the walk-in well and sizable reservoirs mentioned earlier, a canal system issuing from a spring source 6 km away was designed partly to recharge the community tanks (refer to figure 4.18).

Farther south in Mexico, the evidence for canalization of the scale suggested by the Hohokam region is limited (Doolittle 1990a). Woodbury and Neely (1972; also, Neely 2001a) have identified extensive canalization in the Tehuacán Valley of highland Mexico at least by AD 700 (see figure 4.43). Nevertheless, canalization systems as complex as those reported in southern Arizona are in little evidence. Two exceptions exist. Palerm (1955:40) indicates that the Aztecs dammed, diverted, and finally

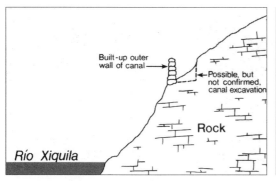

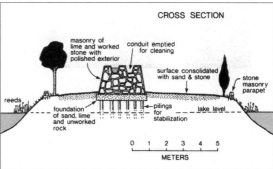

Figure 4.44 Aqueduct at Tehuacán, reprinted by permission of the University of Texas Press from W.E. Doolittle (1990).

Figure 4.45 Aztec aqueduct, reprinted by permission of the University of Texas Press from W.E. Doolittle (1990).

redirected the Cuauhtitlán River of the Basin of Mexico to a newly widened channel 2 km long, nearly 3 m wide, and about 3 m deep. Recently, Hatch (1997) and her colleagues identified the largest canal segment in Mesoamerica, and likely the New World, by 600 BC—3.3 m wide by 5.8 m deep by 1 km long. Issuing from the ancient Lake Miraflores, the canal and its feeders provide water to the field systems of Preclassic period Kaminaljuyu, highland Guatemala.

Until recently, the earliest empirical evidence for New World canalization unassociated with a dam came from the Basin of Mexico at 700 BC (Nichols 1982), although older water systems of this kind were inferred in coastal (Lumbreras 1974) and highland Peru (Burger 1984). Evidence from coastal interior Peru—derived from monumental architectural associations, limited floodplain agriculture access, and a suite of recovered domesticates—now suggests canalization by 2600–2000 BC (Solis et al. 2001). These new dates push back the origins of canalization in the New World by a millennium or more.

The earliest evidence for an aqueduct in Mesoamerica comes from the Xiquila canal south of Tehuacán (Woodbury and Neely 1972), dated by settlement association to AD 400–700 (see figure 4.44). A portion of this canal was forced over and across a natural tributary, suggesting the use of perishable, hollowed-out log segments suspended by a wooden trestle. Aqueducts of this type probably were widespread at that time, but few can be reconstructed. Not until the Aztec period (AD 1150–1519) do well-documented sources reveal the complexity and sophistication of aqueduct construction in the Basin of Mexico (Doolittle 1990a:120–27) (see figure 4.45). An elaborate aqueduct carried waters from the celebrated springhead at Chapultepec Hill across the western embayment of central Lake Texcoco to the island city of Tenochtitlan. Its initial construction consisted of a packed-clay-lined trough of hollowed logs supported by human-made islands. Later, it was secured by stone buttressing of the underlying support islands and made more durable with lime masonry construction of the aqueduct segments themselves (also see Wolf and Palerm 1955).

The Lowland Maya introduced across their low-relief landscape a still-water canalization technique and flow-water channels from permanent, slow-moving rivers

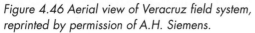

Figure 4.46 Aerial view of Veracruz field system, reprinted by permission of A.H. Siemens.

Figure 4.47 Aerial view of raised fields, reprinted by permission of American Antiquity from A.H. Siemens and D.E. Puleston (1972).

(Dunning et al. 1999, 2002; Scarborough 1983a, 1983b, 1993a, 1993b; Turner and Harrison 1981). The former technique directed runoff into annually replenished reservoirs, from which water was released onto internally draining fields during the dry season. A *flow-water* channel is a water system with an external riverine drainage inlet and outlet. At Pulltrouser Swamp, Belize, during the Classic period, sluice gates leading away from the New River may have controlled the water levels of a huge backwash zone immediately adjacent to the river (Harrison and Turner, eds. 1983).

Although the amount and kind of agriculture practiced in the extensive *bajos* (seasonal, internally drained swamps) remains unclear, drained fields and associated channels are well documented along the perennial rivers of northern Belize. The earliest shallow ditches draining the margins of swamps—an elevated water-table cropping technique—date to c. 1000 BC in northern Belize (Pohl et al. 1996). Pulltrouser Swamp and Albion Island on the Río Hondo/Río Azul system reveal well-documented wetland reclamation projects during both the Formative and Classic periods. Wetland reclamation via shallow canals flanking planting platforms is also reported near Veracruz, Mexico (Siemens et al. 1988) (see figure 4.46). Research there suggests that channelizing efforts occurred by AD 500 and perhaps earlier within the floodplain and backwater margins of the San Juan River basin. Siemens and Puleston (1972) first identified raised fields and associated channels in the Maya Lowlands near the early Postclassic site area of Acalán, southern Campeche, Mexico (see figure 4.47).

Although drained-field swamp agriculture occurred earlier in the humid lowlands of Mesoamerica (perhaps by 1000 BC and certainly by 200 BC), lacustrine soils were also deliberately drained and low-gradient canal systems maintained in interior Mexico (Doolittle 1990a:56). Amalucán, in the Puebla Valley, provides the oldest evidence for valley bottom agriculture in the highlands (Fowler 1987) (see figure

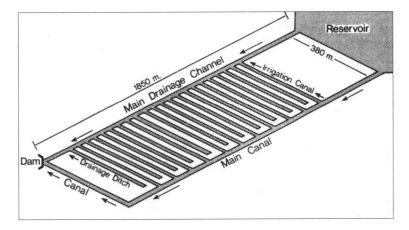

Figure 4.48 Amalucán irrigation, reprinted by permission of the University of Texas Press from W.E. Doolittle (1990).

4.48). Precipitation alone allowed only one crop, but this reservoir-fed system could produce another harvest during the dry season over an area of 70 ha. In the Basin of Mexico, lake margin field systems are suggested as early as the Late Formative (650 BC–AD 1), with well-documented pre-Aztec *chinampa* (raised and drained field plot) systems in the northwestern portion of the lakes region before AD 1150 (Armillas 1971; Nichols and Frederick 1993; Palerm 1955:35). Extensive Classic period (AD 200–900) lake-basin *chinampa* systems have been recently documented in Jalisco, western Mexico (Weigand 1993). Some of our best evidence for *chinampa* systems, however, demonstrates an Aztec period (AD 1150–1519) use and expansion within and around the grand city of Tenochtitlan (Calnek 1972; Coe 1964; Parsons 1991; Sanders et al. 1979) (see chapter 7).

Peru provides extensive data on past canal schemes, some associated with the widespread terracing of the Andean landscape (Donkin 1979; Farrington 1980; Moseley 1974, 1983; Ortloff 1988, 1993; Ortloff et al. 1982, 1985; Solis et al. 2001). The ethnographer Guillet (1987, 1991) has shown that Peruvian terracing was as much an attempt to exploit limited water supplies as it was to create cultivable land. Today, in the semiarid setting of Arequipa, terracing provides the gradient necessary for the careful downslope distribution of canalized water. Although terracing retards soil erosion on precipitous slopes, skillfully manipulating water along terrace end-wall canals permits agriculture. Both the ancient Mochica and their subsequent Inka lords sometimes further managed water systems by lining their main canals with stones to reduce seepage (Ortloff 1988, 1993; Sherbondy 1982). Terracing in Mesoamerica and the Greater Southwest, in contrast, was designed primarily to stabilize planting surfaces using dry farming techniques (Donkin 1979; Doolittle 1985; Doolittle 1990a, 1990b; Dunning and Beach 1994; Hard and Roney 1998; Hard et al. 1999; Turner 1974; Williams 1990).

Ancient and well-defined still-water canalization appears in Ecuador (Parsons 1969), Colombia (Parsons and Bowen 1966), Surinam and Venezuela (Denevan 1970;

Figure 4.49 Raised field system in Bolivia, digital enhancement by C. Erickson of aerial photograph reprinted by permission of the Instituto Geografico Militar.

Parsons and Denevan 1967; Spencer et al. 1994), and Bolivia/Peru. In this last area, it occurs in the highland basin of Lake Titicaca (see figure 4.49) and in the Casma Valley of north-central Peru (Denevan 1970; Erickson 1993; Kolata 1991; Moore 1988; C. Smith et al. 1968). Even though dating difficulties persist, Erickson (1993:389) indicates that raised fields and associated canals date as early as 1000 BC in the Lake Titicaca area (about the time wetlands channeling began in the Maya Lowlands of Mesoamerica). The degree of social complexity associated with raised-field agriculture is debatable (Erickson 1993), but Kolata (1991; Ortloff and Kolata 1989) suggests state intervention and water control from the city of Tiwanaku between AD 400 and 1100. Functioning still-water systems in South America are reported into the historic period (Denevan 1970).

Old World

In the Old World, many ancient canalization projects developed near large permanent rivers. Along the lower Nile (Butzer 1976; Hamdan 1961), the Huanghe and Yangtze (Hsu 1980), and possibly the Indus (see chapter 8), canals helped direct seasonal floodwaters across extensive floodplains in association with early state developments. However, along the Tigris and Euphrates, canalization may have been most widely utilized at an early date.

The best evidence for the earliest canalization comes from Choga Mami (Mandali) in Iraq (Oates and Oates 1976) (see figure 4.50). Resting on the outer slope of the foothills near the limits of dry farming, Choga Mami occupied a triangle of land flanked by two streams. Canal segments dating to the sixth millennium portend in miniature later developments in southern Mesopotamia (Oates 1972, 1973).

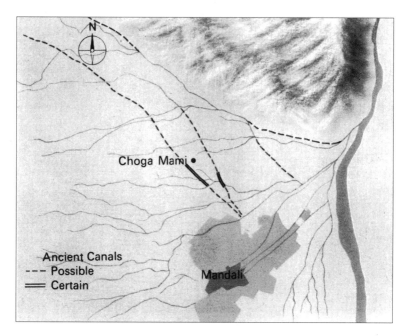

Figure 4.50 Choga Mami, reprinted by permission of Andromeda Oxford Limited from D. Oates and J. Oates (1976).

Furthermore, Helbaek (1969, 1972) indicates that irrigation was necessary at other Samarran communities beyond the range of dry farming. He bases his position on the moisture requirements of domesticated plants identified from these ancient arid settings.

The great attempts at dam and reservoir construction along the Tigris and the Euphrates extend back to neo-Babylonian times (625–537 BC). However, the most massive earthmoving operations are associated with the Sassanians (AD 226–637) (R. McC. Adams 1981). Earlier, King Sennacherib (707–681 BC) is credited with several water management installations, including two 16-km-long canal segments issuing from diversion weirs across tributaries of the Tigris and leading into the city area of Nineveh (Assyria). Furthermore, water was diverted from the Gomel River to Nineveh along a 50-km course, of which a 300-m segment was designed as an arched aqueduct—"12 m wide, 7.5 m high and a conveying capacity of up to about 40 m³/sec" (Garbrecht 1987:7).

At one time, the Euphrates was entirely diverted in an attempt to relocate recalcitrant farmers farther downstream (Fernea 1970). Unlike other great river systems associated with civilization, the Euphrates generated floodwaters during an April peak, too late for winter crops and too early for summer planting. Because of a steep gradient and a low-lying floodplain, as well as overall irregularities in annual discharge rates, the Tigris and the Euphrates required the skillful use of dams and reservoirs in directing water through a canal system.

The amount of canalization associated with the Indus civilization remains unclear, but the later Rig-Vedic scripture suggests significant diversion damming and irrigation by 1100 BC along the margins of the Ganges (Prasad et al. 1987). During both

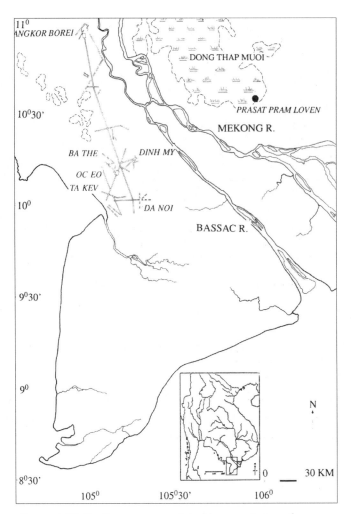

Figure 4.51 Oc Eo system, reprinted by permission of
Cambridge University Press from C. Higham (1989).

the Maurya (325–185 BC) and the Gupta Empires (AD 320–540), the centralizing
forces of an expanding state promoted major irrigation projects. The Moguls (sixteenth to eighteenth century), though, built the most enduring water management
features (see chapter 5).

The extensive canalization systems of Sri Lanka were based on water collection in
large tanks. Replenished from seasonal sources, these tanks released water into canals
immediately below the dam or bund (a diminutive dike) supporting the reservoir.
Similar systems are suggested for Cambodia and Java (Bronson 1978; Higham 1989).
For the period AD 100–550, extensive canals visible from the air bisect and radiate
from the large site of Oc Eo near the delta of the Lower Mekong Valley (Higham
1989:249–53, 246, fig. 5.2) (see figure 4.51). An arterial canal extends for 90 km,
connecting the seaport of Ta Kev with Oc Eo and continuing north to the river's margins at Angkor Borei, a principal town. It probably functioned as a transport channel

Figure 4.52 Guanxian irrigation sceme, reprinted by permission of Cambridge University Press from C. A. Ronan and J. Needham (1995).

as well as an irrigation canal, and its numerous branches also drained and reclaimed unusable marshlands. Although Oc Eo appears to be the most elaborate and extensive canalization effort of the time, throughout Southeast Asia, canal conduits linked numerous towns to a stream or river. Following this period of *mandala* development—the formation of early city-states in the Lower Mekong Valley—the stimuli for statecraft moved north to the Middle Mekong area with the founding of the magnificent Angkor Complex on the north shores of the Tonle Sap (Great Lake).

Early in the ninth century, Jayavarman II initiated Angkor with the construction of the huge Eastern Baray, or rectilinear reservoir, which was later expanded (see chapter 5). Together with subsequent tank excavations, Angkor's reservoirs provided a predictable, canalized source of water for field systems severely affected by the erratic monsoonal rainfall of this zone. Higham (1989:352) suggests that the reservoir and canal system in the Angkor Complex may have sustained as many as 600,000 people. The *barays* functioned as storage tanks to maintain the continuity of supplies, with seasonal rainfall providing most of the water necessary for cropping.[2]

With its tremendous achievements in water manipulation, China inspired Wittfogel's (1957) and Chi's (1936) hydraulic society theory. As we will discover in chapter 5, drainage canals first appeared at Anyang by 1100 BC but were not put to potable or agricultural ends at that early date (Chang 1986). By 250 BC, however, the grand Guanxian irrigation system diverted water to fields from the wild Min River, a tributary of the Yangtze. The governor of Sichuan, Li Bing, initiated this project. Needham estimates that an area of approximately 65 by 80 km was predictably irrigated, supporting a population of five million people (Bray 1986:89; Needham et al. 1971:288–89; Ronan and Needham 1995:202–10) (see figure 4.52). The simple but ingenious "fish snout," or division head, made this system possible by separating a

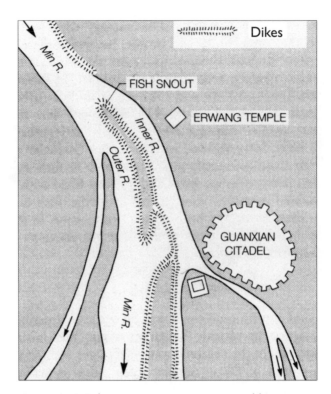

Figure 4.53 Fish snout at Guanxian, reprinted by permission of the author from E. Bray (1986), based on a diagram in Wuhan Hydroelectric Institute, A Brief History of Water Control in China [in Chinese]. Beijing (1979):68.

portion of the river into two great feeder canals, one for irrigation and the other partially for flood control (Bray 1986:89, fig. 3.7) (see figure 4.53). Constructed of bamboo mats, wooden posts, and gabions filled with stone, the fish snout directed floodwaters into a system of dikes and spillways that automatically prevented devastating crop damage. Because of the marked fluctuation in seasonal river flow, a temporary (seasonal) cofferdam was built across one and then the other of the two huge feeder canals to allow adequate and continual maintenance. The system remains intact and in use today (Bray 1986:90).

Creek irrigation, or the dredging and canalizing of deltaic wetlands, required a coordination of channel depths and resources that only a state could manage. From the Song through the Ming Dynasties (eleventh to seventeenth century), the Yangtze Delta was reclaimed using bunds and *poldered* (reclaimed wetlands) field techniques first identified in texts dating to the Spring and Autumn period (722– 481 BC) (Bray 1986:30, 34). Although polders are usually associated with the Netherlands, the first extensive use of this technology did not appear in northwestern mainland Europe until the seventh and eighth centuries AD (de Jong 1987:81), at least a thousand years after its invention in China. Creek irrigation of the scale shown in the Song period required huge energy outlays, given the expense of removing siltation and the salinization buildup from coastal polder construction, to say nothing of flood repairs. Bray (1986:91) relates an account from the Song *Dynastic History* of AD 1158 illustrating the investment necessary to reclaim an abandoned portion of the delta:

> The estimated cost to restore them [creek-irrigated fields] to their former state was more than 3.3 million man-days, an equal number of strings of cash and over 100,000 bushels of grain. Thereafter, 24 creeks were opened up between the Taihu Lake and Yangzi, and 12 more were opened up directly to the sea; according to the statesman Fan Zhongyan some 6,000 or 7,000 farmer-soldiers were settled in the Suzhou area specially to maintain the system and prevent flooding [Nishioka 1981:127]. (Bray 1986:91)

These historical figures are useful in assessing labor and scheduling costs in other reclaimed swampland settings, especially the Maya Lowlands and Khmer Cambodia.

In a migration story not unlike the Aztecan banishment to the marshy island of Tenochtitlan, Watson (1975) recounts the flight of the Man clan from Mongol expansion into the present-day margins of Hong Kong. Because the best lands were already taken, the Man were forced to use the brackish marshlands of a river delta draining into Deep Bay. By constructing dike systems with locks, they were able to drain portions of the wetlands and reclaim land from the bay. The dike system retained rainwater and separated it from saline-rich floodwaters. The reclaimed land permitted a single annual crop of salt-resistant red rice that produced only average yields relative to other varieties of rice grown in less severe settings. However, the red rice required no fertilizer and markedly less labor than other strains.

Aqueduct conveyance has a long history in the Old World. Han dynastic official Du Shi (c. AD 25–57) alluded in texts to mountain stream waters channeled into bamboo pipes joined end to end and carried across valleys and level ground to distant fields. Open wooden flumes were also used, sometimes with a fine-meshed bamboo basket positioned along the conduit to filter out sediment before it issued to fields (Bray 1986:81–84, figs. 3.4 and 3.5).

Pressure-pipe technology also has a long history in the Old World. Pipe segments were made in graded diameter reductions for this purpose. Joined tightly to prevent leakage, they formed a pipe that generated pressure as gravity flow moved water through it. In Europe, this technology is suggested on Crete by the second millennium BC. There, a pipeline of tapered terra-cotta segments, a portion of which may have been pressurized to accommodate a fountainhead, carried springwater to the palace at Knossos (Evans 1928, 1930; Fahlbusch 1987:115) (see chapter 5). At Late Bronze Age Mycenae and Pylos (1500–1150 BC), terra-cotta pipes carried water from nearby springs to the respective citadels, although considerable debate continues (T. Smith 1995:115–24). The first clear evidence for an aqueduct, however, comes from Lemnos in 575 BC. Additional evidence indicates extended lengths of pressure pipe along the Syracuse aqueduct (491–447 BC) and siphons at Pergamon by the third century BC (Crouch 1993:119).

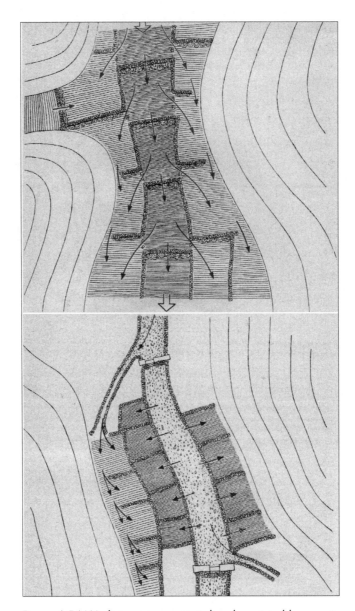

*Figure 4.54 Wadi terraces, prepared and reprinted by permis-
sion of the Estate of Eric Mose from M. Evenari and D. Koller
(1956), courtesy of* Scientific American.

Roman canal construction resulted in arched aqueduct sections of 10 km or more
leading into Rome between 312 BC and AD 226 (Ozis 1987:36). Eleven major canals
supplied the urban requirements of Rome, totaling nearly 500 km of channel length
and providing a flow rate into the city of 13.5 m³/sec. Channeled waters terminated
in a circular distributional basin structure, or *castellum,* and then were redirected into
the city through pressure pipes, often made of lead (Fahlbusch 1987:118).

Early terracing and water channeling in the Old World were not elaborate, except
where they were associated with rice production in eastern Asia. Carter and Dale

(1974:71) have suggested that extensive Phoenician terracing by 1500 BC spread throughout the Mediterranean and the Arabian Peninsula, but this simple technique probably extends back to the origins of Near Eastern agriculture. The Nabataeans produced the most sophisticated wadi (arroyo or gully) runoff diversion systems ever. Hammond (1967) reports that ceramic pressure pipes were connected to spring and diversion dam outlets during the first century BC at their capital city of Petra, Jordon. Evenari et. al (1971; also, Evenari and Koller 1956) have shown the ingenuity of Nabataean erosion control and water-diversion terracing systems and associated spill-ways, as well as expedient weir construction (Evenari and Koller 1956:42) (see figure 4.54). Evenari and Koller (1956) and Shaw (1984:146–47) note that wadi-runoff systems encouraged "controlled erosion." Sediment washed from higher elevations, exposing bedrock and accelerating runoff while allowing thick lenses of soil to accumulate in shallow broad terraces within and adjacent to wadi bottoms.[3] Water retention behind sediment-laden terraces was clearly an end as well. In most cases, however, terracing was designed to facilitate dry farming on steep terrain by preventing soil erosion and conserving moisture and nutrients.

Although the preceding attributes were also important for East and South Asian terrace systems, terraced rice paddies and related field systems required the significant retention of channelized runoff water for the extreme moisture demands of rice, a labor-intensive investment. Most contemporary rice terrace systems demonstrate a labortasking economic orientation emphasizing heterarchical, or highly interdependent, economic and political relationships within and among groups (see chapters 2 and 3). Furthermore, ethnography frequently notes the heightened importance of ritual among labortasking groups and ritual's unifying effects on their interpretation of the agricultural cycle (Scarborough 1998). The advent of intensive and extensive rice terracing in northern Luzon (Keesing 1962:312), Yunnan and Malaysia (Bray 1986:28–34; Donkin 1979), and Bali (Liefrinck 1969; Lansing 1991; Scarborough et al. 1999, 2000) remains poorly dated, but it heavily influenced these areas' ideological constructs. Wheatley (1965:135) goes so far as to reverse that causality, asserting that religion as much as agricultural demands inspired the megalithic terracing of Gio-Linh in Quang-Tri Province of North Vietnam, perhaps dating to 2000 BC (also Bray 1986:30).

The foregoing classification of water management features as wells, reservoirs and dams, and canals is a heuristic device of traditional merit to categorize and describe the key components of functional water systems. Nevertheless, as shown here, these categories considerably overlap in function and complement one another; definitional difficulties arise when we attempt to separate them from their interconnectedness in the real world. Because water management at its various levels of abstraction is a set of systems, component parts cannot easily be isolated from their context.

This discussion does not explicitly separate the functional water components by topography or climate, but individual systems are given such contexts. Another common dichotomy not employed here is that of systems emphasizing a scarce water supply and soil preservation (arid regions) versus systems designed for excess water and drainage (humid regions). At a functionally descriptive level, this is not a very fruitful separation, given the seasonality—and, many times, erratic arrival—of precipitation and runoff in both arid and humid regions. Nevertheless, this very dichotomy becomes highly useful for culturally assessing water management and land use globally (see chapters 2 and 3). I develop this separation further in the archaeological case studies described in chapters 7 and 8.

Figure 3.1 Balinese terraced rice paddies, photograph by V.L. Scarborough.

Figure 3.2 Water temple at Sebatu, photograph by V.L. Scarborough.

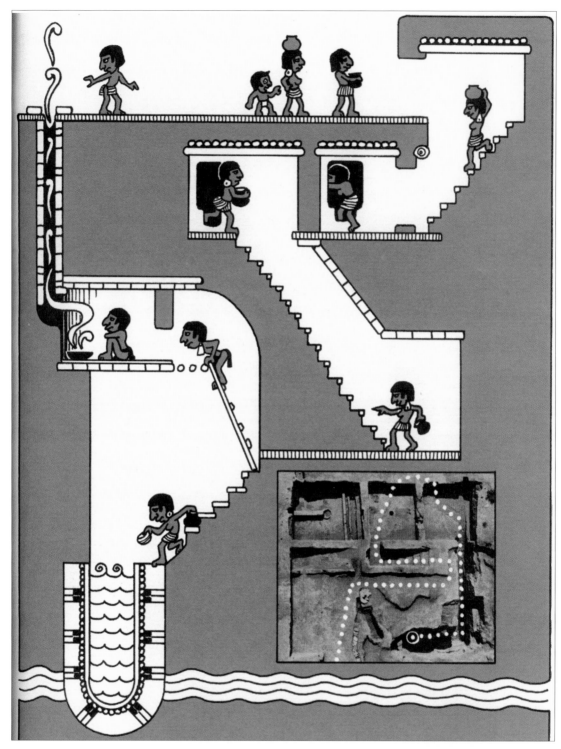

Figure 4.5 Walk-in well at Casas Grandes, reprinted by permission of Northland Publishing from C.C. Di Peso, J.B. Rinaldo, and G.J. Fenner (1974).

Figure 4.9 Karez village, photograph by V.L. Scarborough.

Figure 4.10 Inside Karez, photograph by V.L. Scarborough.

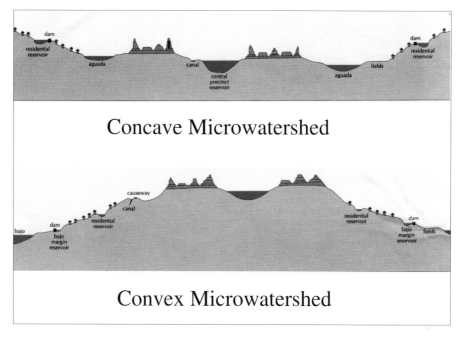

Concave Microwatershed

Convex Microwatershed

Figure 4.24 Microwatersheds in the Maya Lowlands, copyright 1994 and reprinted by permission of the National Geographic Society from V.L. Scarborough, Research and Exploration 10:188.

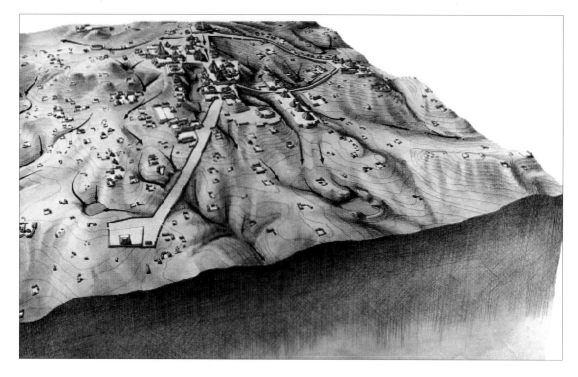

Figure 4.26. Tikal isometric map, copyright 1994 and reprinted by permission of the National Geographic Society from V.L. Scarborough, Research and Exploration 10:188.

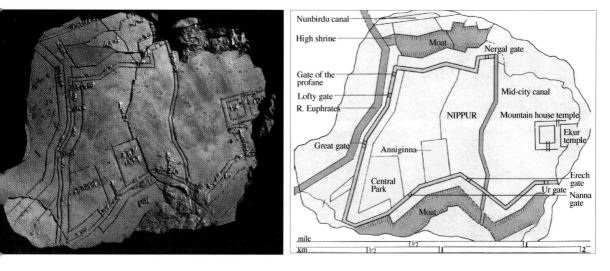

Figure 5.1 Nippur canals, reprinted by permission of the author from J.A.J. Gowlett (1993).

Figure 5.4 Great Bath at Mohenjo-daro, photograph by
V.L. Scarborough.

Figure 5.5 Covered drainage canals
at Mohenjo-daro, photograph by
V.L. Scarborough.

Figure 5.10 Palace gardens at Versailles, reprinted by permission of Tim Bienze (2003).

Figure 5.9 Alhambra Palace garden, photograph by V.L. Scarborough.

Figure 5.14 Shalimar Gardens, photograph by V.L. Scarborough.

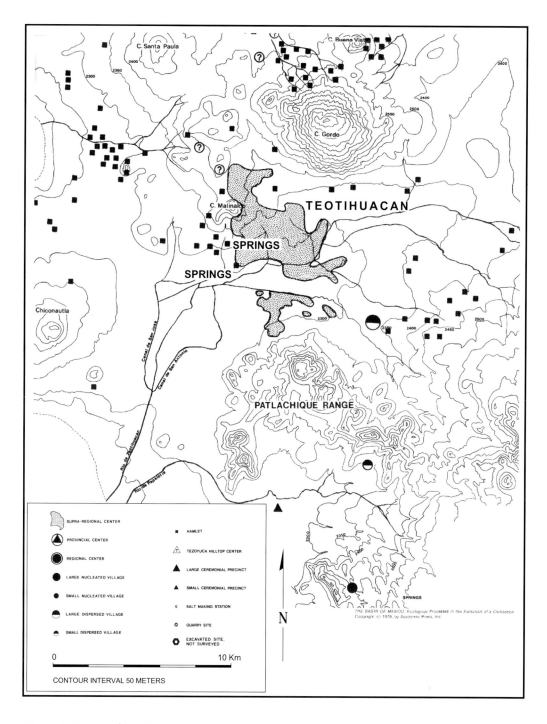

Figure 7.7 Map of Teotihuacan, showing springs, prepared by Sarah Stoutamire after W.T. Sanders, J.R. Parsons, and R. S. Santley (1979), by permission of Elsevier.

Figure 7.8 Teotihuacan mural of chinampa, reprinted by permission of Dumbarton Oaks from A.G. Miller (1973), prepared by Felipe Dávalos G.

FIVE

Nonagricultural Aspects of Water Management

In the temple dedicated to the latter {Li Erlang of third-century BC Sichuan},
there are a series of stone-cut inscriptions, probably of no great age themselves,
but perpetuating certain old key phrases, some attributable to the Qin, such as
"Dig the channel deep, and keep the dykes (and spillways) low," and "Where
the channel runs straight, dredge the centre of it; where it curves, cut off the
corners."

—Ronan and Needham (1995:190–91)

Through the availability of water, ancient complex societies promoted several kinds of activities and facilities in addition to food production. Most material remains identifying nonagricultural water features, though, are neither clearly distinguishable from those put to agricultural ends nor separable from mundane access to potable water sources. Frequently, water management systems accommodated multiple uses, including transportation, defense, drainage and flood control, nomadic/sedentist symbiosis, and ritual.

Transportation

Water has served as a medium of communication and transportation since the first maritime voyage, probably in the colonization of Australia some 40,000 years ago (Keegan and Diamond 1987). Riverine navigation is clearly as ancient. Maritime exchange between Harappan cities along the Indus and Persian Gulf states of Sumer is chronicled as early as the third millennium BC (Possehl 1982; Wheeler 1968). In the fifteenth century, the Aztec island capital of Tenochtitlan within the lake region of the Basin of Mexico received massive amounts of tribute, as well as locally marketed goods (Palerm 1955:41). Transportation canals made a celebrated appearance in Italy (Venice) and Flanders (Bruges) by the 1300s (Singer et al., eds. 1954:442). The earliest recorded transport canal existed by 130 BC and terminated in the Han capital region of west-central China. Approximately 124 km long, it facilitated grain shipments, and irrigation was practiced along its length (Hsu 1980:101, 259). Riverine, lake, and canal navigation was very important in early states.

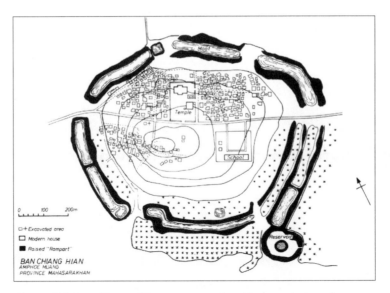

Figure 5.2 Ban Chiang Hian moat, reprinted by permission of
Cambridge University Press from C. Higham (1989).

Defense

Ancient states skilfully manipulated water to protect and defend themselves. Water-
related defences were of two types: moats and deliberate inundations.

The medieval castle of western Europe (Wilson 1985) best exemplifies a moat surrounding a redoubt, but in a clay model of the Sumerian city Nippur, dating to 1800
BC, a moat outlines the city's perimeter (Gowlett 1993) (see plate 5.1). The technique
also has deep roots farther east. Spectacular examples dot the Mogul landscape of
western India and Pakistan by the thirteenth century AD. The Angkor Complex of
Cambodia contained moats by the eighth to twelfth centuries (Briggs 1951; Higham
1989). Perhaps the earliest evidence for a moated community in Southeast Asia comes
from the third-century BC site of Co Loa, 15 km northwest of Ha Noi, Vietnam, on
the floodplain of the Red River (Higham 1989:193–94). Although moated towns
also may have been widespread by this time throughout portions of Thailand and
Cambodia, dating concerns linger. The moated community of Ban Chiang Hian, one
of several in the Mun-Chi drainage basin (Thailand), encloses 38 ha; an estimated
100,000 m^3 of earth was excavated in the moat's construction (Higham 1989:210,
212, 219, fig. 4.14) (see figure 5.2).

In the New World, the Maya constructed ditch and rampart systems by the second
century AD. Webster (1976) argues that the dry ditch circumscribing Becán in
Campeche, Mexico, did not hold water in the past, in spite of a pond (*aguada*) immediately above it. Drainage contours and precipitation rates indicate otherwise.
Interestingly, the plan and scale of the moat at Ban Chiang Hian (Thailand) is nearly
identical to that found at Becán, suggesting similar functions (see figure 5.3). A
longer but discontinuous ditch at Tikal, Guatemala (Puleston and Calender 1967),
also may have carried water (Patrick Culbert, personal communication, 1996).

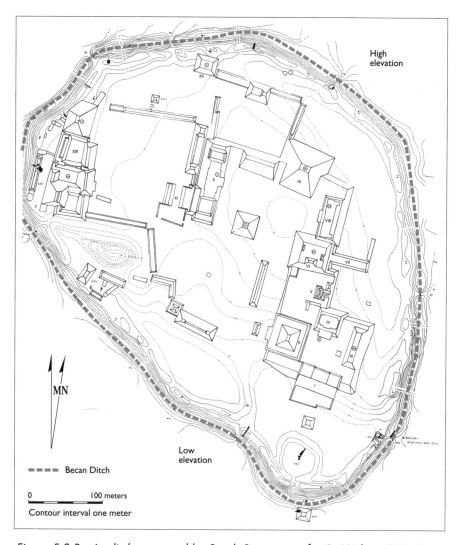

Figure 5.3 Becán ditch, prepared by Sarah Stoutamire after D. Webster (1976), courtesy of the Middle American Research Institute, Tulane University.

At Cerros, northern Belize, a drainage canal 2 m deep circumscribed 38 ha of civic and residential occupation, implying both agricultural and defensive functions (Scarborough 1983a, 1991b). Outside the Maya area, the Aztec capital of Tenochtitlan, on an island in Lake Texcoco, enjoyed a clear defensive advantage, although its location was not initially selected for this advantage.

Sometimes irrigation systems served as deterrents to outside aggression. In the Maghrib, Shaw (1984:145) indicates that a North African lord or chief diverted floodwaters into a Roman (Byzantine) encampment by shutting off the system of diversion weirs, designed to spread water, along a cultivated wadi system. Glick (1970) has shown that deliberate flooding of canal systems in medieval Valencia, Spain, disrupted invading armies. The Aztecs almost drowned the Spanish at Ixtapalapa in the Basin of Mexico by opening a set of dikes to flood the city (Díaz del

Castillo 1956:344). The Maya of Acalán employed a similar strategy when the Spanish attempted to subjugate the dispersed populations of the southern Maya Lowlands (Freidel and Scarborough 1982).

Drainage and Flood Control

Some scholars argue that all water manipulations are forms of drainage control, even where water is scarce (cf. Doolittle 1991a:136–43). Here, however, *drainage control* refers to the storage or diversion of damaging excess water. Wittfogel (1957) argued that severe flooding was the major stimulus for the hydraulic state in China and other Old World civilizations occupying the great seasonally inundating rivers. The extreme flooding along the Yangzte and Huanghe Rivers, coupled with the advent of statecraft along their tributaries, demonstrated to Wittfogel water management's primal role in the archaic state. In southern China and Southeast Asia, rice cultivation ideally suited the diversion and management of excess waters where labor was also abundant.

The earliest evidence for drainage channels in China comes from Anyang, dating to 1100 BC (Chang 1986); these ditches were unrelated to agriculture. Other Old World examples of drainage control are less spectacular. At several Harappan sites (2550–1900 BC), lined drainage canals and sewer systems have been documented (Allchin and Allchin 1982). These same adaptations occur some 2,000 years later at Taxila, in the same geographic sphere as the earlier Harappan communities (Marshall 1960). In the agora (marketplace) of Morgantina, Sicily, the fifth-century BC Greek occupation established the oldest known covered drainage system in the West (Crouch 1993:29), although earlier open canal systems are well reported. Crouch suggests that storm waters flushed out latrines and sewers, carrying the effluent to irrigated fields, especially tree crops.

At the Olmec site of Teopantecuanitlan (1200 BC) in the state of Guererro, Mexico, a *possible* drainage canal issues from a dam and debouches into a floodplain field of a few hectares. Another Olmecan community, San Lorenzo (1150–900 BC), Veracruz, which lies more than 50 m above the surrounding floodplain, used lined drainage channels probably to direct excess runoff away from the core area of the community (Coe and Diehl 1980). At the Andean type site for the Chavín Horizon, Chavín de Huántar, Peru, drainage canals date as early as 850 BC (Burger 1984).

Nomadic/Sedentist Symbiosis

Water has often provided the interface between sedentary villagers and mobile pastoralists. Although the interactions of these mobility-opposed adaptations are often very tense, their symbiosis has enabled their mutual survival in many parts of the world (R. McC. Adams 1978; Barth 1961, 1969; Fernea 1970; Scarborough 2000). For centuries, these groups have exchanged meat, milk, and wool or hides for domesticated plant resources and town-crafted trade goods. The neutral ground associated with a permanent water source, such as a well or reservoir, within an otherwise arid environment may provide the staging arena for such events. At Jericho, during the Pre-Pottery Neolithic (8000–7200 BC), a sizable spring was maintained outside the main wall and tower enclosing the town (Bar-Yosef 1986). Although the towns-people had the architectural capabilities to include a portion of the spring behind the wall, thereby securing a major source of potable water otherwise unavailable during siege, they did not do so (Kenyon 1981). Instead, the actual design may have pro-moted pastoral exchange at a neutral location away from the threatening enclosure of the town proper but near enough to ease the fears of vulnerable urbanites.

The capital investment for constructing a cistern or reservoir is most readily pro-vided by a sizable sedentary population capable of maintaining the water source. The deliberate placement of several of these features across an arid landscape could estab-lish a controlled and predictable mobility round for pastoralists and also benefit the scheduling and defensive requirements of settled townspeople. The *hafir* (reservoir) system of the Butana grasslands in northeastern Sudan, dating to Meroitic times (350 BC–AD 350), may have established just such a dependency relationship between pas-toralists and sizable towns (Crowfoot and Griffith 1911; Shinnie 1967).

Ritual

As the most precious of natural resources controllable by humans, water affects every-one, every day. The way a group's daily activities and decisions affect water access, in turn, strongly influences the extent and kind of ritual it performs. Unlike beliefs, symbols, or myths—the "conceptual blueprints" for ritual—*rituals* are the habitual actions essential for publicly defining an ideology (Bell 1992:19). Stated more gen-erally, rituals are the prescribed, repetitive activities of a religion or ideology within society. All hierarchical levels of society perform rituals and frequently draw their inspiration from such mundane, everyday experiences as water use.

> It is rather too easy to reply, when asked about religion, that it is concerned with all the things that technology and science cannot deal with, man's spiritual and moral nature. That is true, but it is only part of the answer. Religions are also down to earth, and we believe it is this contact with the material world that explains the continued existence of religions in all coun-tries.... (Reynolds and Tanner 1995:8)

These everyday tasks and activities are grounded in the landscape from which groups make a living.

All societies performed water rituals. Religious appeals to supernatural forces for adequate quantities of water escalate during periods of extended drought. In drought-stricken medieval Valencia, for instance, not only did the incidence of interpolity warfare increase but also interest in Catholicism (Glick 1970). Frequently, water also serves as an unction (holy water) in symbolic healing rites or as a libationary offering to deities. Its cleansing properties make it an appropriate symbolic medium for bathing the soul. A manipulative elite's ritual appropriation of the mundane, daily activities associated with water use is broadly evident in ethnographic and ethnohistoric examples from Madagascar (Block 1987), to Bali (Lansing 1991), to highland Chiapas in Mexico (Vogt 1968, 1969), to northern New Mexico (Rodriguez 2002), and elsewhere (see Scarborough 1998).

Symbolic Statements

Symbolic water statements by elites are static investments that on first inspection would seem to yield little immediate economic return. Deeper examination, however, reveals that symbolic and ritual use of a water system reinforces socioeconomic inequalities and solidifies elite dominance. Material metaphors convey to a constituency that those in power have not only the authority to construct such works (implied by most monumental structures) but also the privilege of lavishly consuming this precious resource. Conspicuous consumption is a major lever in controlling others and their resources (Veblen 1934; cf. Schneider 1974). Such elite displays cultivate a social distance between commonality and aristocracy.

Unlike other public architecture associated with complex societies, symbolic water management facilities usually require great planning to construct and maintain. Although built as static and permanent fixtures and as an index of elite control—generally a quality of civic architecture (Price 1982:731; Trigger 1990)—water monuments require a careful layout to accommodate the physical properties of fluidity and gravity flow. Accordingly, many hydraulic features were built in their entirety in a short time (contra Leach 1959). This characteristic makes water management systems a better measure of an elite's power and control than lofty pyramids that may reflect many generations of labor (cf. Kaplan 1963).

One example of a symbolic appropriation of social control incorporating water is the public bath system. Public bath use by the governing elite of ancient Greece and Rome is well known (Crouch 1993; Herschel 1899), but civic architecture dedicated to bathing dates at least two millennia earlier in Pakistan. At Mohenjo-daro (2550–1900 BC), the Great Bath, situated on the elevated reaches of the Citadel, probably drew from the canalization of surface runoff, as well as from well water (Wheeler 1968) (see plates 5.4 and 5.5). A citywide design to remove human excreta by way of bathrooms and sealed sump pits may have kept runoff clean. Positioned 12 m above the surrounding floodplain and even more removed from the underlying water table, the Great Bath measured 12 by 7 m and approximately 3 m deep. Built of fired brick, like most structures in the city, it was entered by a set of inset stairs placed at either end and drained by a high, corbel-vaulted passage debouching near the Citadel's margins. The floor was constructed with finely joined bricks placed on edge, with a layer of bitumen sealant sandwiched between an inner and outer course (Wheeler 1968). More important than the technology involved or the Great Bath's capacity was its location atop the access-controlled Citadel. Many groups on the

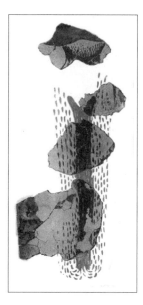

Figure 5.6 Knossos water mural, from S.A. Arthur (1928).

Figure 5.7 Greek atrium, reprinted by permission of Oxford University Press from D. P. Crouch (1993).

South Asian subcontinent valued ritualized cleansing, so this feature's connection to the seat of administrative and ceremonial activity was highly significant. Access to ritualized bathing both conferred and reflected elite status.

Perhaps the most celebrated sacred space of Western antiquity is the Oracle at Delphi, "navel of the universe." Well documented for the period beginning a few hundred years after the demise of the Late Bronze Age Greeks (1500–1150 BC), the Oracle and other springheads were also the stage for involved ritual activity during the earliest Mycenaean, or Late Bronze Age, times (Andronicos 1976; Burn and Burn 1980; Crouch 1993). Traces of Mycenaean activity are apparent at Kefalari and Delphi, to name only two springheads. My recent work at Midea in the Argolid suggests that the great city-states of the Bronze Age Argolid—Mycenae, Argos, Midea, and perhaps Tiryns—were founded upon and partially dependent on the region's geological faults; spring activity frequently accompanied the upthrusted faulting of the folded hills on which the citadel fortresses were placed (Scarborough 1994b). The ordinary use of water near spring sources was ritually elevated in at least some cases. Even today, the small Orthodox chapels dotting the countryside throughout the Peloponnese are frequently associated with springs or wellheads.

Palace gardens with fountain construction probably date to the very beginnings of statecraft. The earliest published reference to such a fountain is Evans's (1928:460–63) description of the House of Frescos at Knossos, Crete, for the early second millennium BC. He suggests that reconstructed fragments of a Minoan wall painting reveal a kind of fountain (see figure 5.6); nearby physical evidence of pressure pipes strengthens the argument. By the third century BC, the Greek atrium, frequently associated with a water-collecting *impluvium* (shallow, flat-bottomed basin) canted to

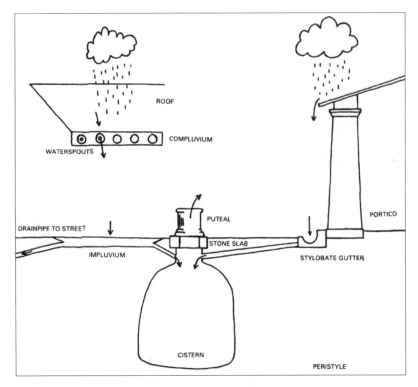

*Figure 5.8 Greek impluvium, reprinted by permission of the author from
G.C.M. Jansen (1991).*

fill sizable cisterns, was an established architectural design within elite houses
(Crouch 1993:231, fig. 16.16; Glick 1970) (see figures 5.7 and 5.8). Persian Persepolis
(600 BC) also suggests the importance of enclosed private garden space for the aristocracy. The concept of a palace garden with fountains was disseminated widely by the
Islamic jihad (post-AD 700) (Wilber 1979) and introduced into thirteenth-century
Europe in a spectacular manner within the walls of the Alhambra at Granada (see
plate 5.9). Later, in the late seventeenth century, Louis XIV commissioned the palace
gardens and fountains at Versailles (see plate 5.10).

In South Asia, the Sinhalese of Sri Lanka engineered some of the most spectacular
waterworks. By the mid-third century BC, they constructed several ornamental pools
at Anuradhapura. Two examples, with ornamental *makara* (Hindu/Buddhist water
monster) gargoyles and lion-headed spouts, were lined with stone and fed by channels filtered through silting tanks (Vann 1987:168). By the third century AD, every
monastery and park within and near the city contained ornamental pools, and the
royal pleasure gardens were positioned immediately below the great Tissawewa dam
(5 km long by 8 m high). However, the most spectacular water gardens were located
75 km south of Anuradhapura, at Sigiriya (see figures 5.11 and 5.12). Built by King
Kasyapa I (AD 473–491), Sigiriya was planned rather like the great *wats* of Cambodia,
with the entire rectilinear complex symmetrically oriented on an east-west axis. With
carefully positioned swimming pools, reflecting ponds, fountains, and conduits

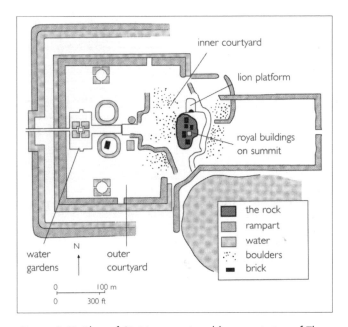

Figure 5.11 Plan of Sigiriya, reprinted by permission of Thames and Hudson from C. Scarre (1999), drawn by Philip Winton.

Figure 5.12 Sigiriya, showing tank complex, reprinted by permission of Thames and Hudson from C. Scarre (1999), photograph by R.A.E. Coningham.

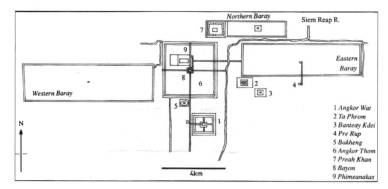

Figure 5.13 Angkor Complex, reprinted by permission of Cambridge University Press from C. Higham (1989).

leading from a massive moat system, the formal water gardens were the largest in Asia (Vann 1987:171).

Throughout ancient South Asia, monumental architecture and the plans of entire cities manifested Hinduism and Buddhism. Perhaps the archetype of symbolism was the "hydraulic city," the eighth-to-twelfth-century capital of the Khmer Empire, the Angkor Complex (see figure 5.13). Built to reproduce the churning sea surrounding Mount Meru (home to the gods), huge reservoirs flanked the palace and temple-mausoleum complex (home to the kings). Here, the functional was little separated from the symbolic. The tanks provided necessary water storage for the irrigation of vastly altered landscapes under rice production. They also significantly structured the plan of the heavenly patterned city—the *mandala,* a circular design of concentric geometric forms, symbolizing the universe, totality, and wholeness in Southeast Asian Hinduism and Buddhism.

The Moguls of South Asia (sixteenth to eighteenth century AD) made some of the most extravagant and imposing architectural statements in history. Through the private and public use of water, the Mogul nobility attempted to create an earthly paradise. Shan Jehan, most renowned for commissioning the Taj Mahal, was the period's architect-king, even though elaborate terracing and enclosed gardens had been introduced two centuries before he ordered the construction of the Shalimar Gardens of Lahore in the seventeenth century AD. Three receding terraces embraced a rectangular area of more than 16 ha enclosed by a high wall. More than four hundred symmetrically placed fountains graced the lavish setting, and marbled pavilions and causeways connected the tiers. A canal is said to have brought water from a pure source more than 160 km away (Rehman 1981; Taylor 1965) (see plate 5.14).

Mogul royal palaces, usually within massively fortified redoubts, also contained gardens. At the Mogul palaces of ancient Rajasthan, as well as their maharaja satellites, we find royal baths, reflecting pools, and methods for cooling rooms that were often constructed of white marble. Woven curtains of a sweet-smelling marsh grass draped across arched entranceways. Delicate earthenware pipes punctured with small holes spanned the doorways, dripping water to moisten a braided mat. Thus, with a draft from an open window, these items created a simple but elegant evaporative cooler. The scent of the aerated plant fiber further sweetened this opulent surrounding (personal observation, Amber Palace, Jaipur, India; cf. Taylor 1965).

At a comparable time in the New World, the Aztecs created splendidly altered landscapes for manipulating water. At the palace of Tetzcotzingo (Texcoco) near present-day Mexico City, King Nezahualcoyotl is credited with building a resort involving a significant investment in canals, aqueducts, and terraces in the mid-fifteenth century AD (Doolittle 1990a:127–35; S. Evans 2000; Palerm 1955:36; Wolf and Palerm 1955). On the island city of Tenochtitlan, King Moctezuma Ilhuicamina (who reigned 1440–1468) established an aqueduct to bring water from the mainland springs at Chapultepec (Doolittle 1990a:120–27). He is further credited with the construction of botanical and zoological gardens with facilities for aquatic plants and animals (S. Evans 2000; Weaver 1981:424).

For the Lowland Maya, we have only limited evidence for baths or palace water systems. Vaulted aqueducts channeled water into the central precinct at Palenque (French 2002; Weaver 1981:315). A narrowing aqueduct channel at the site suggests that the Maya knew how to create and use water pressure. At Becán, a crude plumbing system seems apparent in the architecture of a single elite structure (Potter 1977:44), but no sources from the Maya area refer to palace gardens. On the other hand, elaborate sweat houses have been identified within the central precincts of the largest cities throughout the Maya area. Native Americans practiced ritualized sweat baths, but the Maya appear to have been the first to formalize the institution architecturally. At Tikal (Coe 1967), Piedras Negras (Cresson 1938; Satterthwaite 1936), and Chichén Itzá (Ruppert 1952), steam was directed into sealed masonry rooms. Houston (1996) suggests that the Maya viewed masonry sweat baths as artificial caves, the source of "virgin waters," or *zuhuy ha,* incorporated into ritual activities (Thompson 1959; Brady 1997).

As we will see in chapter 7, the Lowland Maya used elaborate water rituals in the context of their functional reservoir systems to manipulate and control a sustaining population symbolically (Scarborough 1998). Beginning with the Olmec site of Cerro de las Mesas (600–700 BC) (Stark 1999:210–11) in southern Veracruz, Mexico, and continuing into the Late Preclassic and Classic periods (400 BC–AD 800) at several sites throughout the Maya Lowlands, the Maya positioned sizable reservoirs immediately below the grandest temples and palaces. The thin, reflective reservoir surfaces revealed the tension between this world and the Maya's watery image of the next. The elite's mirrored ritual actions strengthened its association with and control over water. Sophisticated hydraulic systems emphasizing functional and pragmatic ends frequently have implicit symbolic overtones for a society. For the Maya, with their characteristically dispersed settlement and land-use adaptation, the centralizing influence of water ritual at great cities was crucial to elite management and control of resources.

SIX ≈≈≈≈≈

Economic Outlays and Political Risks of Water Management

It has been said that in New Mexico, "whiskey is for drinking,
water is for fighting."

—Baxter (1997)

The ethnographic record provides several kinds of information about water management and its effects on both economy and political organization. Chapters 2 and 3 examine the wealth of ethnographic material that bears upon the advent and development of the early state and how cultural anthropology informs my models for water, land, and labor with reference to the origins of statecraft globally. Here, I present a set of factors that implicitly underpin the models and elucidate aspects of the organizational planes composing all social systems.

Costs

In an important article, Hunt and Hunt (1976) pointed out that the manipulation of water toward an agricultural end involves both short-term and long-term costs, or economic outlays frequently associated with political risks. Short-term costs are usually routine tasks or assignments conducted during an agricultural year. They include decisions about water allocation, intragroup conflict resolution, and maintenance of functional features. Long-term costs occur much less frequently and usually require more uninterrupted time, labor, and planning. Construction projects, major repairs, and external conflict resolution constitute long-term community investments. Both long-term and short-term costs depend on whether the hydraulic system is expanding or contracting in scale and complexity. The significance of such costs is most readily evident in studies of historic and contemporary peoples, rather than through an examination of the ancient material record. However, by studying the dynamics of economic outlays and political risks, we can better understand the archaeological record and the forces and relations of production influencing the archaic state.

Short-Term Costs

Water allocation is the principal source of conflict among all water users, whether in small-scale, community-oriented systems or complex, bureaucratically managed ones (Chambers 1980). Users must decide on the area of land to irrigate and the times and amounts of water delivery. For these allocations, ethnographic groups have *traditional formulas* (regulatory principles). Although the formulas vary with the particular ecological and technological constraints, in most societies an impartial *ditch master* is routinely responsible for the daily task of distributing water equitably. Furthermore, during periods of acute stress brought on by unexpected droughts or severe floods, certain other individuals or groups of community elders may become responsible for allocations.

Intragroup conflict generally arises over water allocation disputes—when individual users violate the traditional allocation formulas or the ditch master is unfair. Emotions can be especially volatile during drought periods. An impartial ditch master who speaks for the community can quickly settle most water management infractions. However, if conflict goes unchecked or escalates, a greater jural body eventually intercedes. The latter event usually triggers the less frequent, and more complicated and serious, long-term water management outlays and risks (Hunt and Hunt 1976).

Negligence in maintaining a water system can also cause conflict. For instance, private construction projects lacking community support can disrupt system maintenance. The unannounced construction of a canal can significantly affect the whole group (cf. Vandemeer 1971; Howard 1993), changing water volumes throughout the irrigation scheme and altering sedimentation and discharge rates (cf. Glick 1970).

System maintenance is a periodic task dictated by tradition and sanctioned by a governing body. Typically, routine maintenance everywhere is the responsibility of every single user. Stiff fines are frequently levied against slackers, although a user can sometimes pay to have another perform maintenance tasks (see Crawford 1988). Of course, maintenance requirements vary by landscape and type of water system. Each year in the Tehuacán Valley of Mexico, it is essential to remove the solidifying calcium carbonate accumulation from canal walls and floors (refer to figure 4.43) to maintain the volume and gradient of water necessary for irrigation (Woodbury and Neely 1972). The swampy tail end of the medieval Valencia (Spain) system required the removal of accumulated sediments carried down from the head end of the canal system. The marshy concentration of silts at the tail end promoted a greater incidence of disease than elsewhere (Glick 1970).

Long-Term Costs

Corporate construction projects involving the reclamation of defunct water features or the initiation of new features demand energy and forethought. The community at large often undertakes construction during periods of perceived economic and political mismanagement. In this sense, construction is a form of social repair, correcting unfairness in the old system. Generally, construction outlays come at a time when material resources are scarcest and in greatest demand. For instance, in San Juan, Oaxaca, the canal system's conveyance inefficiency created a critical water shortage, so the community built a dam (Hunt and Hunt 1974, 1976). However, its construction was delayed until local resources were entirely consumed and an external governmental agency intervened to furnish construction resources. In medieval Valencia, Spain, drought stimulated canal building; again, the lack of local construction resources prevented the development of adequate stores of water. Only with an external government change did subsequent public works projects correct the shortages (Glick 1970). Construction costs are also a major determinant of economic change, frequently affecting political organization as well. Such outlays often force an evaluation of the individuals or groups responsible for the decision-making process—before, during, and after construction—promoting or demoting an individual or group into a more powerful or less powerful governing role.

Repairing an old water system following a natural catastrophe, such as flooding or extended drought, represents an attempt to maintain the status quo during a period of resource stress. The repair investment to overcome a widespread disaster may force lasting organizational change; repairs usually salvage not only damaged features but also the social organizational system. Most water management systems have traditional formulas for recruiting laborers for repairs during and following natural disasters.

Long-term social costs also arise from uncontrollable internecine feuding and external conflicts (Hunt and Hunt 1976). Sometimes, recurrent, short-term intragroup fighting escalates as a consequence of poor economic and political management. If the formulas do not resolve the conflict, major institutional changes ensue. For example, uncontrollable conflict in the Teotihuacan Valley of Mexico led to serious disruption among water users (Millon et al. 1962). The old community's traditional formulas for coordinating new arrivals could not accommodate the rapidly growing immigrant population. Until a new, effective organizing principle was introduced to the valley's residents, the water system remained chaotic.

Warfare over control of water and the agricultural or pastoral resources it nourishes has an ancient history. Eva Hunt's (1972) examination of interpolity strife in Cuicatlán, Oaxaca, documents the fluctuating agricultural borders of a Postclassic state affected by incursions from less well-supplied neighbors several hundred years before Spanish conquest. A less socially complex ethnographic example is the settled Sonjo of East Africa (Gray 1963), who have a history of conflict with the pastoral Maasai, partly over access to water. The defensive adaptations made by the Sonjo irrigation agriculturalists include wall fortifications around their villages and clear-cut social organizational differences from their Maasai neighbors.

Expansion and Contraction

The rate and process by which natural resources generally—and water resources especially—are harvested (implying sustainability and renewal of a supply) or exploited (suggesting a less measured use of the supply) can reveal a cultural landscape's over-all stability. Periods of increased group size and resource consumption are followed by periods of contraction, the latter a partial consequence of a scarcity of the very natu-ral resources that formerly allowed growth.

Growing Systems

Water system expansion can result from a slow-growth process (*accretional approach*) in which community organization, ecological constraints, and technology accommo-date population increases. Preadapting the original water system to accommodate change sometimes results in economic shifts. In some agricultural systems, intensifi-cation can develop slowly by employing a growing labor pool (labortasking).

Rapid radical growth (*expansionist approach*) in a hydraulic system frequently occurs during periods in which long-term economic outlays are initiated. It can be stimulated by accelerated population growth, technological innovation, the harness-ing of new varieties of domesticated plants, or the more effective distribution of an old crop. Generally, radical hydraulic growth curves result from an external stimulus such as in-migration or the introduction of new tools or crops. If additional labor is immediately available to a hydraulic system, significant adjustments to the tradi-tional cropping cycle may mean more frequent cropping (involution) and/or an expansion of the cultivated area. Immediate critical needs caused by a hopelessly inad-equate water system trigger long-term costs. Although a small community may struggle to maintain an inefficient water system to preserve its traditional formulas and the autonomy they allow, change must occur at a certain point. Because a system's growth rate varies with the specific condition of the land and water resources avail-able, most societies pass through periods of accretionary stability followed by expan-sionist vulnerability.

Declining Systems

Contracting water systems are frequently victims of climatic or geological deteriora-tion, although unresolved social conflict may also reduce a hydraulic system. Generally, environmental deterioration manifests itself through two forms of radical decline in the water system:

1. The natural elements incite a catastrophic change.
2. The slow, extended effects of human-induced environmental deterioration cul-minate in the rapid abandonment of a landscape.

The principal climatic variable causing catastrophic change is precipitation. Some societies appear capable of accommodating extended periods of cyclic drought (for example, indigenous groups in the U.S. Southwest) or periodic flooding (pharaonic Egypt, for example), but there is a threshold beyond which no group can exist.

The primary geological variable influencing radical hydraulic change is tectonic activity. Along the northern Peruvian coast, a tectonic event reversed the gradient of the Chicama-Moche intervalley canal system and severely disrupted the huge Chimu capital of Chan Chan between AD 1100 and 1200 (Moseley 1983; Ortloff 1993; Ortloff et al. 1982, 1985; contra Farrington 1983; Pozorski and Pozorski 1982). Postulated uplift along the lower Indus during the Harappan period (see chapter 8) may have drastically altered the gradient and the hydraulic adaptations made at Mohenjo-daro (Raikes 1964, 1965, 1984; cf. Possehl 1967). Although Raikes's (ibid.) position has received mixed reviews, his strongest critics have recently championed stream capture precipitated by uplift for the upper and middle Indus. Possehl (1997, 2000) and others argue convincingly that the Yamuna captured the now dry Sarasvati River during the Mature Indus (2550–1900 BC) period, irreversibly altering settlement and agricultural production in a presumed breadbasket region of the ancient Indus.

Too much water can also lead to human-induced deterioration. In arid and semi-arid zones with extensive canalization or sizable reservoirs, the water table under an irrigated area rises. Without proper drainage, swamplike conditions can occur, promoting root rot of some cultigens and the emergence of previously unknown plant and human diseases (Glick 1970). An elevated water table also produces salinization in areas with mineralized runoff. This condition may have been acute along the Tigris-Euphrates, where little occupation is possible even today in areas near the great Babylonian and Sassanian ruins (R. McC. Adams 1981; Fernea 1970; Gibson 1974; Jacobsen and Adams 1958).

Poor management of a canal or reservoir system may increase sediment accumulation. A significant rise in the water table without careful management of the water resource can cause rapid siltation rates and changes in the gravity flow gradient. This condition may have affected early first-millennium BC Mohenjo-daro, Sind, Pakistan (Dales 1965; Raikes 1965, 1984), and the Late Preclassic (400 BC–AD 150) and Terminal Classic (AD 800–900) Maya of the south-central Yucatan Peninsula (Dunning et al. 2002; Harrison 1977; Jacob 1995).

Climatic fluctuations exacerbate water scarcity, a condition influencing most early states. Whether induced by human mismanagement or changes in rainfall patterns, a dropping water table will cripple a dependent population. Seasonal flood damage can produce erosion, and long-term gradient changes in a dropping water table promote erosive cutting of a field area. Left unchecked, erosion destroys a hydraulic system, as is well documented in the U.S. Southwest through late prehistoric and historic times (Dean et al. 1985; Vivian 1974:109; Worster 1985).

In addition to the preceding factors, overly intensified agriculture can lead to reduced food production and the degradation of the water management system. Agricultural systems in Southeast Asia have been described as "involuted" (Geertz 1963) or as having more labor than is efficient (Hanks 1972), given the quantity of food produced. If such a community does not acquire more land or water or better techniques to use the available resources more efficiently, it may experience severe food shortages. Overly intensified use of the land and water resources stimulated by the traditional allocation formulas may eventually lead to collapse or to new formulas embedded in a different economic organization (see chapter 3).

Lees (1973, 1974) suggests that an expeditious centralizing of sociopolitical control frequently coordinates declining small-scale water systems in the short term. At the same time, her work in Oaxaca, Mexico, also indicates that homeostatic imbalances evolving from a rapid centralization response during times of environmental stress (drought, in this case) can lead to greater decentralization of resources over the long term. Decentralization occurs because of the fragility of the agricultural base during environmental stress—frequently exacerbated by poorly centralized management—and the difficulty in coordinating access to water. The consequence of decentralization in this context is either the development of effective allocation formulas, in accordance with new environmental parameters, or the system's collapse, followed by markedly increased state control of the water system.

Allocation

Even before Hammurabi's famous code of laws (1850 BC), the concepts of proportional distribution and collective responsibility to a greater irrigation community existed in Babylonia (Glick 1970). Roman water law (c. AD 1–300), less concerned with irrigation and clearly having a greater antiquity, had defined the basic doctrine of riparian rights. An individual living on the banks of a water source had the right to divert water as long as doing so did not harm those below. The present-day notion of water "turns" evolved from this code (Glick 1970).

As they did in the past, water allocations in a simple irrigation system today involve

- The size of the area to be affected
- The amount and timing of the release
- The established rules and traditional formulas affecting distribution

When water is a scarce resource, risk of crop failure exists to some degree. Although each agriculturalist is responsible for the immediate decisions affecting the allocation of water across a plot of land, the community is responsible for the amount and timing of the release. These tasks are usually delegated to the ditch master. In communities little influenced by privately controlled water sources or the forces of coercive elites, the job of ditch master tends to be a rotated position with little economic attractiveness (Crawford 1988; Gray 1963; Hunt and Hunt 1976). Because the post takes time away from an individual's field work, he may be granted compensatory access to additional land or water. Where land and water are not distributed equally, the ditch master's role is compromised. He must give the appearance of representing the greater community while supporting the demands of the larger landowners or landlords.

Water allocation inspires cooperation as much as social conflict. Because water is

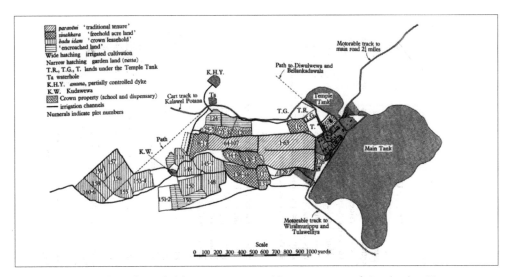

Figure 6.1 Sri Lanka village field system, reprinted by permission of Cambridge University Press from Leach (1961).

a shared community resource needed daily by each member, the rules for distributing water reveal core aspects of social, economic, and political behavior. In this regard, Chambers (1980) has drawn attention to the differences between an analysis of water management through the eyes of an elite (the *top-down* view) and an analysis through the eyes of the ordinary agriculturalist (the *bottom-up* view). The top-down perspective involves dichotomizing the hydraulic system into private (elite) and public (community) sectors. Private water schemes incorporate symbolic systems, such as baths and gardens, but may also include the exploitation of water resources from a public domain. Control and manipulation of private water sources usually impinge on the public hydraulic system, causing shortages when water is most needed.

The bottom-up view evaluates a water supply in terms of costs, adequacy, convenience, and reliability (Chambers 1980:32). Although these factors are considerations in a top-down view, they figure less importantly because of the elite's power to coerce work, frequently from a disenfranchised labor pool. Economic outlays are simply assumed in a top-down view. On the other hand, even under a coercive elite, the bottom-up view evaluates the distribution of a reduced water supply in terms of traditional allocation formulas and equitable allocations to the greater community.

At least two key types of water allocation, or broadly encompassing traditional formulas, exist. In the *Syrian model,* the quantity of water available to each user is directly proportional to the amount of land under cultivation. This ideal system demands that agriculturalists at the head end of a canal receive the same (or proportionate) amounts of water as their counterparts at the tail end. In the *Yemenite model,* water distribution is not tied directly to parcel size but is allocated on a fixed, time-released basis, frequently dependent on elite control through the sale of water.

One of the greatest individual advantages in any moving water system is the positioning of a plot at the source. In southern India and Sri Lanka (Chambers 1980; Leach 1961) (see figure 6.1) and in the Philippines (Coward 1979) (see figure 6.2), an

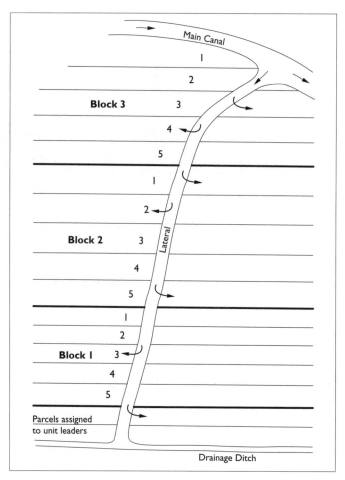

Figure 6.2 Philippine field system, prepared by Sarah Stoutamire after Coward 1979.

individual's cultivable land is parceled equally between the head and tail ends of the canal system. This ingenious distribution of land, sanctioned by tradition, permits the maintenance of the Syrian model. Water allocation abuses are considerably less likely if access to the head end of the canal is shared equitably.

A similar adaptation is apparent in southern Peru. Guillet (1987, 1991) indicates that the allocation of water over the Colca Valley terrace system is usually controlled in vertical strips (see figure 6.3). Water is released from an elevated main canal above each vertical strip sequentially. The individual terraces within a strip are usually owned by families who attempt to keep strip holdings intact (unsalable) within the kin group. This land-use and water-use adaptation, or traditional formula, requires that the same individuals securing access to the head end of the main canal be directly accountable to their immediate family members for losses to tail-end plots. The South Asian, Philippine, and Peruvian cases clearly represent bottom-up views of water distribution, in which indigenous custom and community sanctions direct the water needs of the greater community.

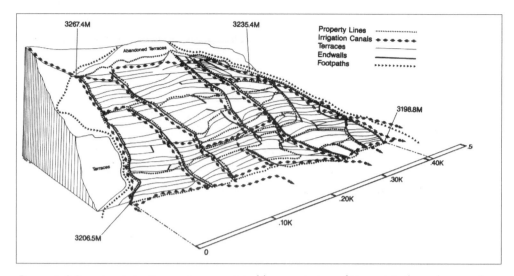

Figure 6.3 Peruvian irrigation system, reprinted by permission of Current Anthropology *and the University of Chicago Press from Guillet (1987).*

In the strict Yemenite model, a tail-end user is penalized by the conveyance loss resulting from his distance from the main canal. Evaporation and seepage can severely diminish an initial allotment made by a time-controlled rationing arrangement. The amount of discharge into feeder canals at the tail end of a trunk canal is always less than at the head-end locality, even with identical periods of timed release. During extreme drought, a tail-end user is unlikely to receive water.

Under any allocation model, extended drought is especially difficult for the small-plot agriculturalist. Even under the equitable Syrian model, an allotment of water proportional to the amount of land that a small agriculturalist may have under cultivation could be so reduced as to make cultivation untenable. Add to this any tendency by larger, better-positioned head-end users to surreptitiously extract just a little more during periods of water scarcity, and tail-end users are completely ruined. The Yemenite model probably arises from periods of natural calamity, even when an earlier Syrian adaptation may have been in place.

In the Cuicatec and Teotihuacan regions of Mexico, a Yemenite model was operative in the private sector, and a Syrian model ordinarily governed community lands *(ejido)* (Hunt and Hunt 1974, 1976; Millon et al. 1962). Nevertheless, during extended drought, a Yemenite allocation model prevailed on community lands. A few users can take sociopolitical control at this time of vulnerability, and dependency relationships rapidly develop.

Still-Water versus Moving-Water Systems

Whereas moving-water distributional systems have been studied extensively, still-water systems almost completely constructed by humans—such as reservoirs or raised-field basin canals (see chapter 4)—have received little research attention. In still-water systems, allocation decisions remain important, but other factors weigh more heavily. Because water collection is a deliberate action requiring construction and maintenance in still-water systems, organizational principles differ from those of irrigation (moving-water) systems. In areas of the world dependent on reservoir sources, entire watersheds were created to accommodate the water demands of a thriving community. For example, the Classic-period Maya Lowland hilltop cities of Tikal and La Milpa were extensively paved, partly to prevent precipitation from seeping away into the jungle floor but mainly to direct runoff into seasonally recharged reservoirs (Harrison 1993; Scarborough and Gallopin 1991). The ancient Sinhalese made adaptations representing another, perhaps grander watershed experiment (Gunawardana 1971; Leach 1959). Note that the elevated seepage rates of the Maya Lowlands karstic terrain made site paving absolutely necessary, whereas the Sinhalese of northern Sri Lanka adapted to the paucity of water by damming small rivers to produce huge collection tanks (see chapters 4, 7, and 8).

Unlike canal distributary systems, which require the overall availability of water from a faraway and sizable watershed, reservoir/catchment-basin systems demand immediate persistent attention to a watershed. Accordingly, the physical positioning of goods and people across the landscape differs in the two systems.

Another kind of still-water management is the modification of lake margins and internally drained, seasonally inundated wetlands. Because access to acceptable water levels and water purity depends on landscape engineering, these systems require an immediately available water source and an economic outlay for a sizable reclamation project investing in raised or drained fields. How water is stored in the still-water channels between fields is critical. Too much water floods the fields; too little results in plant desiccation. Accelerated sedimentation rates or uncontrolled mineralization are as much a concern to still-water managers as to moving-water (irrigation) managers.

Storage is an important component of any still-water system. The seasonal availability of water, coupled with its sometimes erratic occurrence even during the rainy season, makes the physical preparation and maintenance of the rainfall runoff catchment area critical for storing sufficient quantities of water.

The organization of labor for the construction and maintenance of an engineered watershed differs from that of a purely distributary system. When a community is located within a circumscribed, partially built watershed, a communitywide investment in watershed maintenance is necessary across a wide variety of spatially separated areas—unlike the maintenance organization associated with a ditch master's obligations to fixed points along narrowly defined stretches of canal. The runoff draining across an engineered watershed and into the associated reservoirs built to receive that water is not accessible or divisible until these reservoir waters are canalized away. Still-water reservoir systems emphasize communitywide activity, whereas irrigation (moving-water) systems are more readily exploited by the special interests of an individual or a group.

The task demands for the maintenance of a reservoir system are legion. Although certain times of the year are especially demanding in terms of monitoring flows and generating water stores, maintenance of the seepage-proof catchment surfaces and removal of debris must be done even during the dry season. Heavy rainfall periods require community coordination to make sure that runoff is directed to reservoirs and that the scouring action of moving water is minimized. In the case of the southern Lowland Maya, the entire site was the catchment surface, with each household having a direct, immediate interest in maintaining the quality and quantity of water community wide.

Both the ecological (human-land) relationships and the fundamental organizational outlooks (societal regulatory principles) are significantly different in reservoir/catchment (still-water) systems than in canal distributary (moving-water) systems. In the still-water cases, people probably do not travel great distances from a reservoir or circumscribed catchment area to plant, maintain, or harvest their agricultural plots. Although reservoirs can reach sizable proportions, they are finite in capacity. The farther a field is from a reservoir, the greater the likelihood that households closer to it will exhaust the water supply. Thus, the adaptation is primarily to the immediate margins of the reservoir; the larger its capacity, the larger the population nearby.

Canal distributary systems encourage field plots at greater distances from the water source and frequently away from sizable labor aggregates, given the abundance of a perennial riverine setting. When positioned on a plain, ancient cities were frequently horizontally gridded. This was in keeping with the original and regular layout of the irrigation system, with its set of fields following the riverine course as far as the transportation networks would accommodate. Communities compacted themselves at periodic intervals within the riverine system but still maintained their field plots some distance away. Because of the potential distances between communities and field plots, canal agriculturalists could operate more independently than could agriculturalists using a reservoir system. Early states frowned on this independence and developed both coercive and cajoling methods to integrate their sustaining population. As Wittfogel (1957) stated (overstated, actually), a fledgling bureaucracy was frequently necessary in a canal distributary system to control land and water allotments and to prevent abuses.

These two adaptations (reservoir/catchment and canal/distributary) existed to varying degrees in each of the earliest states. Even so, we can assume that a community relying on catchment runoff reservoirs demanded tighter intragroup integration than one associated with outfield canalized plots, for the reasons just stated.

As suggested elsewhere (Scarborough and Gallopin 1991), reservoir dependency centralized the prehispanic Maya water resource and may have influenced their political organization. The Maya did not nucleate into large urban aggregates like those of some early states based on canal distributary systems. The organizational outlook associated with Maya water systems emphasized reservoir and watershed construction and maintenance. It also entailed

- A less routinized scheduling of labor, because of imprecise knowledge of when the rains would actually fall on the human-made watershed
- A tendency toward dispersed settlement to maintain and deploy a labor force

over a wide catchment area, although the watershed's natural contours partially determined the settlement pattern

Even though factors other than water influenced the ecological relationships and
regulatory principles of Maya economy, watershed maintenance was a significant
organizing principle—less apparent in many riverine-based, canal-dependent states
(see chapter 7).

Political Organization

The influence of water management on sociopolitical organization has been hotly
debated. Wittfogel (1957), Steward (1955b), and Sanders (Sanders and Price 1968)
championed a deterministic view in which controlled irrigation schemes triggered
early state development and complex bureaucratic organization. R. McC. Adams (1966,
1974), Leach (1959), Millon (1971), Gray (1963), and others have severely challenged
that position. However, Wittfogel's thesis did force a timely reflection on the effect
of water manipulation upon early state development. Furthermore, despite the many
problems associated with Wittfogel's (1957) hydraulic society model, most early
states did develop sophisticated water management schemes. Wittfogel's top-down
view limited his approach to understanding water manipulation, however. Other factors, not incorporated in his hydraulic hypothesis, remain pivotal to an understanding of the archaic state.

The cooperative bond established by water users sharing an irrigation system
appears to stimulate a territorial alliance mainly where well-developed traditional
formulas for water allocation are present. Strong in-group associations evolve,
although intragroup conflict may continue to follow clan or lineage lines. Such associations are well defined in closed-corporate communities such as the Sonjo of East
Africa (Gray 1963), the Pul Eliya of Ceylon (Leach 1961), the Zanjera Danum of the
Philippines (Coward 1979), and the Quinua of central Peru (Mitchell 1976). In con-
flict-ridden regions such as Cuicatec (Hunt and Hunt 1974, 1976) and Teotihuacan
in Mexico (Millon et al. 1962), immigration and lack of well-developed traditional
formulas for water allocation have worked against strong associations.

Both isolated and interconnected irrigation systems across a region usually maintain intervillage territorial alliances. In medieval Spain (Glick 1970), Peru (Mitchell
1976), Japan (Beardsley et al. 1959), and Bali (Geertz 1973; Lansing 1987, 1991),
well-established rituals coupled with periodic markets helped to bind the associated
communities and stem conflict.

Viewed by the agriculturalist in the field, state interference and control represent
meddling with a community's traditional formulas for resolving water problems
(Flannery 1972). State control can provide the capital necessary for long-term construction and restoration, and the state's authority and power can quell conflict.
However, this control introduces the element of domination and potential coercion.
Long-term, regionwide state investments may pose a considerable threat to an individual community. For example, the construction of a dam may be advantageous to

the residents of Mexico City, but its immediate effect on the water supply of farmers in the Teotihuacan Valley may be disastrous (Millon et al. 1962).

State control frequently attempts to integrate complex social organizations through an imposed bureaucracy, often at the expense of organizational efficiency. Many insular communities react against this top-down approach, preferring their own traditional formulas for water distribution. Rulers of early states certainly would have been aware of such resistance, but truly despotic regimes could have forced communities into submission by controlling the sluice gates to their fields. The kinds and degrees of control used by early states differed markedly (see chapters 7 and 8).

One index for assessing the influence of early states on water management is the degree of boundary concordance between the two (Hunt and Hunt 1976). Wittfogel's (1957) despotic hydraulic state should have borders corresponding to those of the irrigation system, a condition apparent in classic and medieval China, according to Wittfogel (cf. Isaac 1993). However, many early states were not organized in this manner. Irrigation schemes can even crosscut state boundaries, as the *qanat* system did in the Tehuacán Valley of Mexico during the Spanish Colonial period (Woodbury and Neely 1972).

Bali has received considerable attention in this regard. Millon (1971) argues that Bali was not a state, despite strong evidence for a sophisticated water manipulation system. As outlined in chapter 3, however, Lansing (1987, 1991) argues that Bali may simply have been a decentralized state (cf. Geertz 1963, 1973, 1980) and that the irrigation system on the island operated independently of state control. Nevertheless, the water system was isomorphic with the boundaries of the state, in his assessment. If Lansing is correct, precolonial boundary concordance between a state and a water management system may not indicate centralized state control.

Rural-Urban Dichotomy

Settlement patterns provide another insight into the influence of water management systems on economic and political organization. Many early states in arid or semiarid settings depended on irrigation or controlled flood recession. They built nucleated communities, often fortified by a wall or protected simply by the imposing density of structures even at the margins of the town or city. Historically, such irrigation communities as medieval Valencia (Glick 1970), the prehispanic towns of Cuicatlán in Oaxaca (Hunt 1972), and the Sonjo villages of East Africa (Gray 1963) were nucleated. In the case of contemporary Iranian villages dependent on *qanat* irrigation (Bonine 1996), nucleated settlement growth follows the grid patterns of displaced canal segments, filled and reclaimed as streets and alleys by residential expansion. The water resource associated with these semiarid, irrigation-dependent communities made their relative prosperity attractive to outsiders, perhaps forcing a nucleated and defensive posture.

An interpretive model dichotomizing urban dwellers and country folk has existed at least since the Greek concept of the polis, or city-state. It reflects an urban detachment from the rural hinterlands and from the support population supplying many economic needs of a town or city. In a nuanced assessment drawing upon the early first-millennium Roman period, Shaw (1984:133) distinguishes between the often elaborate urban consumptive water systems and the less monumental rural productive water systems. The latter provided the primary food supply for the entire society. Shaw suggests that early cities (especially Roman colonies) were ordered around abundant water supplies made available at a limited number of geographic nodes. To accomplish this focused availability, water was diverted and redirected from hinterland rivers, streams, and springs to serve a densely concentrated population at the terminus of a masonry channel or large-scale aqueduct. From the management perspective of a bureaucratic state, many advantages accrued from concentrating people into controlled urban spaces created, in part, by focused water access. Furthermore, cities are defined to some extent by the presence of sometimes ostentatious monuments, including waterworks. Elaborate consumptive water systems take on a prestige value that may overlook functional utility in an attempt to elevate the urban elite's political aspirations and its need for appearing central to the organization of a region or state.

If the separation between consumptive and productive water systems is pronounced, it can shorten the longevity of the early state, especially if urban water demands deplete hinterland resources. This situation is most likely in an arid environment, such as the Maghrib during its historical Roman colonization (Shaw 1984) or, perhaps, in the prehistoric and protohistoric lower Tigris and Euphrates drainages. In the latter case, overuse of the hinterlands may have resulted in severe field salinization (Gibson 1974).

On the other hand, a small heterarchical state system, even one developing in an arid setting, will manifest a weak dichotomy between consumptive and productive water-system users. The small Nabataean state, occupying sizable portions of Jordan, Syria, and Israel away from riverine access (but trading with the expanding Roman Empire), constructed a dispersed but coordinated seasonal system of wadi terracing. Here, the consumptive and productive difference was much less exaggerated because the system was based on the accretional harvesting of water and land resources and a sustained use of the desert (see chapters 3 and 4).

The view that civilization is spatially pitted against a surrounding wilderness—the source of base raw materials for processing the refined goods consumed by the city—is one model for the state. Perhaps a uniquely Western perspective today, it has considerable antiquity, as demonstrated by the fortifications enclosing the world's first city, Uruk, in southern Iraq by the Early Dynastic period (c. 2700 BC) (Redmond 1978:264; cf. Stone 1997). The concept was also well developed in Classical Greece, although the division changed over time (Morris 1997; Small 1997). Less divisive separations between urban and rural are apparent in other models of civilization.

For the great Khmer state, the ancient Maya, and perhaps the ancient Sinhalese, the city was not the dense concentration of ordered controllable humanity that it was in some of the more arid, riverine-dependent primary states. Bray (1986:73; after Groslier 1974) indicates that the Angkor Complex within the Khmer state did not distinguish between urban and rural because it equated the hinterlands with the positive forces of nature, incorporating the gods of water, soil, and fertility. These elements strongly defined the political and ritual center, also. The tank systems operating within Angkor, in the Lowland Maya city of Tikal, and in the Sinhalese capital of Anuradhapura reflect a less consumptive water system than those featured in the ancient city-states of Iraq or Greece (see chapters 4, 5, 7, and 8). Tropical cities and their associated rural aggregates exhibit less dichotomous population densities than are apparent in more arid primary state settings, allowing greater potential for integration between center and periphery. In ethnographic Bali (Geertz 1963, 1973), Sri Lanka (Leach 1961), and the Philippines (Coward 1979)—each dependent on ponded water features designed for rice production—a more dispersed settlement pattern is reported than in contemporary water management systems with small-scale, unterraced irrigation systems without significant use of tanks. In short, the deployment of reservoirs and tanks across a landscape opens the hinterlands to more people while preventing huge population aggregation at any single urban node.

Archaeological Case Studies—New World

Among the wonders unfolded by the discovery of these ruined cities, what made
the strongest impression on our minds was the fact that their immense popula-
tion existed in a region so scantily supplied with water.

—John Lloyd Stephens (1843, II:165)

The accounts of water management among contemporary or historic peoples provide a richness of detail generally not retrievable from the archaeological record. Nevertheless, archaeology is the only vehicle for long-term comparisons of the growth, maintenance, and decline of water systems in various parts of the world, enabling us to identify ecological and cultural constraints on water management. The Old World and New World examples presented in this chapter and the next reveal the tension between hierarchically controlled water systems and those of the insular village. The juxtaposition of arid and humid settings in these chapters also illustrates the variability and complexity of ancient water management systems.

The New World examples are taken from Mesoamerica and the U. S. Southwest (inclusive of northern Mexico). They afford a focused assessment of three environments and the organizational adaptations characterizing them (see figure 7.1). I emphasize the distinctive organizational aspects of each group in identifying the variability in water management systems. Nevertheless, when we understand the limitations of the landscape, the organizational outlooks (regulatory principles) of these societies exhibit considerable consistency in decision making and problem solving. At the same time, lowland and highland systems manifest notable organizational and causal differences. For instance, I emphasize the ritualized elements guiding water systems in the Maya Lowlands but concentrate on the natural environmental influences affecting hydraulic decision making in highland Mexico. This is not to say that the political economy or ritual was not involved in water management solutions in the Mexican Highlands. Rather, the organizational planes (see chapters 2 and 3) of these two cultures emphasized different themes at different times, changing with modifications to the landscape and the water systems deployed.

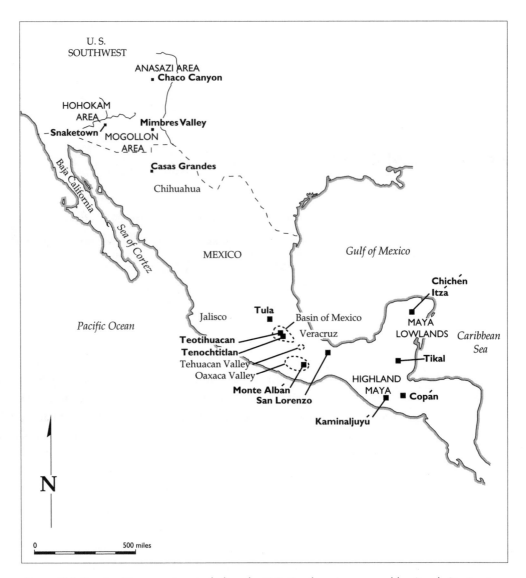

Figure 7.1 Greater Mesoamerica, including the U.S. Southwest, prepared by Sarah Stoutamire.

Southern Maya Lowlands (400 BC–AD 900)

The environmental seat of Classic Maya civilization (AD 250–900) was the heavily vegetated, limestone surface of the lower Yucatán Peninsula (see figure 7.2). In the southern Maya Lowlands (the focus of Maya state development), rainfall is highly seasonal, with a four-month period of annual drought. Precipitation rates today range from 1,350 to 2,000 mm/year in north-central Petén, Guatemala (Bronson 1978; Puleston 1973). Major surface drainage is lacking, although the Usumacinta River on the west and the Río Hondo on the east permit some riverine discharge from the ancient Maya heartland. Far from being desertlike, though, the setting is a semitropical forest area, slightly on the dry side. The thin soils are fertile on the hills and

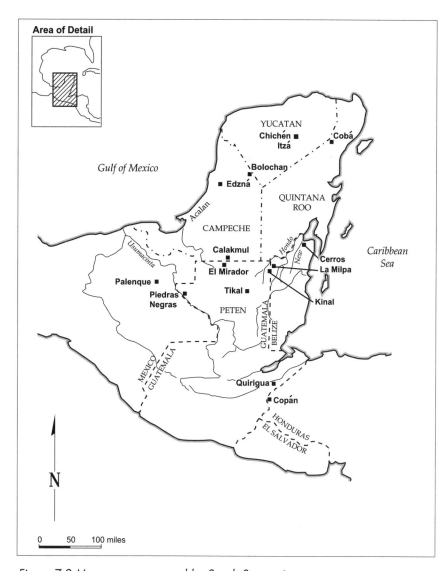

Figure 7.2 Maya area, prepared by Sarah Stoutamire.

better-drained flatlands *(mollisols),* but thick viscous clays *(vertisols)* presently limit utilization of the low-lying *bajos* (seasonally inundated, internally draining swamps). *Bajo* covers approximately 30 percent of the area. More than 40 percent of the most densely occupied zone—from Tikal to Río Azul—was *bajo* during the Classic period (Culbert et al. 1989). During the dry season, water is costly because of the paucity of springs, permanent rivers, and streams.

Of the external drainages in the Maya Lowlands, the western Usumacinta drainage carries the most water, but its incised channels and poorly defined floodplain preclude extensive canalization. The eastern Río Azul/Río Hondo system allows slow-moving, backwash floodplain channelizing. However, because of the absorption/dispersion characteristic of the porous limestone watershed, fluctuation in annual water level is somewhat unpredictable (Siemens 1978). This former characteristic permits a slow-release discharge during both dry and wet seasons, generally preventing yearly flood-plain sediment renewal and prohibiting the deployment of complicated water diversion techniques. This does not mean that the meandering course of the Río Hondo or its tributaries has not yielded evidence of intensive forms of agriculture based on water manipulation. To the contrary, the annually stable water levels enabled drained-field and raised-field agriculture to flourish in northern Belize (Harrison and Turner, eds. 1983; Scarborough 1991b; Siemens 1978, 1982; cf. Pohl, ed. 1990; Pope and Dahlin 1989). Nevertheless, standard forms of riverine canalization or pre-dictable flood sediment deposition have not been found in the Lowland Maya area.

Reservoir Dependency

Drawing on an earlier position taken by Cooke (1931) and Palerm and Wolf (1957), Harrison (1977) posited that many of today's internally draining *bajos* were lakes or modified reservoirs that have silted in. A recent article by Jacob (1995) argues that these depressions were instead *civales,* or "marshy areas of perennial wetness," provid-ing an extremely fertile matrix for agriculture. At any rate, poorly coordinated slash-and-burn agricultural systems practiced on higher ground adjacent to the *bajos* have accelerated sedimentation into these depressed settings since their disuse more than a millennium ago. Recent work in northwestern Belize also suggests that the *bajos* were perennial wetlands or shallow lakes during the Late Formative period (400 BC–AD 150) and that they infilled during the Classic period (AD 250–900), precipi-tating a significant settlement shift (Dunning et al. 1999, 2002). Other surveys and excavations further suggest drained-field agriculture in *bajo*-like settings in Quintana Roo, Mexico, and northern Belize (Gliessman et al. 1983; Harrison 1977, 1982, 1993; Harrison and Turner, eds. 1978; Scarborough 1983a, 1983b, 1993a, 1994a).

In addition to the possibile *bajo* "tanks," numerous reservoirs are reported in more elevated settings, associated with ancient communities of all sizes (Scarborough 1993a, 1994a). Perhaps modified from natural depressions or limestone quarries, these basins could reach immense proportions. At the Campeche city of Edzná, Mexico, Matheny (1976; Matheny et al. 1983) has identified several monumental canal basins dating as early as the Late Formative period (400 BC–AD 150) (refer to figure 4.23). More than 1.75 million m^3 of fill was removed in their construction— more than the volume of the Pyramid of the Sun at Teotihuacan.

Tikal is the best-documented large community in the Maya Lowlands (W. Coe 1967, 1990). At several elevated locations within and immediately outside the cen-tral precinct, reservoirs were formed behind well-defined causeways, or *sacbeob* (refer to figures 4.25, 4.26, and 4.27). These causeways connected various portions of the compacted temple core but also served to dam water within a sizable catchment area (Carr and Hazard 1961; Scarborough 1993a, 1994a; Scarborough and Gallopin 1991). Nearly dry today, these tanks likely held considerably more water in the past. Controlled release from these elevated reservoirs to the downslope flanks and adjacent *bajo* margins supplied household and agricultural water during the dry season. In physical appearance, the Tikal tank system is strikingly similar to the tanks of south India and Sri Lanka (see chapters 4, 5, and 8).

Causeways functioning as dikes are not limited to Tikal. Such a dam or dike crossed the water-filled basin in one of the large lakes, or reservoirs, at the Classic period site of Cobá (Folan, Kintz, Fletcher 1983). At Late Formative period Cerros (refer to figure 4.21) and El Mirador, causeways *(sacbeob)* traversed low-lying swamp or lake settings near the central precincts (Dahlin 1984; Graham 1967; Scarborough 1983a, 1991b, 1993a, 1994a). The Cerros hydraulic system suggests that an elevated road or dike separated water into communitywide agricultural sources on one side and private-household potable sources on the other (Scarborough 1983a, 1991b) (refer to figure 4.22). Canalization also was well developed in the slow-moving, internally drained Cerros system.

Emphasis on water sources and the kinds of landscape modifications in the southern Maya Lowlands evolved through time, induced by increased population densities and possibly climate fluctuations (see Folan, Gunn, et al. 1983; Gill 2000; Gunn et al. 1995; Hodell et al. 1995; Messenger 1990). As outlined in chapter 4, Late Formative period (400 BC–AD 150) Maya positioned their communities at the margins of swamps *(bajos)* or related depressions. Subsequent Classic period (AD 250–900) cities adopted a land-use strategy requiring construction of their largest and most densely concentrated civic structures at the summit of elevated hillocks or ridges (refer to figure 4.24). The Formative landscape adaptation resulted in *concave microwatersheds*—passive water systems requiring expeditiously excavated drainage channels located to shed runoff from the canted pavements of large plaza and courtyard groups into artificially enlarged or otherwise modified depressions. The Classic-period, built-urban environment was more deliberate, characterized by sizable but elevated reservoirs. Excavated for the fill produced in constructing the monumental architecture of the great centers, these reservoirs were designed to receive the large quantities of runoff flowing seasonally over the great plazas, pyramids, and palaces (refer to figure 4.26). During the dry season, their *convex microwatersheds* permitted the directing of water downslope to residential consumers and *bajo*-margin agricultural plots. Despite the change from concave to convex microwatersheds, however, the basic secular trend persisted: a slow, accretionary development of the engineered landscape.

The history of water management in the Maya Lowlands demonstrates the general principle that water must be considered an independent variable in any land-use study. If it can be assumed or predicted along a stream course or canal system, other variables can take on greater significance. In the Maya Lowlands, ultimate source could not be assumed, but greater predictability for the resource developed as reservoir technology evolved. Nevertheless, this dependence on capturing rainfall from diminutive, immediate catchment areas (microwatersheds), which directed runoff into depressions or tanks, established water as the unequivocal independent variable for survival in the Maya Lowlands.

Settlement

It is generally agreed that Maya cities had relatively dispersed (as opposed to densely compacted) populations. The largest of the well-mapped cities had densities of little more than 900 persons/km^2 (Culbert and Rice, eds. 1990), markedly less than urban densities in Classic-period highland Mexico, Middle-Horizon Peru, Shang China, Sumer, Harappa, or even the towns attributable to Old-Kingdom Egypt (Fletcher 1986). At the same time, though, the sustaining population outside the urban core in the Maya area did not abruptly decrease as the cities grew, as it tended to do in cases of semiarid state formation tethered to permanent water courses. Rural population densities during the Late Classic period (AD 550–900) averaged 180 persons/km^2 (inclusive of vast tracts of swamp, or *bajo*), among the world's highest for preindustrial states (Rice and Culbert 1990:26).

Because the Maya seem so different from the primary temperate civilizations, researchers ever since V. Gordon Childe have tended either to particularize their interpretations of the early state or to generalize, with a caveat about this one anomaly, the Maya. "Hence, the minimum definition of a city, the greatest factor common to the Old World and the New, will be substantially reduced and impoverished by the inclusion of the Maya" (Childe 1950:9).

The earliest Maya may have tethered their settlements to streams, initially colonizing the southern Maya Lowlands by migrating up the slow-moving seasonal streams flanking the Yucatán Peninsula's interior (Puleston and Puleston 1971; Scarborough 1994a). However, subsequent populations were less inclined to accept this settlement adaptation. Because of the heavy rainfall during eight months of the year, people could venture away from riverine settings and occupy the margins of natural sinks (*aguadas*) and swamps (*bajos*). Where human alteration enhanced the water-retaining character of a natural depression, long-term residency was possible. Furthermore, the construction of formal reservoirs and diversion features by the Late Formative period (400 BC–AD 150) opened the landscape in ways that simply did not occur in semiarid state areas. Reservoirs at the household and village level permitted ready access to collected water, but village size depended on the tank's capacity.

At the same time, dense population aggregates comparable to those at Teotihuacan in highland Mexico or Chan Chan in Peru were impossible. In the semitropical ecosystem, species diversity in the Maya Lowlands was high, but concentrations of any single species at any one location were minor—preventing the large natural harvests associated with more temperate environments. Because that ecosystem quality was coupled with a lack of predictable surface water, human populations naturally tended to disperse.

Economic Outlays

The economic outlays for establishing the water systems in the Maya area may not have been as severe as those in other parts of the world. The ancient Maya adapted to an accretionary harvesting of resources (see chapters 2 and 6), given the ecosystem's fragility for human use. Overexploiting portions of the environment was possible, but the threshold for ecological disaster was so much more immediate than in semiarid and temperate settings that only the slow, measured use and modification of the environs was practical. The relative ease with which limestone was quarried to produce reservoirs and dams (causeways), as well as the need for construction fill in erecting monumental architecture, resulted in an approximate 1:1 relationship between reservoir volumes and temple/palace/house mound volumes in some communities (Scarborough 1983a, 1991b). Furthermore, the greater rainfall associated with a semitropical forest enabled small, insular communities to construct and maintain their own reservoirs, independently of larger cities.

The Maya tank, or reservoir, systems (excluding reclaimed *bajo* settings) probably functioned in a manner akin to those documented in southern India and Sri Lanka (see chapters 4 and 8). Within the insular community, water allocation likely followed a Syrian model until resources were severely stressed. Although the state almost certainly would have meddled, most maintenance and internal conflict resolution connected with water distribution probably occurred within the community.

If the present-day swamps *(bajos)* were ancient lakes, however, state regulators would have controlled salinity rates and lake levels, as indicated in the lake basin of Aztec-period highland Mexico. Raised fields, such as the Aztecs' *chinampas,* required a significant corporate investment to establish and maintain. The early utilization of the swamps *(bajos)* is evidenced by the causeways leading into these depressions at the Late Formative city of El Mirador (Matheny, ed. 1980) and more widely in the Petén (Graham 1967; Folan 1992) and by aerial photographs of drained fields in southern Quintana Roo (Harrison 1978, 1993). This evidence suggests large agricultural tracts regulated by controlled water levels. Foot survey and excavation in far northeastern Petén and Quintana Roo (Culbert et al. 1989; Harrison 1978) indicate that water levels fluctuate seasonally within these swamps today but that rainy-season drainage devices and dry-season conservation measures permitted at least two crops per year in antiquity. Sizable diversion dams are suggested along the Río Azul (R. E. W. Adams 1984), and floodgates are postulated immediately off the New River (Harrison and Turner, eds. 1983). In these latter examples, water appears to have been diverted from a river to an adjacent floodplain and backwash setting for raised-field agriculture.

Maya water systems allowed several simultaneous functional adaptations. The seasonality of rainfall and the lack of significant external drainage permitted the control of water reserves at several sites. Tikal and other elevated sites with artificially altered, convex microwatersheds controlled several sizable tanks, doubtless under elite authority. Large communities such as Tikal would have required complex water bureaucracies if the elite used these reservoirs to manipulate the adjacent swamps *(bajos)* for agricultural ends. On the other hand, even small autonomous communities were capable of constructing reservoirs adequate for domestic (nonagricultural) use. More generally speaking, the difficulty of controlling a dispersed population in a tropical rain forest (Scarborough 1998; Scarborough and Gallopin 1991; Scarborough and Robertson 1986) and the relative ease of constructing a reservoir system from the limestone relief meant that absolute elite control of water was never possible.

Ritual and the Semitropical Setting

Maya society was highly ritualized, perhaps more so than other case examples that follow. Richard Fox (1977) has suggested a categorization of complex sociopolitical organization that some researchers have used in typing the political structure of many Mesoamerican states, particularly the ancient Maya (Sanders and Webster 1988). According to this categorization, the Maya had "regal-ritual" state systems. This means a weakly developed, centralized administrative apparatus associated with highly public, complex rituals performed by nobility to recruit labor and obtain resources. As in the case of Geertz's (1980) Balinese "theater state," some researchers continue to view the Maya as having less developed state systems than the primary states in semiarid environments. However, to paraphrase Lansing (1991:4), if the kings did not control the economy, who did?

The Maya were never centralized in the manner of the modern nation-state and even less so than some of the earliest primary states in either the Old World or New World. As we saw in chapters 2 and 3, centralization is a process in which resource control is concentrated in varying degrees; in response to this, focused (centralized) power waxes and wanes. The Maya offer an important perspective on the centralization process because they never commanded the size and type of resource concentrations suggested by the densely occupied urban centers of primary states elsewhere (cf. Sanders and Price 1968; Sanders and Webster 1988). Nonetheless, they were great architects and artisans and developed the most advanced form of writing in the New World. What the Maya provide is a different perspective on the centralization process and the kinds of forces acting to decentralize any state.

The Maya were less centralized than other primary states because of their natural environment—the karstic, wet-dry tropical ecosystem defined by species diversity (limited concentrations of any one species, however). In tropical and semitropical settings such as the Maya area or Sri Lanka (see chapter 8), the dispersed character of organic resources influenced a set of regulatory principles culminating in less centralized landscape use. As indicated in chapter 3, an ecosystem's limitations can frequently direct a society's organizational outlook, especially in the formative stages of social complexity. Through time and environmental alteration, a different—frequently unanticipated—and highly engineered landscape may develop from the decisions filtered through the original traditional land-use and water-use formulas. The inheritors of such altered ancestral landscapes frequently use past formulas that are poorly adapted to the newly built environment.

Most semiarid archaic states show a rapid exploitation of the environment precipitated and accommodated by *technotasking,* the rapid consumption of newly understood resources, based on technological advances. Because of rapid change, the formulas used in this organizational outlook were conducive to overexploitation and were frequently short-lived. In contrast, the ancient Maya were less obliged to modify their pioneering land and water management strategies significantly, because of the slow rate and process of environmental change in the lowlands. Although the Maya evolved into a complex civilization, their traditional formulas for deciding how to alter the landscape were rooted in an earlier adaptation based on the fragility of the tropical forest setting. Clearly, resource overexploitation occurred, but the careful husbanding and harvesting of fragile resources in an accretionally altered ecosystem most heavily influenced Maya institutional organization. Because they manipulated the environment less drastically from the outset, compared with semiarid states, the Maya were able to maintain much of their original organizational outlook, which was fashioned on the model of labortasking.

Because Maya populations and their resources were dispersed across their semi-tropical setting, they devised organizational strategies to coordinate labortasking. In this context, ritual helped keep groups tethered to urban nodes. However, neither ritual cohesion nor the centralizing efforts involved in constructing and using sizable reservoirs at the summit of most Classic-period centers could prevent Maya populations from spreading centrifugally. Minor centers, even clusters of seemingly less coordinated households, frequently commanded economic resources fundamental to maintaining a complex society. To attract a permanent, loyal support population to principal centers, elite managers would have appropriated everyday ritual activity, especially water ritual, to manipulate deeply held traditional formulas relating to water use (Scarborough 1998) (see chapters 3 and 5).

The Maya case permits entrée to segmental and heterarchical organization, as defined in chapter 2. Many hinterland communities were resource-specialized and economically organized to produce a few things well. Typically, a rural nobility occupied the Maya countryside but was inextricably linked to the primary monumental centers through a set of interdependencies including both economic exchange and ritual attraction. Such linkages enabled the movement of information and goods within the dispersed settlement pattern and allowed the economic and political flexibility necessary in a fragile, though highly engineered, environment (Scarborough and Valdez, in press).

Highland Mexico (100 BC–AD 750)

The Basin of Mexico was the seat of great civilizations (see figure 7.3). Although canalization is well reported by 700 BC (Nichols 1982), clear associations between the state and the construction and maintenance of formal irrigation systems do not become evident until the Late Aztec period (AD 1350–1519). Like the Maya area, the Basin of Mexico lacked significant external drainage. The closed system of five connected lakes, along with the expanded lake margins during the rainy season (the Lake of the Moon), covered an area comparable to the swamp *(bajo)* and small-lake system between Tikal and Río Azul in northeastern Petén, Guatemala. Rainfall in the basin is 700 mm/year, far less than in the Maya Lowlands, and frosts severely affect the agricultural year (Sanders et al. 1979). The basin's soils are fertile, characterized as either chernozem or chestnut. Today, crops such as maize and beans are particularly successful on the piedmont slopes above frost-damaged alluvial settings.

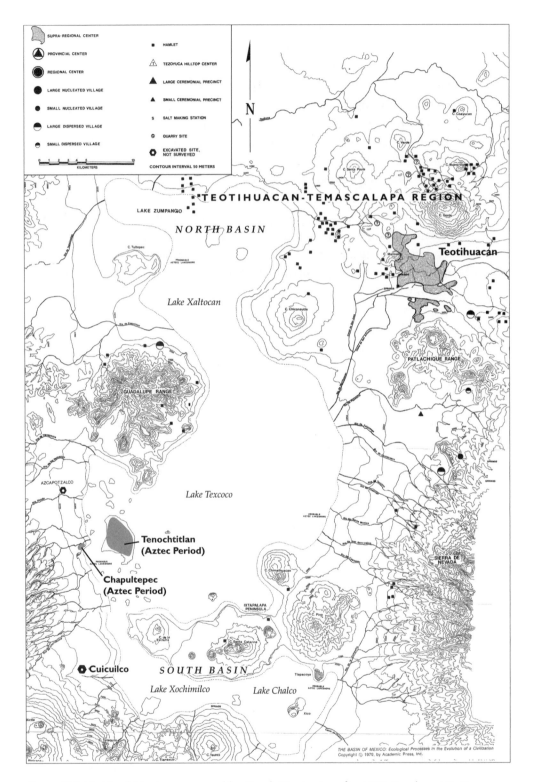

Figure 7.3 Highland Mexico, prepared by Sarah Stoutamire after W.T. Sanders, J.R. Parsons, and R.S. Santley (1979), by permission of Elsevier.

From a very early date, settlement pattern data suggest extensive canal irrigation systems within central highland Mexico (Angulo 1993; Doolittle 1990a; Fowler 1987; Nichols 1987; Sanders et al. 1979; Sanders and Price 1968; Sanders and Santley 1977; Woodbury and Neely 1972). In the basin, these irrigation communities were relatively small, although a single drainage might share its waters with several adjacent communities (cf. Millon et al. 1962). In contrast to the Maya area, a mountainous watershed created permanent streams that eventually issued into the closed five-lake depression. However, the rugged topography and the distances separating small drainages made state control of large tracts of the irrigation systems difficult. Against this ecological backdrop, the gigantic Classic city of Teotihuacan arose explosively by AD 1, an event repeated in the Postclassic rise of Aztec Tenochtitlan beginning c. 1325.

Chinampa *Agriculture and Settlement Patterns*

Sanders and his colleagues (Sanders and Price 1968; Sanders et al. 1979) indicate that large-scale *chinampa* (raised and reclaimed swamp) and lake-margin agriculture was entirely a Late Horizon or Aztec-period (AD 1350–1519) development. They suggest that *chinampa* field plots supported half a million people at this time. Therefore, they concluded that Aztec civilization was a "true" hydraulic society in Wittfogel's (1957) sense of the word. In part, they based their case for state centralization on the highly regular, rectilinear patterning of the *chinampa* field networks and the implied planning necessary to coordinate such construction. Early Colonial accounts also allude to the significance of *chinampas,* but Sanders's strongest argumentation is buttressed by archaeological settlement density data and the implied correlation between settlement location and the agricultural utilization of that zone.

Although the precise inception of lakeshore *chinampa* agriculture remains unclear, Palerm (1955) provides historic accounts demonstrating its widespread use during the Aztec period. Parsons's (1991) settlement data also corroborate Sanders's position. Nevertheless, unstable lake levels and elevated salinity rates severely limited the potential for extensive *chinampa* agriculture. Because the basin was closed, heavily mineralized sediments accumulated in the lakes, making the waters nitrous and harmful to plants and humans. In addition, unchecked fluctuations in stream discharge rates, coupled with periodic droughts, radically altered lake levels, resulting in flooded or dry *chinampa* plots.

To prevent damage by floods or salt contamination, dikes or causeways spanned portions of the lakes. The spectacular island city of Tenochtitlan was made possible, in part, by a dike controlling the floods of nitrous water into the western embayment of Lake Texcoco (see figures 7.4, 7.5, and 7.6). Effectively separating the embayment from the greater body of the lake, the dike promoted *chinampa* cultivation and the development of potable water supplies. Sweet water from Chapultepec and other springs on the mainland flowed by aqueduct into the cordoned-off embayment, eventually diluting the saline concentration. In addition, the dike's sluice gates were used to control water levels within the dammed area (Palerm 1955).

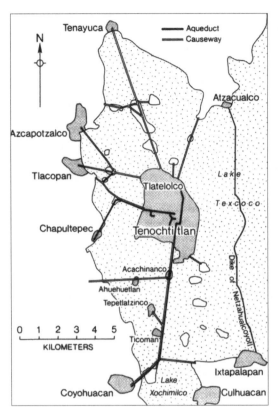

Figure 7.4 Aztec lake embayment with Tenochtitlan, reprinted by permission of the University of Texas Press from W.E. Doolittle (1990).

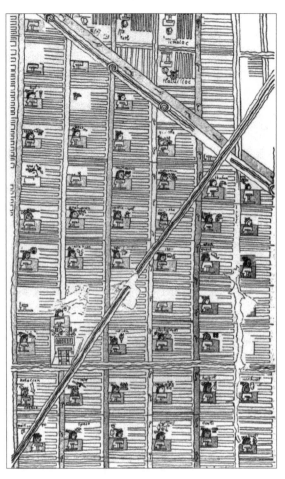

Figure 7.5 Chinampa fields in vicinity of Tenochtitlan, prepared and reprinted by permission of the estate of Eric Mose from M.D. Coe (1964), courtesy of Scientific American.

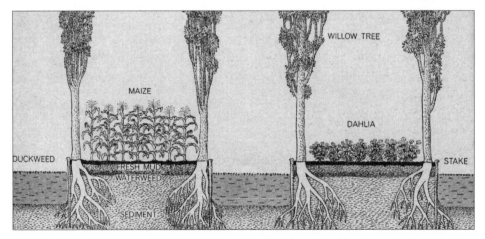

Figure 7.6 Cross section of a chinampa, prepared and reprinted by permission of the estate of Eric Mose from M.D. Coe (1964), courtesy of Scientific American.

Although received wisdom argues for the late appearance of *chinampa* agriculture, settlement data from the Southern Basin—the most productive *chinampa* zone during the Aztec period—may suggest otherwise. During the Second Intermediate Period (AD 750–1350), immediately before Aztec occupation, 69 percent of the population resided on the lakeshores. By Aztec times, however, only 44 percent, including the huge island population of Tenochtitlan (Sanders et al. 1979:192), lived on the shores. If the greatest population density in *chinampa* settings occurred before the well-documented Aztec period of *chinampa* cultivation, how much earlier was this form of intensive agriculture practiced?

According to the figures of Sanders et al (1979:192), lacustrine-adapted families settled in at least 27 percent of the Chalco and Xochimilco area, the focus of the Southern Basin, during the First Intermediate Five/Middle Horizon (AD 100–200). This is the interim period associated with the final days of Cuicuilco—the only other large center in the basin at this time—and the ascendancy of Teotihuacan on the basin's northern edge. Intensive *chinampa* agriculture in the Northern Basin area within the greater Teotihuacan-Temascalapa region is poorly documented, for two reasons:

1. Methodological difficulties in identifying any ancient agricultural feature
2. The tremendous implosion of regional population into Teotihuacan—the most influential city in Mesoamerica by AD 500 or earlier—obscuring *chinampa* field systems near, if not within, the city

During the Middle Horizon (AD 300–750), nearly 155,000 people lived in the Teotihuacan-Temascalapa region (Sanders et al. 1979:204); 125,000 resided in the 23.5 km^2 of Teotihuacan (Millon 1970, 1973).

Teotihuacan arose swiftly on the outer edge of the Northern Basin, some 60 km from the Southern Basin's marshy, swampy lakeshores—famous for *chinampas* during the Aztec period, more than a millennium later. This fact has deflected attention from the possibility of *chinampa*-type raised fields during Teotihuacan times (AD 1–750) (see plate 7.7). Indeed, it has led many scholars to assume that this type of agriculture not only was unimportant to Teotihuacan but also did not even exist in the Basin of Mexico before the Aztec period (AD 1350–1521). Nevertheless, we have just seen that sizable pre-Aztec (AD 750–1350) lakeshore populations already existed in the Southern Basin's Chalco-Xochimilco area—*chinampa*-rich during the subsequent Aztec period. Furthermore, Palerm (1955:35), M. Coe (1964), and Armillas (1971) point to the construction of *tlateles* (islands), now thought to be ancient *chinampas,* on the lake margins of the Southern Basin as early as 150 BC, the date of initial settlement at Teotihuacan in the Northern Basin (Cowgill 1992:90-92).[1] (These *tlateles* were probably the subsistence base for Teotihuacan's early southern-lakeshore rival, Cuicuilco, before its catastrophic abandonment.) In short, *chinampa* agriculture has a considerably longer history in the Southern Basin than previously thought. As we shall see, there is good reason to believe that this form of agriculture was also practiced in the Northern Basin at the very inception of Teotihuacan there, c. 150 BC, and was important to the great city's ascendancy and regional dominance (AD 1–750).

Teotihuacan occupies a basaltic tongue, part of the lower piedmont, but projects into the alluvial plain that Sanders et al. (1979) propose was significantly altered by irrigation schemes. Within the Teotihuacan Valley, Sanders et al. (1979:252–53, 277, and maps 1, 13, 14, 24) argue that 1,000 ha (10 km^2) of swampy terrain were reclaimed during the late First Intermediate period (no later than 150 BC) around the 80 to 100 springs near present-day San Juan Teotihuacan—along the western and northwestern urban margins of Middle Horizon (AD 300–750) Teotihuacan (see plate 7.8). The transformation of this swampy terrain may have permitted the diversion of water into an extensively irrigated alluvial plain to supply the concentrated urban population at Teotihuacan. More likely, though, this reclamation project was carried out to construct *chinampas.* What better way to reclaim a swampy 10-km^2 zone with scores of active springs than by ditching it and relocating the fill to nearby, agriculturally preadapted raised plots? Of course, after this sizable area was reclaimed, some springwaters may have been directed to a canalized alluvial plain.

In the past (Scarborough 1991a), I suggested that Teotihuacan was located specifically to tap the abundant natural resources at the northern reaches of the basin's lake system, as well as to access obsidian quarries and related production sites. I was probably incorrect on both counts. First, John Clark (1986) has challenged the causal significance of the obsidian trade in Teotihuacan's growth and regional dominance, a position championed widely by Sanders and his students (Sanders et al. 1979; Sanders and Santley 1983; Santley 1983, 1984). Second, the use of the lake system in the Northern Basin—the portion of the lakes closest to Teotihuacan—for *chinampa* agriculture during the Middle Horizon is unlikely because the dams or causeways necessary to control lake levels in this area were probably not in place until the Aztec period. This lack of north-shore intensive agriculture, however, in no way negates the posited dependency of Teotihuacan and other communities in the greater Basin of Mexico on *chinampa* agriculture at this time. As just noted, the inhabitants of Teotihuacan likely excavated their own *chinampa* system near the city's abundant springwaters, located several kilometers from the lakeshores (refer to figure 7.3). Whether a *chinampa* system was in place even before the initial settlement at Teotihuacan c. 150 BC—influencing or even determining its location there—is an open question. For the Lake Xaltocan area, immediately west of the city, recent research has produced absolute dates associated with relict *chinampas* that fall within the Late Formative (650–150 BC). The excavators responsible for this work remain uncomfortable with these early dates, however, and prefer to associate the fields with a later, pre-Aztec context (Nichols and Fredrick 1993).

The existence of springs and reclaimed swampland and the related potential for *chinampas* very near to Teotihuacan support the idea of a complex connection between intensive agriculture, population growth, and strong centralization. As Sanders has stated on several occasions (Sanders et al. 1979; Sanders and Price 1968; Sanders and Santley 1983), social complexity and limited means of transport—no wheel, sail, or beast of burden—caused nucleated settlement near crucial resources in the highlands. In this regard, the *chinampas* on the Southern Basin lakeshore were likely too far from Teotihuacan to augment its food production significantly, nor would these southern *chinampas* have influenced the city's initial location.

It is important to point out that canal irrigation was probably not a significant aspect of Teotihuacan's development. Even acknowledging the irrigation canals under the Oaxacan Barrio on the city's western periphery at AD 1–100 (Nichols et al. 1991) or the postulated canals in its southern section at 300 BC–AD 150 (Nichols 1988), the amount of land demonstrably farmed by formal irrigation of the alluvial plain is small. In fact, utilization of the alluvial plain southwest of Teotihuacan by employing conventional canalization schemes would have likely spread the population, resulting in a less nucleated community than actually existed.

One unique characteristic of Teotihuacan's ascendancy was its blurring of the urban-rural distinction. Only 7.5 percent of the Teotihuacan Valley population resided outside the city during the Middle Horizon (AD 300–750) (Sanders et al. 1979:204), even though nearly two-thirds of its inhabitants were agriculturalists who commuted to and from their fields. Given transportation limitations and the city's huge, highly nucleated population, perhaps the most parsimonious explanation for Teotihuacan's location was its initial dependency on local *chinampas*. Irrigation systems may have increased community food supplies, especially by recycling potable water leaving the city (to the south and west of the city's margins, precisely where we find the best evidence for early canalization). However, these systems could not have provided the same geographical focus and immediate field access as intensive *chinampa* agriculture. Without a more advanced transport technology than was available, farmers would have spent as much time walking to their canalized plots as farming them. The density, scale, and rigidity of the city plan at Teotihuacan strongly suggest a state order capable of directing the movements of a rural support population to produce the most food possible within the state's technological limitations.

Definitions of City

The truly nucleated character of Teotihuacan's urbanism, with its highly ordered grid layout, is unusual in the prehispanic New World. Planned central precincts are apparent at many large centers; some were also ordered on a rectilinear grid. Seldom, though, was a community true to a common orientation throughout its urban limits. Nucleated cities half the size of Teotihuacan were rare enough, and the attention to spatial layout makes it unique. What forces may have enabled these characteristics to develop?

As Sanders and Price (1968) convincingly argued years ago, transportation limitations on Mesoamerican communities were severe (also see Drennan 1984a, 1984b; Drennan et al. 1990). Because the resources necessary for making a living are seldom naturally concentrated, groups disperse and locate near the most significant resources to exploit them more advantageously. Exchange networks coordinated by a village or town center then supplement household resource requirements. Nevertheless, a city the size of Teotihuacan overcame most of these settlement limitations. Charismatic leadership and the manipulation of power symbols may be causal agents in Teotihuacan's florescence (Millon 1992; Pasztory 1988), but economic explanations are also possible. To assess Teotihuacan's uniqueness, we must examine how land and water resources were exploited.

As already mentioned, the 10-km^2 area of swamp initially reclaimed by Patlachique-period (100 BC–AD 1) residents was responsible for the density and size of Teotihuacan's population. The other extremely dense population center of scale— Tenochtitlan, six centuries after Teotihuacan's collapse—was positioned within the basin's lake system. Canoe traffic in bulk goods and the immediate proximity of *chinampa* fields offset this situation's transportation and resource limitations (Calnek 1972; Santley 1986). The strict grid layout of Classic Teotihuacan (AD 150–750) doubtless reflects a desire and capacity for the spatial regulation of a vast support population controlled partially by a compelling ideology. However, the ordered rectilinearity of Postclassic Tenochtitlan (AD 1325–1521) suggests a possible additional factor influencing urban planning at Teotihuacan. The urban layout of Tenochtitlan may have been a consequence of *chinampas* within the island core (Calnek 1972) (refer to figure 7.5), even though the widespread presence of field systems on the island is now in doubt (Calnek 1973). Nevertheless, if a small portion of the island were initially devoted to *chinampa* agriculture, the grid pattern of these fields would have strongly influenced settlement layout. Also, canalization at the expanding city's margins, to carry potable water through the developing city or to supply irrigation schemes, artificially gridded the suburban landscape. As the city expanded outward, certain canalized space would have been reclaimed for residential purposes, with house lots and related streets adhering to the earlier canal grid.

Angulo's (1987) water management investigations at Teotihuacan demonstrate the existence of an elaborate street drainage (*otli-apantli*) system formed by a network of gridded canals. The system drained excess waters away from public and residential buildings and toward agricultural lots scattered within the city. These canals were sometimes substantial, as suggested by a Teotihuacan mural showing a canoe on one of them (Angulo 1987:fig. 9) (refer to figure 7.7).

Ethnographic cases in which initial canalization precipitated an urban grid layout, as suggested for Teotihuacan, are easy to find. Towns and cities in contemporary Iran expand into adjacent irrigated lands as population pressures force urban residential growth.

> Most settlements in the central plateau exhibit a rather distinctive orthogonal or rectangular network of streets and houses. This grid pattern has resulted from the rectangular irrigation and field system. As villages (and even cities) expanded, they filled in adjacent rectangular fields and orchards.... Major streets and many blind alleys already existed with the field patterns

before houses spread into these areas. Even the sizes and shapes of new houses are governed by the pre-existing system of fields and passageways. (Bonine 1996:198–99)

The foregoing (on Iran) is one of several useful analogies between the Old and New Worlds, but care must be taken in their application. The first Sumerian city-states are frequently compared with incipient urban nodes in the Basin of Mexico because Early Dynastic Uruk (c. 2700 BC), near the southern Euphrates River, also experienced a population implosion within a walled 4-km^2 area surrounded by a res-identially empty, agriculturally rich hinterland (Adams 1981:85; Redman 1978:264; cf. Rothman, ed. 2001). On the other hand, early archaic states along the Tigris and Euphrates Rivers had permanent (but not totally predictable) water sources for irri-gation schemes and made use of wheeled vehicles, beasts of burden, and navigable waterways within a much less topographically dissected region. An early city as large and complex as Teotihuacan is even more astonishing in the absence of these inven-tions that facilitated urbanism in the Old World.

Economic Outlays

Truly urban conditions prevailed in the civilizations seated in the Basin of Mexico. State planning and control directed water manipulation near the large cities. The island city of Tenochtitlan (AD 1325–1521) likely had some of its own *chinampas* and certainly had immediate access to *chinampa* fields on the southern lakeshore margins (Monjarás-Ruiz 1980: 117–18, 134–38, 156). Clearly, *chinamperos* were at the mercy of the state bureaucracy, for only the state could control and regulate water levels. A statewide Syrian water allotment system (equitable water distribution based on allot-ments proportional to the amount of the land cultivated) would have been unavoid-able, however, given the characteristics of lakeshore agriculture.

The small size of the drainages feeding into the basin and the absence of conjoined interdrainage areas make regional hydraulic control unlikely. Generally speaking, irrigation organization was villagewide and sometimes drainagewide. However, according to Palerm (1955:40), the Cuauhtitlán River emptying into the lakes was dammed, diverted, and finally redirected into a newly widened channel 2 km long and nearly 3 m wide and 3 m deep during the Aztec period (AD 1350–1519). Obviously, such focused energies required state action to mobilize the numerous vil-lages that Palerm's figures suggest. However, the state was likely a temporary player called upon for long-term economic outlays that may or may not have been beneficial to an individual village (cf. Hunt and Hunt 1974), a situation precipitated by a water crisis with regional consequences. Reduced quantities of water, induced by natural drought or increased numbers of consumers, probably resulted in considerable con-flict. Under these conditions of severe shortage, I would predict a Yemenite allotment adaptation (unequal water allocation based on timed releases) favored the local elite and triggered widespread tension.

Although conventional wisdom has highlighted the intensive lakeshore agriculture of the Aztec period, we have seen that Classic-period Teotihuacan (AD 150–750) was arguably more dependent on *chinampa* fields than previous assessments indicate. Such dependency by a city of its scale would strongly suggest state management of the *chinampas*. Given the nearness of the *chinampa* fields to the city and the transportation costs of exploiting fields farther away, I would argue that the state had everything to do with Teotihuacan's *chinampa* system. Furthermore, I suggest that a Syrian allocation system was operative there, even though considerable variation in water control would be expected during the seven hundred years in which Teotihuacan thrived.

Millon's (1992) recent assessment of the political/ideological history of Teotihuacan reveals a set of very strong rulers, beginning with the founding of the great center (AD 1–100) and the establishment of the Avenue of the Dead (ca. AD 50) and the Pyramids of the Moon and the Sun and ending with the construction of the Cuidadela, the Great Compound, and the Feathered Serpent Temple (AD 250–300). The centralized intensity of state monument building (AD 1–200) probably correlates with swamp reclamation and early *chinampa* construction. The political economy was decentralized for most of the city's remaining reign (AD 200–750) over the basin (see Cowgill 1997). Those 450–500 years following AD 1–200 are characterized by much more modest building activities, indicating to Millon (1992) a "suppression of personal rule." This posited collective leadership (AD 200–750) appears less autocratic than that exercised during the earlier formidable building boom (AD 1–200), indicating that highly centralized resource control at Teotihuacan lasted for only about two hundred years. Except for the last one hundred years of occupation, the city thereafter maintained a less hegemonic political economy. The severe, colonizing exploitation of the landscape during AD 1–200 likely gave way to more extensive, varied water and land use, perhaps incorporating more of the alluvial plain in the manner outlined by Sanders et al. (1979).

The Lowlands and Highlands Compared

The close-fitting technology associated with internally draining, closed-basin, raised-field agriculture and the *chinampa* lakeshore systems probably existed in both the Maya Lowlands and the Basin of Mexico as early as the Late Formative period (300 BC–AD 150). Canalization at the insular village level was elaborated in the Basin of Mexico where permanent streams flowed. In the Maya Lowlands, without permanent water sources but with greater precipitation, both villages and cities focused water management on reservoir construction. Dispersed populations characterized even the largest cities. In both village and city, the potential for state control in the lowlands was limited to swamp *(bajo)* or lakeshore hydraulic management. The more dispersed, autonomous villages would have managed their own water needs, unless the state intervened during a regional water catastrophe.

Why didn't a more conventional form of urbanism—one with much higher population densities—appear in the Maya Lowlands, given the proximity of vast productive swamp margins for raised-field agriculture to feed densely populated regions? One possible explanation is that it was precisely the highly diverse, widely dispersed suite of lowland resources that prevented a focused exploitative effort at any one location, as in Teotihuacan. Because most natural resources are highly dispersed and limited in number in a tropical or semitropical setting, human populations likewise dispersed, preventing the highly centralized urbanism occurring in the Basin of Mexico.

U.S. Southwest (AD 150–1400)

The U.S. Southwest developed complex social institutions, but not the state (see figure 7.9). Accordingly, this area's water management systems afford an interesting comparison with those of the Mesoamerican state areas. Some of the best evidence for prehispanic canalization in the New World comes from the U.S. Southwest. Although water control may have stimulated tenth-century Chacoan political developments in the Anasazi heartland of northeastern New Mexico (Sebastian 1992; cf. Vivian 1990), it was the Hohokam (AD 600–1450) of the northern Sonora Desert in Arizona who established extensive canal systems. They did so near the Gila and Salt Rivers (see figure 7.10). Both are considered perennial, although segments of each may have carried little surface flow during drought cycles (Crown 1987b). The rainfall in the Salt-Gila Basin averages less than 250 mm/year, but more than 500 km of major canal length have been identified (Masse 1981), dating from the Pioneer period through the Classic (AD 150–1400) (Nicholas and Neitzel 1984). In passing, I should note that Mabry (2000) has recently identified early canalization in the Tucson Basin by 1000 BC, but the degree of social coordination in this system is unclear.

Physical Water Management Systems

Howard (1993) demonstrates that canalization of the Salt River involved an earlier, more explosive set of construction events than is frequently argued. According to Howard, the traditional idea (Woodbury 1961) that Hohokam irrigation systems resulted from an unplanned accretionary process carried out by an acephalous social organization does not explain the levels of complexity attained. Simply lengthening a trunk canal significantly alters the larger system's discharge capacity, affecting sedimentation rates and flow velocity and immediately causing systemwide malfunction—ruling out the unplanned, noncomplex accretional model.

Using a combination of approaches based on formal hydraulic-engineering tenets and in situ dating of canal sections (archaeomagnetism), Howard (1993) reveals the explosive construction of irrigation systems during the Colonial period (AD 600–900) and the labor-intensive maintenance of the extensive canal networks through the Sedentary (AD 900–1100) and Classic (AD 1100–1450) periods. Howard's breakthrough in canal segment dating confirms not only an early rapid construction

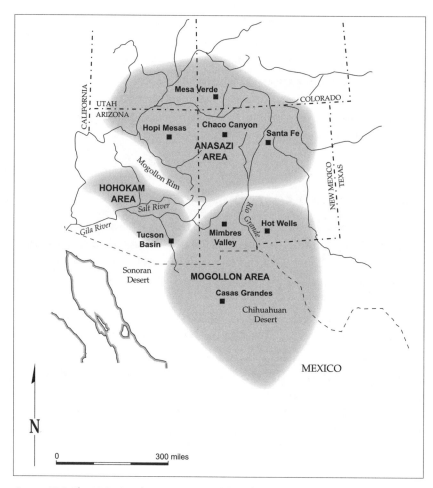

Figure 7.9 The U.S. Southwest, prepared by Sarah Stoutamire.

history but also the necessity of frequently rebuilding segments. Even main canals had a use-life of no more than 50–100 years, and major flooding events would have precipitated the mobilization of numerous laborers to maintain the water system. To Howard, this sizable complicated canal investment indicates a much higher level of sociopolitical complexity than formerly assumed.

In the Salt-Gila Basin, canalization promoted intervillage cooperation in constructing and maintaining the water management system (Wilcox 1979). Crown (1987b) has shown that "irrigation communities" settled along main canals issuing directly from the Gila River. These may have included several platform-mound villages and may have interacted independently of similar neighboring single-main-canal irrigation communities. This autonomy is further attested in the Salt River valley, where "patterned regularity in the spacing of major villages along a series of parallel canals at 5 km intervals appears to reflect territorial spacing" (Howard 1993:310; Howard and Wilcox 1988). Generally, the village at the head end of a canal system had the largest platform mounds and was the most prominent and controlling (cf. Nicholas and Neitzel 1984).

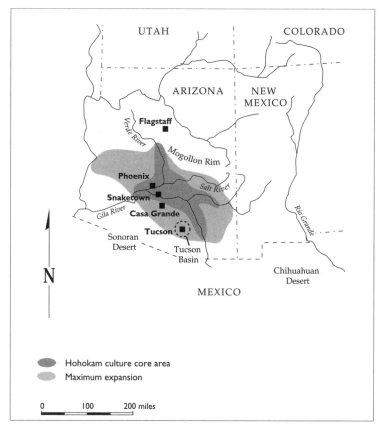

Figure 7.10 The Hohokam area, prepared by Sarah Stoutamire.

Water storage in reservoirs during droughts was attempted throughout the Southwest (Crown 1987a; Scarborough 1988a), but sparse rainfall, high evaporation rates, and less dependable drainages prevented this technique from operating as effectively as in the Maya Lowlands. Nevertheless, the Hohokam did colonize desert lands away from the principal riverine and irrigation settings, most notably during the Classic period (Bayman and Fish 1992). The "marginal" zones were reclaimed by non-canal agricultural techniques, including floodwater and surface runoff diversion and deep reservoir construction and maintenance. These adaptations opened the interior desert away from irrigable riverine lands and facilitated the integration of the greater Hohokam region. Elsewhere in the U.S. Southwest, however, reservoir technology was highly expedient, with only shallow tanks identified. Sizable surface areas, or evaporation exposures, were coupled with relatively small tank capacities (Scarborough 1988a).

Political Economy and Settlement

The irrigation community on a single main canal was a well-integrated social unit. The Hohokam platform-mound site of Casa Grande in Arizona is especially illustrative. Casa Grande was located at the tail end of its canal, even though it was the largest town on the channel and cultivated the most land (Crown 1987b). For Casa Grande to receive the amount of water necessary to irrigate its fields, a controlling elite within a greater irrigation district must have enforced the equitable allocation of water to this tail-ender. Because smaller villages upstream had the opportunity to divert water, the size and needs of Casa Grande suggest a Syrian allocation model (equitable water distribution based on allotments proportional to amounts of land cultivated). Even during droughts, it seems unlikely that a Yemenite distributional model (unequal water allocation based on timed releases) could have been enforced. Casa Grande—the most powerful town on the canal—would have attempted to receive the lion's share of the resources. Lacking state sanctions, however, it probably could not prevent head-end villages from drawing their allotments during droughts.

Nevertheless, the obvious centralized planning and maintenance requirements of the irrigation system outlined by Howard (1993) suggest a degree of complexity not unlike some formative states. As Doolittle (1990a) shows, the extent of canal used by the Hohokam exceeds the length of most canals in ancient Mexico. The scale of public architecture and the population size of Hohokam towns were small compared with the complex states of Mesoamerica. However, the canalization efforts during the Hohokam Colonial period (AD 600–900) evidence the same kind—if not degree—of complexity spike noted in the Basin of Mexico (Teotihuacan) during the first century AD.

Furthermore, this enormous investment in canalization coincides with the widespread expansion of formal ball-court architecture in Hohokam towns (Wilcox 1991), reflecting the integration of a political economy driven, in part, by intensive forms of irrigation. Here, the ritualized rubber ball game reflects formal institutions for conflict resolution and greater group mediation (Scarborough and Wilcox, eds. 1991). Howard (1993) indicates that the periods following the Colonial (AD 600–900) threshold for irrigation expansion were ones of stabilization and perhaps refinement of the original investment. During these periods, platform mounds replaced ball courts and their integrative political characteristics, for reasons I will soon explain. This same kind of explosive growth, followed by stasis, is described in Millon's (1992) interpretation of civic architectural construction and population scale at Teotihuacan (AD 1–200).

I am not saying that organizational change and creative resource management did not develop beyond these initial bursts of cultural energy. For the Hohokam, the late Sedentary and early Classic periods (AD 1000–1100) were ones of unification and aggregation of population along the Salt and (upstream) Gila Rivers. Howard (1993:316–17) suggests that this trend reflects a greater degree of sociopolitical integration among the irrigation communities, precipitated by attempts to control conflict and regulate water capture, especially during periods of low canal-flow rates. A centralizing administration operating at the irrigation-community level during the Colonial period (AD 600–900) reinvented itself by further consolidating populations around platform-mound complexes.

During the Preclassic period (AD 150–1100), Hohokam settlements were dispersed. A more aggregated village settlement evolved during the late Sedentary period (c. AD 1000) at Snaketown, and room space aggregated behind compound walls at Casa Grande during the Classic period (AD 1100–1450) (Wilcox 1979). In addition, Howard (1993) shows that the consolidation of shorter canal segments into major canal systems occurred much earlier than was previously thought (Nicholas and Neitzel 1984). The coincidence of greater village aggregation and the continued adjustments made to the engineered landscape probably indicate a renewed effort at resource centralization. The Sedentary/Classic (AD 1000–1450) social investment in village solidarity along a shared canal length resulted in village compaction. The defensive advantage gained by settlement compaction may also reflect heightened competition for well-watered resources.

The Hohokam example illustrates the extent to which water systems can be built under even the most severe environmental constraints. Canalization involved a set of long-term corporate work projects, even though state organization was not achieved. Perhaps greater complexity and scale eventually would have emerged if the multiple main canals issuing from the Salt River into single platform-mound sites had continued to exist. On the other hand, it appears that the initial rapid growth of the irrigation system during the Colonial period (AD 600–900) covered the potentially canalized landscape, given the existing technology and organizational outlook. If greater scale and complexity were to have evolved, it most likely would have been at this initial juncture. Instead, the organizational outlooks (regulatory principles) guiding expansion during the Colonial period were fulfilled by the initial abundance of the resources exploited by the new technology. Without new techniques for increasing water availability or marked changes in the organizational outlook, neither greater expansion of the water system nor further development of social complexity was possible. Later, the Sedentary/Classic transition (AD 1000–1100) saw a modification of the regulatory principles through greater aggregation and a focus on centralized platform-mound construction. It provided for the continuation of Hohokam society by overcoming the increasing political and economic stress caused by a four hundred-year-old management style grounded in dispersed settlement, aging canal segments, and a political ideology involving ball courts as an integrative social mechanism (Scarborough and Wilcox, eds. 1991).

I should mention that there is no evidence in the U.S. Southwest of the conspicuous water consumption suggested by the Gardens of Netzahualcoyotl in the Basin of Mexico (S. Evans 2000; Wolf and Palerm 1955) and the masonry sweat baths of the Lowland Maya (see chapter 5). Perhaps such conspicuous consumption is an indicator of elite power and early statecraft.

World Comparisons

The New World case studies capture the variability in early complex societies and in their water and land use. None of the New World primary states, though, evolved in proximity to the hemisphere's great rivers, as did several archaic states in the Old

World. As Wittfogel's (1957) work implies, the reasons for this difference may include the lesser aridity of the regions through which the Mississippi and the Amazon flow (compared with the Tigris-Euphrates, the Nile, and the Indus) or the levels and kinds of technology that developed in the New World. In any case, only exceptionally in the New World did large urban settlements develop upon broad flat tracts of land, as they did in the Old World on the great floodplains of the Tigris-Euphrates, Indus, Huang-he, and, to a lesser extent, the lower Nile. In the Basin of Mexico, the great cities developed on flat land, but an ancient lacustrine environment—not the abundance of a permanent river—facilitated urbanism there. Even the great center of Chan Chan on the north coast of Peru depended on a canalization scheme very different from the Old World systems (Moseley 1983; Ortloff 1993). At Chan Chan, a relatively small, incised river knifing through a tectonically active environment forced frequent canal abandonment and a heavy investment in excavated water-table fields (sunken gardens). Only the U.S. Southwest canals resemble the early canal systems of the Old World. Even so, adequate water storage for expanding the economic base was limited, compared with Old World waterways.

Some of the earliest urban forms in the two hemispheres warrant additional discussion because the resources stimulating their growth were rooted in their water management systems. The most ordered, planned city in the New World was Teotihuacan (AD 150–750) in central Mexico. With a density of 5,000 people/km^2 and a population of more than 100,000 inhabiting a gridded plan, it was one of the most condensed urban environments ever associated with an archaic state. Although Early Dynastic Uruk (c. 2700 BC) of Sumer had an estimated population of 50,000 within the walled city of 4 km^2, a density of 12,500/km^2, its layout was not nearly as ordered (R. McC. Adams 1981; Redman 1978). More comparable to Teotihuacan was the great city of Mohenjo-daro, associated with the Harappan civilization (ca. 2550–1900 BC). This was one of several cities in the Indus Valley organized by a tightly prescribed grid plan. Highly concentrated, Mohenjo-daro covered 2.5 km^2 and had a population estimated at 40,000, or 16,000/km^2 (Fairservis 1971) (see chapter 8). What forces and relations of production permitted people and resources to be concentrated in such circumscribed organized nodes?

Although Old World city populations seldom approached the numbers inferred for Teotihuacan, they sometimes reached urban densities higher than in Teotihuacan or any other New World city. Their higher densities are partly a consequence of the wheel, domesticated beasts of burden, and the navigability of the rivers and streams near which Old World civilization flourished. The greater ability to travel longer distances with less energy expended meant that the concentration of people at a few urban nodes was an efficient adaptation in many environments. Effective transport of people and resources also enabled more control over an engineered landscape and the possibility that cities would evolve as the coordinating nerve centers.

In contrast to most Old World cases, Teotihuacan immediately accessed land and water in concentrated abundance at the city's margins, creating a food resource based on highly productive *chinampas* (raised and drained plots). Given the strictly human-carrier transport available in Mesoamerica, population concentrations on the scale of Teotihuacan depended heavily on exceptionally productive resource concentrations in immediate proximity.

Compared with other Mesoamerican communities, what makes Teotihuacan unique is its population size, along with its strict rectilinear layout. Such spatial and architectural order suggests a highly routinized set of regulatory principles grounded in the intensity of *chinampa* exploitation. In the Old World, the Harappan city of Mohenjo-daro (2550–1900 BC) evidences a similar rigidity of form that translates into a highly conservative set of regulatory principles. Its exploitation of the agricultural landscape involved an intensity approximating that of Teotihuacan, although the means of transport available to Mohenjo-daro permitted an even greater density of people.

The Lowland Maya, the other state-level New World case presented in this chapter, displayed a highly dispersed demographic adaptation economically grounded in reservoir construction and drained-field and terrace agriculture. Unlike Teotihuacan or the classic irrigation civilizations of the Old World, the Lowland Maya did not support dense urban aggregates. Rather, their cities were spread out. For example, Tikal enclosed a population of 65,000–80,000 in an area of 120 km^2 bounded by a great ditch and a natural swamp margin, a density of roughly 550–650/km^2 (Puleston 1973; Puleston and Callender 1967; cf. Rice and Culbert 1990:21). Because of the semitropical setting, resources and the people harvesting them maintained a dispersed distribution. Unlike the peoples occupying the semiarid Mexican Highlands or the arid zones of the Tigris-Euphrates, the Nile, or the Indus, Lowland Maya populations seldom nucleated into huge cities. When they did, it was generally late in their cultural trajectory (post-AD 1100) and only in the semiarid northern portion of the Yucatán Peninsula.

The southern lowland tropical ecology influenced and perhaps limited the kinds of organizational outlooks possible within the developing state. Resource centralization occurred with the management of reservoir waters within the largest urban communities, but a myriad of centrifugal forces pulling at the environs and society prevented more nucleated cities. Because of the human-powered transportation systems of the New World, the Maya initially (400 BC–AD 150) positioned their communities at the margins of the largest swamps, close to the potential productivity of raised-field and drained-field agriculture. Relocating their towns and cities at the summits of the adjacent hillocks during the Classic period (AD 250–900) enabled an efficient water catchment system but prevented the grid layout apparent in other highly structured archaic states. As noted elsewhere (Scarborough et. al. 1995), their urban plan took on a "verticality" affected by the movement of water from central-precinct reservoirs to the swamp margins below.

The Hohokam of the U.S. Southwest demonstrate a land-use pattern more akin to Old World canal systems. Although resources were consolidated during the Hohokam Classic period (AD 1100–1450), inadequate water supplies prevented complexity on the order of an archaic state. However, that the Hohokam cultural system was less complex than any others examined in this chapter does not diminish the importance of its advanced irrigation systems in an assessment of the environmental and cultural variables affecting water and land use. The enormous growth by the intricate Hohokam irrigation system indicates a level of coordination and degree of centralization perhaps more typically linked with incipient statecraft. The regulatory principles at work in Hohokam society were less flexible than those of the Maya state but more flexible than those of highland Mexico. If additional water resources had been available to support the further growth of Hohokam society, increasing its overall scale and organizational complexity, the resulting coordination and centralization very possibly would have produced state development.

EIGHT

Archaeological Case Studies—Old World

And sure enough, if we look at Sinhalese history, we find that the great kings
have reputations as irrigation engineers rather than as conquerors or as builders
of cities.

—Edmund R. Leach (1959:10)

Archaeology focused most of its earliest interests in primary state development on the Old World archaic states tethered to the banks of major river systems. In many respects, these states are unlike the New World case studies presented in chapter 7. Because of the early and sustained archaeological work conducted along the Tigris and Euphrates, the canalization of floodplain and riverine margins became the yardstick for sociopolitical complexity and water management. We now know that the riverine adaptations influencing early developments in statecraft varied widely. Nevertheless, riverine waters remain fundamental to any discussion of early intensive agriculture, economic surplus, and transportation systems in Old World archaic states.

The case studies in this chapter reveal that the primary data available on the water management systems of the earliest Old World states are inferior to the data on comparable New World examples. Reasons include the greater antiquity of primary states in the Old World and poor preservation of buried and subsequently disturbed landscape features, especially the fragile ones associated with early water manipulation. This situation is also a historical consequence of the differing archaeological strategies in the New World and Old World. Although the discipline was long grounded in site-centered excavation in both hemispheres, an early emphasis on recovering prehistoric settlement patterns in New World archaeology—inspired by Julian Steward's (1955) development of cultural ecology and Gordon Willey's (1953, Willey, ed. 1974) interest in archaeological survey—resulted in greater sensitivity to questions of landscape use. In the Old World, only Robert Braidwood (1960; Braidwood and Willey 1962) and R. McC. Adams (1965, 1966, 1981; Adams and Nissen 1972) pioneered the same trajectory for research, focusing on cultural ecology à la Steward and settlement survey as established by Willey, in the Near East. It is no accident, then, that the best evidence in the Old World for water and land use, to say nothing of economy, comes from the greater reaches of the Tigris and Euphrates. For that very reason, I have drawn the following case studies from regions outside the Near East. R. McC. Adams and his students have already provided a series of well-known books and articles regarding early water management and its cultural implications in the Near East (R. McC. Adams 1955, 1965, 1966, 1974, 1981, 1982; Adams and Nissen 1972; Neely and Wright 1994).

North-Central Sri Lanka (AD 1–1200)

Sinhala (ancient Ceylon), perhaps the oldest of the great Southeast Asian tropical civilizations, had particularly elaborate water systems. Its reservoir technology was second to none (see figure 8.1). The capital city, Anuradhapura, was occupied from approximately AD 400 to 1000. Both the time period and environment are comparable to the Classic period Maya Lowlands. Only slightly drier than the latter's north-central Petén (1,500 mm of rain per year), the dry zone also lacks navigable drainage. The soils are reddish-brown earths, thin on the unirrigated uplands but deeper and more fertile for rice production today in the island's low-lying depressions (Bronson 1978; Panabokke 1976). Unlike the early states featured in chapter 7, ancient Ceylon was a secondary state generated by colonization from India's states in the last half of the first millennium BC (Murphey 1957; Gunawardana 1981). Linguistic associations and limited Harappan textual remains suggest a link between the earlier Harappan civilization of Pakistan and northwestern India (2550–1900 BC) and the present-day Dravidians of southern India (Parpola 1986). Several centuries after the Harappans' demise, the Dravidians colonized ancient Ceylon, which may have involved the one-way diffusion of water management practices from the temperate (desert) Harappan state to this tropical civilization.[1]

A Landscape of Reservoirs

Today, as it was in the past, north-central Sri Lanka is a landscape of reservoirs. Most are ancient and reclaimed (Leach 1959:8). Because of the long dry season, sizable reservoirs were constructed, some fed by runoff from enormous catchment areas and others by *anicuts* (diversion weirs) placed across small streams (Gunawardana 1971; Murphey 1957:184). In addition, the kings of Anuradhapura and neighboring Polonnaruva commissioned enormous masonry embankments, or dams. Some rose to heights of 27 m over a length of 14 km. Leach (1959:9) estimates that the Kalawewa tank was nearly 65 km in circumference and fed a canal system extending approximately 90 km. Although Leach does not emphasize the amount of labor necessary to construct these public works through centuries of earthmoving additions, these embankments reflect statelike control systems comparable to those discovered elsewhere in the ancient Old World or New World (cf. Gunawardana 1971). Repair was expensive, and flood damage and siltation accumulations necessitated periodic maintenance by a sizable workforce. The major reservoirs within or immediately outside

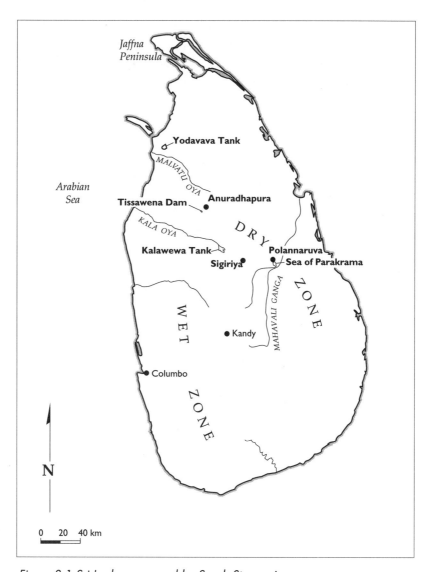

Figure 8.1 Sri Lanka, prepared by Sarah Stouramire.

the capital cities symbolize elite power and conspicuous consumption. The largest artificial lake, Parakrama Samudra (Sea of Parakrama I), provided water piped to several royal baths in the later capital of Polonnaruva (Murphey 1957:193).

Similarities to the Maya Lowlands are striking, probably because of the semitropical environments that first ordered relationships in these two settings, being landscapes of reservoirs. In contrast to the Maya area, colonization—whether Indo-Iranian, Dravidian, or another origin—introduced an organizational outlook designed for a much more arid ecology. The extremely dry margins of the Indus River stimulated early tank technology, attested by the mature Harappan period (2550–1900 BC) at Lothal, Gujarat, in the lower Indus region (see the section "Lower Indus Valley"). In the context of early Sri Lanka, Harappan reservoir technology was likely modified to accommodate the new set of local ecological demands and an evolving set of imported-water regulatory principles. Although Sri Lanka and the semi-tropical Maya Lowlands were alike, the landscape in Sri Lanka's dry zone was much flatter. The soils were less fertile than those available to the Lowland Maya, with fewer swamp settings for reclamation and little limestone except on the northern Jaffna Peninsula.

Thanks to a richly inscribed history—some of it literally carved in stone—we know that initial modest canalization of the most predictably perennial drainage, the Mahavali Ganga, occurred within the first century BC and that reservoir construction was begun by the first century AD (Gunawardana 1971:5). Even at this early date, the texts distinguish "village tanks," "large tanks," and "feeder tanks." The feeder tanks functioned as storage reservoirs for filling other tanks in the vicinity via canal linkages.

In one of the island's driest areas, the north-northwest, historical accounts attribute the Yodavava tank to the fifth century. This tank formed behind an embankment extending for nearly 11 km and was fed by seasonal flow from a canal 27 km long. Because of the flat terrain, excavation was futile without a technology for lifting the water from the depression. Dams of marked height and length, however, could back up and elevate enough tank water to permit a significant flow gradient. During this period, dams were placed across seasonal drainages. The Culavamsa chronicle indicates that a great weir, or dam, was constructed across the Mahavali, containing its permanent flow. Perhaps the greatest engineering feat of its day, this dam was located near a cataract of granite quarried to form the massive 3-ton square blocks used in its construction but now in ruins (Gunawardana 1971:8).

At the end of the fifth century, dam length and height were the principal limitations on irrigation schemes and water management. The head of water behind these increasingly sizable dams made controlled release difficult. Perhaps the most profound innovation was the incorporation of the *bisokotuva,* or "cistern sluice" (see chapter 4). This routed irrigation water under the dam, whereas traditional sidewall sluice gates released water and water pressure. The cistern sluice made dams as mighty as the one associated with the Kalawewa tank (as noted by Leach) possible.

The technological breakthrough of damming entire drainages by raising a dam's height markedly increased the complexity of Sinhalese society. Gunawardana (1971) suggests that the island's two "nuclear areas" developed the necessary resources (principally rice) for a highly centralized political economy by using the tank technology. Anuradhapura, the first and largest capital city of the Sinhalese state, was situated to control the northwestern portion of the dry zone. The sister city of Polonnaruva engineered the southeastern portion and by the ninth century was the principal capital of the entire island. The harnessing of the dependable, predictable Mahavali River for rice irrigation established Polonnaruva as the chief urban node.

Throughout recorded history, Ceylon has been subject to colonizers and invaders. These outsiders have introduced new organizational strategies and technologies, some adaptable to the organizational outlooks already established by the indigenous state. Equally important to the development of the Sinhalese state was a political economy flexible enough to accommodate these repeated incursions, which were frequently military. One adaptation involved less dependence on major tanks and canal systems in the use of much of the dry zone between the two nuclear areas. With a more dispersed settlement pattern than the nuclear areas and a different land-use/water-use strategy, hinterland populations were seldom overpowered by the outsiders who caused havoc in the sizable centers. At the turn of the twentieth century (Codrington 1939), British colonial administrators reported this historical land-use pattern of "one tank–one village" (Gunawardana 1971:4), still present in these zones today.

When the state is incapable of centralizing most of a hinterland population and its resources, a protected status envelops aspects of the political economy and insulates it from drastic change, even during short-term conquest. Invading preindustrial armies seldom have the concentrated resources to subjugate an entire society based on a different set of organizational outlooks, regardless of environmental setting. Populations within a naturally dispersed resource ecology of a semitropical environment, however, are especially difficult to subjugate and control.

Monumentality and Organization

Careful settlement survey of ancient landscapes is still lacking for Sri Lanka. Nevertheless, reasonable estimates suggest a population during the eleventh century of two to four million within an area of perhaps 30,000 km^2 (Murphey 1957:186), or an occupation density comparable to that of the Maya Lowlands during the Classic period. Anuradhapura and Polonnaruva were massive civic architectural complexes containing shrines, temples, and palaces; two stupas (domed Buddhist shrines) at Anuradhapura contained more than 500,000 m^3 of solid brickwork (Leach 1959:12). Drawing on less substantial resources, several smaller communities also existed. A dispersed settlement design is posited, following the Maya settlement model, in which centers of varying sizes are distributed over the landscape, each associated with one or more tanks. Less centralization of resources around a center or set of centers occurred outside the regional reach of the two primary cities, Gunawardana's (1971) nuclear areas. Water management there was more autonomous. It depended on the immediate tank system, not on the canal conduits moving stored water from vast reservoirs buffering the cities from drought.

Little evidence exists for despotic control over Sinhalese hydraulic works. However, the skilled engineers and functionaries who built the largest reservoir and canal systems did develop a hydraulic bureaucracy (Gunawardana 1971:21). As in the ancient Maya case, where centripetal forces drawing populations to sizable centers offset the decentralizing forces, an ideological mechanism embedded in the Sinhalese organizational outlook promoted the concentration of labor and resources at their centers. Through ritual and public theater against the backdrop of dramatic monumental architecture, the Sinhalese elite appropriated the resources and commanded control of the sustaining population. Leach (1959:10) notes that the chronicles judge the greatness of kings not by military exploits or the building of cities but by the size of their waterworks. The last great king, Parakrama Bahu I, who reigned from AD 1164 to 1197, invaded India and Burma and reunified Ceylon. However, he is remembered most for his grand construction and restoration of the Sinhalese tank system.

Smaller cities and towns within and away from the nuclear areas reveal the centrifugal forces influencing land and water use. Considerable control of land, labor, and water was in the hands of both a landed gentry and extremely powerful monastic estates. The latter, a feudal-like institution, kept the agricultural implements (means of production). Hoes, spades, and axes were viewed as a monastery's "indivisible communal property" (Gunawardana 1971:20). By offering private landholdings, the state gave additional power to both the gentry and the monasteries. The state's centralized resources, acquired by the cities of Anuradhapura and Polonnaruva, ebbed and flowed according to the vagaries of the organizational planes (see chapters 2 and 3). Of course, centralization is a relative condition in any nonindustrial complex society (see chapter 3).

Most authors emphasize the role of "king's labor" (corvée) in discussions of political economy and the ancient Sinhalese. A sizable portion of the population was engaged in corvée labor. This included not only the construction of reservoirs and monuments but also individual specialty tasks—making pots or washing clothes for a noble or a portion of a noble's community. These activities did not necessarily benefit the king (Leach 1961).Corvée labor led to a much less centralized economy than that of later states but still carried out construction and frequent maintenance of the complicated hydraulic system. As long as this organizational outlook continued, the state and the feudal lords embedded in the political economy operated effectively.

What caused the demise of the Sinhalese state and its grand investment in water management by AD 1200 remains unclear. Possible explanations include soil exhaustion, climate deterioration, tank siltation, foreign invasion, and malaria (Murphey 1957). This list nearly duplicates that proposed for the Classic Maya collapse c. AD 900. The Sinhalese state evolved in a less accretional manner with respect to the engineered landscape than did the ancient Maya state, partly because of frequent foreign military incursions. However, during certain periods, the landscape underwent slow alteration, most evident in the hinterland zones. Invading armies made less impact here (their focus being the capitals of the nuclear areas). Also, the dispersed resources of the "one tank–one village" pattern prevented immediate ruinous exploitation. The relatively rapidly built brickworks within the huge sister cities of Anuradhapura and Polonnaruva reflect the centralized economy.

As Howard (1993) has suggested (see chapter 7), the building of canal systems tends to be an explosive investment across a landscape. In Sri Lanka, canalization and the construction of enormous dams across the dry zone's seasonal streams and rivers resulted in a tremendous effort expended in the regionally built environment within the nuclear areas. The very scale of water management, however, made these areas vulnerable to severe disruption, especially from outsiders. Any number of mechanisms (Flannery 1972) may have caused the system's eventual collapse, but neglecting the hydraulic system for an extended period would have made reclamation nearly impossible, given the scale of the investment.

Nevertheless, Parakrama Bahu I (AD 1164–1197) is credited with just such a recovery following a series of his own foreign adventures. The revenue obtained from his exploits funded an unprecedented expansion of waterworks. The following will give us an idea of the enormous labor involved. In 1739, a Dutch governor inquired about restoring a large tank in the northwestern nuclear area. The villagers said that it would take five hundred men five months to fix the main breach and another one thousand men two years to repair the entire tank (Brohier 1935:37, cited in Murphey 1957:194). Such figures are not easily evaluated, but the scale of such a reclamation project is apparent from the numerous tanks across the ancient landscape and Sinhalese dependency on them. The grand success of these engineering feats, however, led eventually to maintenance demands that doomed the water- and land-use adaptation. Even king's labor and king's support could not prevent the collapse of a system too large and complicated to maintain.

Tank and canal systems of the magnitude reported in ancient Ceylon were designed, in part, to irrigate land that was not otherwise routinely cultivable. Within the sphere of control of city-states such as Anuradhapura and Polonnaruva, the state managed water allotments in a manner not unlike the lake systems of the Basin of Mexico or the postulated swamp (bajo) settings of the Maya Lowlands. In both the Maya Lowlands and Sri Lanka, the storage of seasonal rainfall in much smaller reservoirs (also see Morrison 1993) made insular village tank systems possible. The manipulation of water located away from the large cities probably resembled that described today by Leach (1961) and Chambers (1980). Villages are not interconnected by canal systems and retain their autonomy by the singularity of their community tank. The villages rest immediately below the embankment, between the tank and irrigated fields, and sluice works lead first into the residential community (refer to figure 6.1). The ancient settlement pattern around these tanks is little known, but the adaptation made today is one of small-scale, dispersed settlement near the tank.

Village access to dependable sources of water during periods of extended drought or community mismanagement may have made the Sinhalese state hydraulic works—and subjugation by an empowered elite—more acceptable to a peasantry. Unlike the Mesoamerica landscapes on which the state affected raised-field, lake-leveling adaptations but seldom promoted canalization, the Sri Lankan landscape was frequently altered by irrigation canals sanctioned by the state. As we saw in chapter 6, such canal systems may operate in an equitable *Syrian* distribution (water allotments proportional to the amount of land cultivated) or a less equitable *Yemenite* manner (unequal water allocation based on timed releases). The turbulent history of ancient Ceylon suggests that the state manipulated water in Yemenite allotments much of the time (Gunawardana 1971). Nevertheless, in the small villages, water was probably more fairly distributed, a situation that continues today (see chapter 6). The presence of sizable temple tanks, sometimes still maintained by the community, reflects the strong influence of Buddhism on the Sinhalese, now and in the distant past.

Buddhism's tenet of equality implies an ancient Syrian allocation model for the sometimes sizable temple tanks in small villages. Away from the large cities, it is unlikely that the state could meddle successfully in most insular village water management affairs.

Lower Indus Valley (2550–1900 BC)

Harappan civilization (2550–1900 BC) was tethered to the Indus floodplain (see figure 8.2). Like other primary states of the Old World—Sumer, Old Kingdom Egypt, and the Shang dynasty—Harappan civilization arose on the banks of a great river flowing through an otherwise arid environment. Today, the Lower Indus Valley receives less than 200 mm of precipitation a year (Johnson 1979), even less than the U.S. Southwest. However, the Indus carries an abundance of water, as well as a heavy silt load, along a very shallow gradient following a precipitous plunge from the Himalayas. Before the British introduced the most extensive canal irrigation scheme known for any single river drainage, great annual floods blanketed the ancient floodplain. Although salinization and waterlogging of soils have severely altered the productivity of many areas formerly occupied by Harappan cities, pre-Vedic occupation (1900–1500 BC) tapped an extremely fertile, annually inundated setting.[2]

The earliest evidence for water management in Pakistan and western India is found west of the Indus in Baluchistan (Raikes 1965, 1984). Massive walls of uncut stone climb as high as 2 m to form diminutive dams across intermittent streambeds and along the parallel margins of these drainages, creating agricultural terraces. Called *gabarbands,* these features are associated with pre-Harappan materials and probably have had a long, uninterrupted use, continuing into the present (Wheeler 1968).

The Environment and the Indus River

Like the other great rivers influencing primary state developments in the Old World, the seasonally turgid Indus carried a load of nutrient-rich sediment that was a blessing and a bane. At Mohenjo-daro, ancient fluvial deposits lie nearly 12 m below the present floodplain and are associated with cultural occupation throughout. Entirely buried and featureless on the vast plain is a mud-brick embankment more than 13 m thick. Placed at the margins of the community early in the citadel's history (Wheeler 1968), this bund presumably held back the floodwaters and their ever-encroaching sediment load. The water table has risen more than 9 m since the site's initial occupation. Some of this rise is a result of recent irrigation schemes and the saturation of the water table, obvious in the damage inflicted by salinization everywhere at the site.

Some students of ancient hydrology suggest that catastrophic uplift immediately south of Mohenjo-daro significantly altered the sedimentation rate along the lower Indus during Harappan times (Raikes 1965, 1984). Combined with oscillations in recent worldwide sea level, this change continues to have consequences. Clearly, such eust-atic imbalances would change cities inextricably tied to the riverine resource.

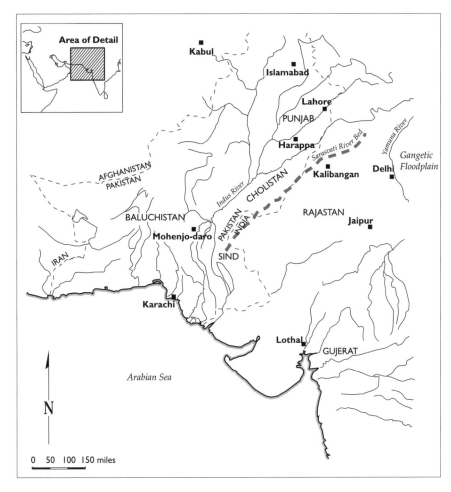

Figure 8.2 The Indus Valley, prepared by Sarah Stoutamire.

The well-reported effects of *stream capture* (the natural rerouting of a drainage or watershed from one set of streams and rivers to another) along the northeast margins of the Harappan sphere further attest to the severity of culture change induced by natural forces (see the next section, "The Indus and Agricultural Intensification"). Considerable debate persists about these environmental changes and how they influenced the course of Harappan society (Miller 1985; Possehl 1967, 2000).

The Indus and Agricultural Intensification

Both Sumer and pharaonic Egypt relied heavily on the sediment loads of their respective rivers, but the Indus received even more alluvium from the nearby precipitous and geologically recent Himalayas. Unlike the preserved remains of canals along the Tigris-Euphrates (R. McC. Adams 1981), the ancient *gabarbands* and related agricultural water control features have been buried by the Indus's wide braided courses. In Cholistan, the sites dating to this period (2500–1900 BC) provide the best opportunity to evaluate the economic base for the Harappan state and its riverine dependency. These are concentrated along the presently dry Indian streambeds of the ancient Sarasvati and Drishadvati Rivers (Mughal 1982, 1997) on both sides of the international border (Possehl 2000; Possehl and Raval 1989:20–24).[3] The abandonment of numerous Harappan sites in this area is coincidental with the apparent desiccation of these Indus tributaries, a natural geomorphological process triggered by the headwater capture of these drainages by the much younger Yamuna River to the east (Possehl 2000; Possehl and Raval 1989:21).

Water manipulation along the Indus has a long history. However, scant empirical evidence exists for extensive canalization, except for the covered brick-lined drainage channels found or inferred at a few larger cities and especially well defined at Mohenjo-daro (Allchin and Allchin 1982; Scarborough 1988b). Primitive floodwater farming without the aid of diversion technology allowed double-cropping of the fertile alluvium—apparent among present-day populations in the state of Sind, Pakistan (Lambrick 1964). However, the Harappans' highly structured organization suggests more intensive land use for supplying cities as large as Mohenjo-daro. Although separated from the Harappans by several hundred years (cf. Renfrew 1987; Kenoyer 1997), the later Rig-Vedic scripture (associated with Sanskrit and Indo-European language origins) suggests diversion dams and intensive irrigation schemes by 1100 BC in the nearby Gangetic floodplain (Prasad et al. 1987). By analogy, today's cities are highly dependent on the irrigation systems initiated by the British, not on the floodwater cropping yields from rural Sind. Still, conventional canalization systems were not well suited to settings as intractable as the floodplain of the Indus, suggesting the practice of other intensification methods. Sophisticated tank technology, evidenced by the ancient reservoir at Lothal (Gujerat state, India)—well within the spatial core of Harappan society—occurred earliest among the Harappans. This technology perhaps precipitated the subsequent evolved systems of bund and reservoir irrigation documented for ancient Ceylon. The inherent difficulties in canalizing the Indus were not resolved until the 1850s, when the British introduced gated barrages to manage the floodwater silt load and permit the canalization of zones immediately outside the floodplain (Johnson 1979; Taylor 1965).

Despite the deeply buried disposition of the Harappans' ancient field system, some direct evidence does exist for the kinds of agricultural tools and farming techniques used. Building debris at the ancient Harappan city of Kalibangan (Punjab state, India) preserved the furrow marks left by an *ard* (wooden plow), indicative of the kinds of tools used in farming the floodplain sediments. Allchin and Allchin (1982:192) show that the furrows were oriented at right angles—"closely spaced in one direction and more widely spaced in the other"—a cropping practice used today on irrigable lands. Nevertheless, few actual implements resembling farming tools have been unearthed from Harappan contexts. Is it possible that the highly structured, conservative regimen of Harappan society—like the monasteries of ancient Ceylon—controlled the tools of production? Are the missing tools concentrated in portions of these great sites yet to be sampled?

Precipitous Development and Cultural Homogenization

Possehl (1990) has emphasized how rapidly Mature Harappan (2550–1900 BC) urbanism arose from its relatively humble Early Harappan origins (3200–2550 BC), both in Baluchistan and along the Indus Plain. Within 150 years, such major cities as Mohenjo-daro and Harappa emerged as complex centers evidencing social stratification, public architecture, writing, highly standardized weights and measures, and an extremely sanitized, controlled urban environment. The grid system was as formal as that at Teotihuacan in highland Mexico (AD 1–700). Although Possehl (1990) does not fully explain why this explosive set of events occurred, the indigenous origins of Harappan civilization during the Early Harappan period may hint at the process. Ideological orientations, such as purity and social conformity, stimulated some unique aspects of the Harappan state (Miller 1985), but the Harrapans were economically grounded (see the section "Social Distance and Purity").

Unfortunately, we understand very little about how the Harappans fed themselves, aside from the agricultural production associated with the Baluchistan *gabarbands* (diminutive dams and agricultural terraces) and the furrow marks noted at Kalibangan. Although we know what they ate—millet, rice, wheat, barley, cattle, goats, sheep—we do not know how they processed their food and organized their economic base. Partially because of how easily trade items can be inventoried, we know much more about these, especially the exotica, than about the subsistence economy. Nevertheless, the riverine positioning of the nine hundred or more Harappan communities recorded within the 125,000-km^2 area of the Indus drainage (Possehl 1990) strongly suggests an intensive agricultural manipulation of the floodplain.

Why the precipitous growth around 2500 BC? I suggest that it involved the institutional organization and formalization of earlier agricultural techniques for controlling the annually flooding, massively silt-laden Indus. These resembled the processes that sped canalization and the effective exploitation of the Tigris and Euphrates area during the Early Dynastic Period (c. 2700 BC) in Sumer (Scarborough 2000). We can hypothesize that systematizing agricultural tasks and scheduling labor to match the natural seasonal rhythms of inundation enabled the Harappans to harness the Indus. The structured routine of repeated economic activities gave Harappan civilization its highly formalized appearance in the material record.

The excavated data suggest a high degree of differentiation and stratification indicative of state complexity in most other portions of the world (contra Miller 1985). Nevertheless, this differentiation is suppressed in the material record by a marked absence of both monumental architecture and elaborate public art. According to Trigger (1990), these are the most important traits for identifying a state elite. As Morrison and Lycett (1994) point out, however, there is considerable confusion in interpreting the archaeological record about an elite's statements using monumental architecture. Is the elite making a claim to power it may not actually have, or does the elite have the power and a desire to announce it? The Harappan case may present a third choice available to a well-established set of elite managers, namely, maintaining power but not wishing to announce it, viewing such ostentation as disruptive to the underlying political economy and social conformity.

What processes cultivated such austere conformity in the material culture when compared with kingly hierarchies elsewhere, with their bold displays of singular control through highly illustrative political theater dramatically carved in stone? Teotihuacan in Mexico shares some conservative tendencies linked to a faceless elite (no portrait monuments) and a highly ordered urban plan reflecting a constrained, routinized labor force. Clearly, Mohenjo-daro and Teotihuacan were not organized identically; for one thing, the Pyramids of the Sun and Moon at Teotihuacan dwarf most monumental architecture everywhere except pharaonic Egypt and Formative Peru. Nevertheless, the organizational outlook suggested by the swift development of a tightly ordered city plan at both centers and the shared suppression of the personification of a king or ruling family surely reflect related processes. Given that Harappan cities developed rapidly and in the form that they did, could the economic adaptations made by Teotihuacan (but not its precise agricultural methods) share similarities with a yet unearthed, intensive agricultural scheme for the Harappans?

Social Distance and Purity

Harappan society poses difficulties for a simple model of hierarchical control based on a vertically exaggerated, socially stratified pyramid. Standardization and mass production of artifacts are frequently attributed to centralized administrative controls and elite management (Blanton et al. 1993). However, other aspects of the Harappan material record do not support facile interpretations of hierarchical controls. For example, the measurable distance separating the Harappan elite and nonelite within the entire inventory of material culture is less than that reported from other early states. Miller (1985) may overstate the homogeneity of Harappan society, but he provides suggestive evidence for a lack of variability in house sizes and forms (after Sarcina 1979) and an absence of nutritional stress on human skeletons from Harappa (after Kennedy 1982). To Miller (1985), these two features of Harappan society argue for a widely equitable distribution of wealth.

Piggott (1950:168; cited in Miller 1985:60–61) noted that "the whole conception [of Harappan society] shows a remarkable concern for sanitation and health without parallel…[in Asia] in the prehistoric past." Harappan urban ordering and sanitation remain the most accomplished of all the world's archaic states, transcending any early human health standards. According to Sarcena (1979; cited in Allchin and Allchin 1982:177), every house had a bathroom, with drainage channels and chutes connecting it to the street. At Mohenjo-daro, water for accommodating these ends was obtained from more than seven hundred carefully constructed brick-lined wells (Jansen 1989). Furthermore, indoor privies discarded effluent via soak pits dug into and under the streets. This antiseptic formula was complemented by public bathing, especially conspicuous at the Great Bath at Mohenjo-daro (see chapter 5; refer to plate 5.4) but also atop other Harappan main platforms. One example is Lothal's citadel, with its twelve bathrooms connected to large issuing drains (Rao 1979:77). As Miller (1985) convincingly argues, the focus on water and cleanliness and the nondisplay of wealth suggest a deeply embedded ritualism associated with purity and an attempt to promote social homogeneity.

The picture revealed is one of a highly integrated political economy (after Blanton et al. 1993), avoiding ostentatious displays and practicing a monastic-like control of community resources. Although very unlike Classic period Maya states in many ways, the Harappan state also used both mundane and ritualistic controls over water—and, perhaps, over fire (Miller 1985:60)—to unite the populace. Other means were surely employed to cement the regulatory principles guiding society, but water ritual dominated the only truly unique public architecture at the largest sites. Water consumption and purity symbolized the unity and sanctity of mundane functional tasks in maintaining the highly regimented order.

Settlement and Economic Outlays

Harappan cities were nucleated communities. At Mohenjo-daro, the population is estimated at more than 40,000 (Fairservis 1971) within an urban area of approximately 2.5 km^2 (Wheeler 1968). This adaptation is more similar to ancient highland Mexico than to neighboring Sri Lanka. Nevertheless, there is no present evidence for complex irrigation systems. Hydraulic investments in functional and symbolic urban contexts—especially in the technical knowledge necessary to manage gradient control across expanding tell cities growing vertically and horizontally—indicate that the technology was available for a highly ordered, intensively exploited agricultural system. The nondisplay of wealth and the evidence for only slight nutritional differences among individuals suggest a Syrian allocation model (equitable water distribution proportional to the amount of land cultivated) for both the subsistence base and the known manipulation of water in urban settings.

For both Harappa and Mohenjo-daro, Wheeler (1968) postulated sizable public granaries near the summits of their main citadels, implying that the state partially controlled foodstuffs. More recent examinations, however, reveal no evidence for granary platforms at any Harappan site (Fentress 1978; Jansen 1979; Shaffer 1982). Direct control of surplus—a principal tenet in Wheeler's centralized state model and supported by analogy with the temple stores of Early Dynastic Mesopotamia—cannot be argued. Indeed, evidence for state control of stored food surplus is largely lacking for any of the world's primary states (although secondary states—from Inka to Aztec to Old Testament Egypt—frequently attest to such stores, historically and archaeologically). On the other hand, the state likely meddled to some degree in agricultural affairs and may have exerted even greater control of inner-city water use.

The resource concentrations stimulated by immediate access to the Indus and its tributaries enabled the precipitous rise of the Harappan state but, contra Wittfogel (1957), probably *prevented* the despotic state. Unlike some other causal agents suggested for engendering statecraft, Harappan water management was probably not a mechanism (after Flannery 1972) for promoting state control. Still, the Great Bath at Mohenjo-daro and the elaborate reservoir at Lothal are monuments to an otherwise suppressed kingship and to a quietly governing elite responsible for their construction—perhaps similar to the collective leadership suggested by Millon (1992) for mature Teotihuacan (see chapter 7). These large elaborate features and the brick-lined functional canals within the largest centers suggest a degree of public architectural investment in water manipulation. The natural abundance provided by the Indus and the technical ability to control aspects of the otherwise seasonally intractable river probably allowed the same degree of agricultural intensification known for other archaic states.

Harappan civilization is the world's most architecturally conservative, artifactually uniform primary state. Extending over an area of perhaps 125,000 km^2, or four times the area of Mesopotamia, the Harappan state grew within 150 years from a series of small villages and towns into a complex urban society. A near uniformity in material culture and a suppression of visible wealth differences accompanied this enormous growth. Its lengthy period (more than six hundred years) of sustained complexity was based on the reproduction of nearly identical or at least highly similar sets of material remains. Future research may reveal greater degrees of social and material change through time (Kenoyer 1997), but the considerable surveys and excavation conducted to date strongly suggest a very conservative set of regulatory principles operative in Harappan society. Although the economic underpinnings of the Harappan state are poorly understood, an examination of the land and water demands in other archaic states suggests an intensive agricultural base dependent on a highly structured exploitation of the Indus.

Mycenaean Greece (1500–1150 BC)

Late Bronze Age Greece (c. 1500–1150 BC) lasted a relatively short time (compared with the longevity of the earlier primary states) but gave rise to one of the earliest complex societies on the European mainland, Mycenaean civilization (see figure 8.3), a secondary state development. Mycenaean civilization spread over peninsular Greece and the greater Aegean islands, with its most concentrated manifestation on the Argolid Plain of the northeastern Peloponnese. The Mycenaeans produced some of the most lavish known tomb offerings (gold, silver, and bronze), invested heavily in monumental defensive citadel walls enclosing the summits of natural hillocks, and likely generated much of the myth and metaphor in Western belief systems relating to the Homeric epic. In spite of a rich, textured knowledge of material remains and a growing corpus of environmental data, we know relatively little about water use in the Late Bronze Age and how it influenced social and political relationships (cf. T. Smith 1995).

The most basic question is this: How did the Mycenaeans make a living and support a civilization in an environment characterized by karstic landforms, thin soils, seasonal drought, and the disturbing absence (today) of permanent natural water

Figure 8.3 Greece, prepared by Sarah Stoutamire.

sources within the largest ancient citadel sites? Clearly, sea resources furnished an important subsistence base less available to the primary states I have discussed, but land and freshwater composed the Mycenaean's fundamental base. One method of using their lands was to exploit springs, a dependency that ultimately caused economic and political vulnerability. Mycenaean temporal and spatial limitations may reflect a problem with access to water (Scarborough 1994b).

In the Argolid Plain (refer to figure 8.3; see figure 8.4), water is the independent variable on which economic development depends. Soil productivity was likely enhanced through terracing, judicious plant selection, and the manuring or composting of fields (Isager and Skydsgaard 1992). Nevertheless, rainfall, surface runoff, and spring access are what permitted agricultural success (Gallant 1991). Today, all the surface water in the Argolid is either intermittent or fed by springs. The location of springheads was of primary concern in antiquity because rainfall was seasonal and sparse, less than 500 mm a year. Because sizable drainages did not exist, canal irrigation was impossible (Gallant 1991:56–57). However, over many generations, landscape modifications designed to improve access to water and extend the period of its availability created a productive environment (cf. Zangger 1994).

Historical and Environmental Background

Both material culture and the Homeric oral tradition depict the political contentiousness of the Argolid Plain during the Late Bronze Age. The cyclopean fortification walls, elaborate armor, slashing bronze sword, and war chariot—together with palace intrigue and avenging wars (especially the Trojan War, mentioned in the Iliad and the Odyssey)—reveal a high level of conflict. The cause remains unclear but probably pertains to the growing population's exploitation of a somewhat fragile physical environment. The poorly understood history of this hostility extends as far back as the Neolithic period (Caskey 1977). Within this combination of ecological constraints and bellicose organizational outlooks emerged the first mainland European city-states.

The Late Bronze Age is defined best by the advent of walled towns perched at elevated defensible settings. Several well-defined communities exist, but the largest concentration of these fortified towns nearly rings the Argolid Plain, which opens to the sea (see figure 8.4). The availability of water was critically important to the positioning of defensible citadel sites, especially during a prolonged siege. Located high on indurated limestone hillocks, these sites overlooked the plain.

Recently, Crouch (1993) compiled much of what is known about pre-Hellenistic and Hellenistic Greek urbanism (c. 900–100 BC) as it relates to water manipulation (cf. Scarborough 1994c). She alludes to Mycenaean achievements but notes that only limited data sets are available for describing the water technology invented during the Late Bronze Age and for determining whether it was handed down to subsequent populations. Two principal ways that Hellenistic groups collected and/or diverted water likely influenced Late Bronze Age water management within the Argolid Plain:

- Collection from roofs and from pavements that sealed otherwise cracked, porous karstic surfaces within communities (not unlike the Maya case)
- Collection from perennial springs and wells associated with the karstic settings that strongly attracted Greek cities

Regarding the latter method, Crouch (1993:63–82) suggests that the Hellenistic Greeks gravitated toward karstic mountains as "gigantic water towers" that stored large quantities of groundwater because of high infiltration rates and the correspondingly reduced surface runoff.

Geologically, the greater Peloponnese peninsula dips from west to east, making the western flank of the Argolid Plain extremely water-rich throughout antiquity. Even today, tremendous quantities of water pour from springheads, many associated

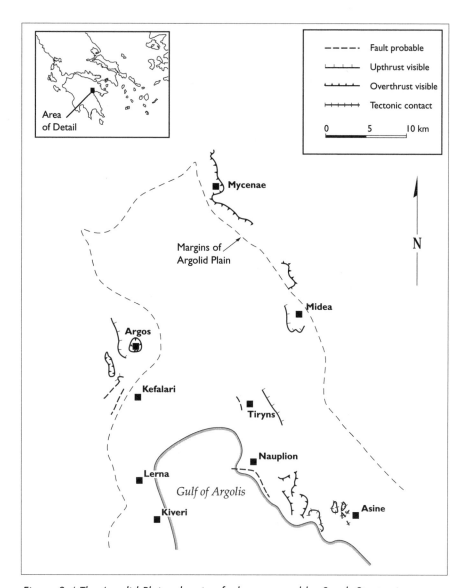

Figure 8.4 The Argolid Plain, showing faults, prepared by Sarah Stoutamire.

with geological fault lines. Drawing from a natural subterranean watershed of 1,000 km^2, extending as far west as present-day Tripoli, discharge rates are as high as 52,000 m^3 per hour near Kiveri (Crouch 1993:78; Travitian et al. 1994)—approximately 4 km south of the well-known springs of the Early-to-Middle Bronze Age (2800–1600 BC) village of Lerna (Caskey 1977). An unusual series of joints in the limestone coalesce to make this discharge possible. Generally, recharge rates from deep wellheads are an impressive 50 m^3 per hour in the Argolid. In the past decade, though, this flow has dropped to 10 m^3 per hour or less.

A similar set of strata, but dipping from east to west, fed the springs on the Argolid's eastern margins. This catchment area, with its associated jointed aquifer, was significantly smaller than that to the west. Today, few perennial springs provide significant amounts of water along the eastern margins, but abundant sources of water were available throughout the Argolid during the Bronze Age.[4]

Following the demise of the Late Bronze Age citadels (c. 1150 BC), centers of power and commerce vanished from the eastern margins of the agriculturally rich plain. Both Mycenae and Tiryns suffered severe settlement setbacks, and Midea was nearly abandoned. Only Argos, on the western edge of the plain, and Nemea, to the north, later evolved into sizable population nodes. The great Roman Bath at the foot of the citadel at Argos (Barber 1988:287–88; Lambrinoudakis 1994:67–93) and the Bath House at Nemea (Miller, ed. 1990) attest to the continued abundance of water on this flank of the Argolid in later antiquity. Although the regional events that spelled the demise of the Mycenaeans and brought the Late Bronze Age to a close also affected Argos, it recovered in later antiquity. Only limited settlement is associated during subsequent Hellenistic times with the other early, sizable citadel sites (Myceanae, Tiryns, and Midea) on the eastern Argolid margins—away from the abundantly watered western margins on which Argos was established.

Earthquakes

Many explanations for the collapse of the Mycenaeans involve geological processes that are well documented in this portion of the Aegean (Doumas 1974). From volcanic eruptions and subsequent tidal waves to the collapse of stone walls and monumental architecture, natural catastrophe has been the explanation for the end of many ancient states (Bawden and Reycraft 2000). Such explanations have generally fallen out of favor in archaeology (Scarborough 2000; Yoffee and Cowgill, eds. 1988). However, one type of environmental explanation, namely, earthquake damage, deserves a fresh examination for Late Bronze Age Greece in light of the *hydrological budget* (the amount of water available).

The principal Argolid citadel sites dating to the Late Bronze Age are located on elevated, frequently isolated hillocks, where ancient *upthrust* (vertical movement) or *overthrust* (angled vertical movement) faults cut through portions of them. Midea and the smaller but elevated Late Bronze Age community of Asine reveal upthrust faulting, and both Mycenae and Argos show clear evidence of overthrust faulting (Scarborough 1994b; Geology Maps of Greece 1970). Tiryns is less convincingly associated with a fault line, but its location within the broad ancient alluvial plain (Zangger 1991), along with its relatively low hilltop relief, may mask buried evidence of faulting. Generally, elevated citadel sites were purposefully located on these fault lines. At Midea, Mycenae, and perhaps Tiryns, these geological fissures likely functioned as conduits for upwelling artesian springs, the only predictable, abundant, potable water source (Scarborough 1994b).

Evidence of earthquake damage has been presented for some of these citadel sites (Mylonas 1966, 1994:79; Demakopoulou 1994). Given that fault localities were selected for occupation because of issuing water sources, even mild earth tremors would amplify through the concentrated architecture within the confines of a citadel site. Earthquakes alone have seldom driven populations away from an entire region or destroyed the social fabric of a civilization, but decreased access to potable water quickly endangers a group's survival. Even a slight drop in the water table following tectonic stressors can spell disaster. Because of Mycenaean society's warlike character and penchant for defensible hilltop citadel sites, communities were extremely vulnerable without a water source within the immediate reach of the cyclopean walls.

Near the end of the Late Bronze Age, population increase (Betancourt 1976) and deforestation in this semiarid area (Well et al. 1993) caused the water table to drop anyway. Enough microclimatic and local landscape modification had occurred to warrant the construction of the Tiryns Dam, which routed deforestation-induced flood-waters around Tiryns (Zangger 1991, 1994). With tremors, adequate water sources for the citadel sites probably disappeared. Precipitation collected off rooftops and paved surfaces might have provided enough recharge to support small populations at these sites, with the former wellhead cisterns deployed as collection basins or tanks. From the beginning, they may have employed this technique to increase water supplies during dry season fluctuations in the water table, but it could not have predictably supported sizable Late Bronze Age populations.

Late Bronze Age (Mycenaean) Greece is a case in which the organizational outlook originating in a history of conflict prevented a group from reinventing itself across a fragile but productive landscape. The organizational outlook restricted occupation to defensible citadel sites, where water access depended on immediate fault lines. The price paid for the combative Mycenaean social environment was a disjunction between environmental processes and the organizational outlook. Decisions concerning the ecology were based on an earlier cultural trajectory (traditional formula) that could not handle the unsettling effects of earthquake damage. A less warlike cultural adaptation might have permitted a longer cultural trajectory.

World Comparisons

The case studies in this chapter reveal the tremendous variability in Old World hydraulic adaptations. This range of land-use and water-use systems was made possible, in part, by the availability of beasts of burden and technologies unused in the New World. Not only did physical distances contract to allow concentrations of resources and services, but also domesticated animals transporting resources that modified and intensified the agricultural landscape introduced engineering options not possible in the Western Hemisphere. Bray (1986) demonstrates the lack of emphasis placed on mechanical techniques in Asian "skill-oriented" economies. Nevertheless, the water buffalo pulling carts and plows and the cattle serving as beasts of burden (not as a principal food source) played a significant role. In rice-based economies from Sri Lanka to South China, the primacy of these beasts in agriculture is as evident today as it was in the ancient past. Harappan terra-cottas and seals feature numerous images of both humpless and humped bulls, the former being especially ubiquitous in the seal depictions (Allchin and Allchin 1982:206–12). Having the wheel and the sail as well, early Old World states were in a position to intensify their landscapes in myriad ways, limited principally by their underlying organizational outlooks.

The complex ecological relationships that captured and redirected the flow of water in Old World states included irrigation systems and the less studied diversion of water from reservoir-based systems. The Old and New Worlds shared certain technologies, although independently invented or discovered. The one European case (Mycenaean Greece) examined here depended on springheads, whereas the spring-fed irrigation systems in the Basin of Mexico case likely supported *chinampa* plots within the principal city of Teotihuacan.

Throughout this book, I have emphasized resource acquisition and consumption in terms of the process by which water resources—and resources more generally—were made available and used and the rate of this process. As implied at several junctures, scale of construction and systemwide maintenance requirements were important factors, too. In the Harappan case, the state was clearly large, controlling, and complex, in spite of its relative homogeneity in material culture. In contrast, the managers of ancient Ceylon directed many more resources toward aggrandizing the elite. Continually, they confronted armed invasions that forced at least the appearance of power through shows of monumental public works, including hydraulic systems. The Mycenaeans followed a similarly contentious cultural pathway, except that they were severely limited by water availability and the organizational outlook guiding their decision making. As in the Hohokam case in the prehistoric U.S. Southwest, water limitations in Late Bronze Age Greece had a debilitating effect on expansion and longevity.

In each of the Old World case studies, a rapid trajectory of state formation is evident. Semitropical Sri Lanka (Ceylon) would predictably have experienced a slower, more measured development—analogous to that of the New World's semitropical Lowland Maya—except that, as a secondary state, it was frequently attacked by state systems as complex as its own, forcing a rapid, reactionary, defensive growth.

NINE

Conclusions

Water, water, every where, nor any drop to drink.

—Samuel Coleridge, The Rime of the Ancient Mariner (1798)

Stephen J. Gould has pointed out that early Paleozoic lifeforms combined elemental chemical and biological relationships that fundamentally directed the course of subsequent evolution. With each new successful, more complex form, the trajectory for life eliminated the possibility of some other, completely unimaginable existence (Gould 1994). Cultural traditions, in contrast, are more malleable. In coping with a changing physical or social environment, people can reach back into an elapsed past to reemploy a long-unused concept or technique. Cultural systems, of course, are as unlikely as natural systems to revert wholesale to a previous adaptation to an earlier environmental setting. More generally speaking, cultural traditions reflect significant aspects of society's relationship with an ancient, less altered landscape and, accordingly, are conservative. Typically, cultures change their traditions slowly, with a temporal lag separating the traditional formulas from the innovations of technology and landscape alteration. This book's primary interest is the pace and process of this separation between the *forces of production* (water and land management and the associated techniques invented or rediscovered) and the *social relations of production* (how society organizes labor to harvest or exploit its natural resources).

To help us better understand the rationale for the arguments presented in this book, I provide a brief intellectual history of water management in chapter 3. To understand our interpretive biases today, we must become familiar with the thinking of those who have synthesized and modeled views of how and why societies alter the landscape and its water systems through time. Because true revolutions in intellectual history are rare, contemporary thinking reflects long trajectories of incremental and additive accomplishments. This intellectual process, too, acts to remove significant variation in attitude and orientation, making historical survey of a little-examined subfield such as water management especially relevant. Intellectual history, then, gives us the opportunity to ask these epistemological questions: How do we know what we know? Why don't we know something else?

Some researchers follow the biological species concept, that re-creating the genetic environment of an extinct life-form is impossible, despite nature's wonderfully creative ventures in convergent and parallel evolution. Unlike them, we can remodel historical trajectories rather than assume that all past perspectives are outdated or simply inappropriate. In part, this book is an effort to examine whether, by refurbishing past perspectives on water management and engineered landscapes, we can take a significantly different path for interpreting ecology and economy.

Theories of Economy and Water Use

One of the several axes aligning this book is a generic concept of the economy (Halperin 1994; Polanyi 1957). Admittedly, it is sometimes difficult to separate human ecology from economy—to sort human-land relationships from the organizational outlooks (regulatory principles) that guide all decision making on a culturally engineered landscape. Nevertheless, the distinction is heuristically useful in conceptualizing the major human inputs to altering the landscape, especially for the purposes of water management.

The economy-ecology dichotomy is heavily influenced by Karl Marx, whose definition of economy, pertaining to water and land, is briefly introduced in chapter 3. Unfortunately, Marx's notion of the Asiatic Mode of Production, viewing the East as ahistorical because (he thought) the economy and associated aspects of the landscape had "stagnated," subverted his clear sense of the economy. An indefensible position today, this outlook nevertheless influenced the deterministic views subsequently championed by Wittfogel (1957) and the cultural ecology advocated by Julian Steward (1955a, 1955b) for complex societies.

The complicated intellectual pathways directing the study of water and landscape management prevent the most influential thinkers on the subject from delineating tightly ordered classification schemes. For example, the early archaeologist V. Gordon Childe, strongly influenced by Marx, viewed the economy as fundamental. Childe (1950, 1951) interpreted the environment in terms of the perceptions of the group occupying it; in other words, he held that "human beings adapt not to real environments but to their ideas about them..." (Trigger 1989:261).[1] Childe (1951) was interested in the pace of culture change and generally adhered to the view that it was very slow. On the other hand, he (Childe 1950) also championed the Urban Revolution, suggesting that external factors could incite major rapid modifications to a culture. This seeming contradiction suggests that he understood the complexity of social evolution and, with his environmental possibilism, grasped that a culture's regulatory principles guided its decision making. Unfortunately, the process he considered fundamental for change was diffusion. Because of this position, subsequent cultural ecologists and cultural evolutionists dismissed his real contribution.

Wittfogel (1957) defined a new trajectory for water-use and land-use studies.

With Steward (1955a), he generated a formidable argument for the origins of the state and definitions of power—of centralization, really. Using cultural ecological theory based primarily on ethnographic examples (ironically, mainly nomadic foragers), Steward constructed an argument supporting a certain ecological determinism for early statecraft, with irrigation as its catalyst. The *hydraulic hypothesis* emphasized a radical social transformation leading to the centralized state at a rapid predictable pace. Viewing cultures uniformly, Wittfogel and Steward described most complex societies as being "preadapted" to an acceptance of irrigation and its associated bureaucracy.

Archaeology was the first field science to assess the determinism of the hydraulic hypothesis. Archaeologists Robert McC. Adams (1966, 1974) and William Sanders (Sanders and Price 1968) came to different conclusions, based on dissimilar data sets and divergent biases. Both were trained in the cultural ecological approach, but Adams viewed culture change as slow and gradual, or "ramp-like" (after Braidwood and Willey, eds. 1962). Gravitating toward Childe's views, he saw process less deterministically than Steward and more varied in its complexity. Sanders, on the other hand, was initially wedded to the determinism of the hydraulic hypothesis (Sanders and Price 1968). In time, though, he replaced irrigation with population pressure as the causal "trigger" (Sanders et al. 1979). His is a continuation of Steward's classic cultural ecology grounded on external factors directing the course of change. Ironically, Adams's position challenges the hydraulic hypothesis, even though his data provide the best evidence for early canalization coincident with statecraft. From the outset, Sanders championed the hypothesis but presented very little empirical evidence for the presence of formal irrigation canals in his study area, Mesoamerica.

Generally speaking, Adams and Sanders's initial attempts to evaluate Wittfogel's ideas drew from an interpretation of culture akin to Steward's (1955b) classic concept, based on homogeneous cores—that the archaic state had a fixed set of attributes everywhere. Although Marx, Childe, and Adams seem to see greater variability in culture than Wittfogel, Steward, and Sanders, the former group's view of culture was also limited in the kinds and numbers of organizational outlooks. Subsequent ethnographic work implicitly grappled with the limitations of the hydraulic hypothesis, initiating a period of careful cross-cultural comparison.

Ethnographers were less divided about the hydraulic hypothesis than archaeologists, perhaps reflecting archaeology's appreciation for the material record and the ease with which artifacts can be measured and evaluated using an ecological approach. Stated differently, archaeologists could focus on recording the material remains of ancient canal systems and might not be pressed to question the underlying social and political organizational assumptions of the hydraulic hypothesis. Most cultural anthropologists immediately took issue with Wittfogel's position, emphasizing the limitations of his interpretation of material remains, especially for addressing fundamental questions about social organization and complexity.

Clearly, Wittfogel's strident tone in discussing centralization or total power has disappeared from most debate. Nevertheless, the elusiveness of such concepts as centralization and power continues to haunt anthropologists, and definitional rigor has been lacking in water management studies. The terms continue to require situational context, a definitional task that Millon (1971) introduced, that Hunt and Hunt (1976) thoughtfully critiqued and developed, and that Kelly (1983) skillfully reintroduced. The rate, scale, and process of culture change must be addressed within an evolving framework of definitions of centralization, power, and political economy—of how a society employs power relationships among groups to organize the use of resources (see chapter 2).

This book proposes a new structure for assessing resource use, partly through an examination of the variability in contemporary thought about water and land management. Even though a continuum does exist, I view the pace of culture change as divisible between *accretional growth* and *exploitative development*. Furthermore, I propose three economic outlooks or approaches affecting rate changes:

1. *Labortasking.* A cultural logic that invests in highly efficient labor divisions
2. *Technotasking.* A cultural logic that invests in novel laborsaving technologies
3. *Multitasking.* A cultural logic in which people diversify the tasks necessary for survival in a less measured routine and without a great demand for technology

Taken together, these three economic orientations provide an initial window into the complexity of landscape and water management issues. The case studies (see chapters 7 and 8) identify the variability apparent in these idealized outlooks.

At a continental level of inquiry, some African systems (see chapter 3) show limited available labor but abundantly useful landscape. Europe, in contrast, has long had greater population aggregates (but densities far lower than Asia) and abundant land (at least early in its history). Asia has had limited land, given its high population densities. These continental differences in the Old World are useful in operationalizing the empirical differences of multitasking (Africa), technotasking (Europe), and labortasking (Asia) economies (refer to figure 2.1). Complex technology did not buffer African laborers from the environment. In Europe, technical innovations and greater exposure to foreign inventions offset labor shortages. Warfare, that consummate spur to technological invention, was a guiding regulatory principle throughout European history, beginning with the Greek city-states and stimulated partly by an unquenchable thirst for technological breakthroughs and superiority (Cronon 1983). Asia's main capital supplied labor and the landscape transformed by that labor.

The rate, scale, and process of culture change embody the fundamental *regulatory principles* undergirding societies. Their physical manifestations with regard to hydraulic systems—their ecological poses—can be dichotomized into

- *Still-water systems* (reservoirs and reclaimed lake margins) emphasizing harvesting/collection and the human construction of water sources
- *Irrigation schemes* emphasizing allocation/distributional decisions

Early tropical states tended to emphasize reservoir management, whereas early semiarid states gravitated toward irrigation management schemes. The archaeological case studies (see chapters 7 and 8) illustrate this division but also show that a model for social complexity must accommodate much variability when put to the test.

Drawing on the intellectual history of water thought, I have proposed a model linking the rate and process of change to the kinds and degrees of centralization, by means of *organizational planes* (refer to figures 3.4 and 3.5). Organizational planes are components of culture: kinship, politics, ideology, and economy (refer to figure 3.4). They are not rigidly separated or mutually exclusive but for heuristic purposes can be seen as loosely divisible parts of culture. For example, Geertz (1959) suggests that every village in Bali has all these planes, each reflecting a uniquely Balinese culture, but some villages emphasize one or two planes, resulting in a kaleidoscope of socio-cultural configurations. In my view, this concept of variability in social order through time and space is a good way to approach centralization, land and water management, and the rate and process of resource use and consumption cross-culturally.

Considerable variation exists within all cultures throughout their history. During some periods, a culture may follow an accretional pathway, but during another period it might take a more exploitative orientation. Even within the same culture area at a coeval moment, one region may take on a more measured, slow utilization of the natural resource base while another region opts for the expansionist approach to the environment. In general, though, the rates and processes of resource management and consumption in the early state correspond to the degree of centralization.

The concept of organizational planes permits us to characterize this variation. The planes can be seen as dynamic and overlapping, with some periods and places revealing an alignment of planes but most times and spaces reflecting a fluidity between planes in nonalignment. Furthermore, because of conflict conditions within each plane—from failed kinship alliances, to economic collapse resulting from drought, to palace intrigue in the political plane—the planes are complicated and fragile. However, a few planes are regularly brought together as a greater unit, united vertically in overlapping alignment. For example, centralization increases when kinship alliances achieve political control in the early state or ancestor veneration knits ideology and kinship over an extended period (McAnany 1995). These two immediate examples exhibit different degrees and kinds of centralization: grand palaces inspired by the wedding of kinship and politics leading to kingship, and towering pyramids with centrally located tombs resulting from the interlocking of ideology, kinship, and an intensified version of ancestor worship. When such organizational planes align, even partially, significant new labor investments in the engineered landscape become possible.

I believe that the highly stratified, hegemonic state is a rare ephemeral phenomenon synonymous with the hypercentralization that occurs when all the organizational planes are vertically stacked and aligned (refer to figure 3.5). Because of the forces pulling the planes apart—for example, palace intrigue, sibling rivalries, ecological degradation—the life expectancy of the hegemonic state is always brief. Nevertheless, total collapse following the separation of the planes is also infrequent. Certain attributes of the hegemonic state may continue, even without its former power and control over a constituency and the landscape. With good dating of pre-historic events on a landscape, we can determine the actual period of control by a hegemonic state, as well as its period as a facade of power. The rate and process of landscape alteration are the keys to this assessment of centralization.

It is important to emphasize that the purview of this book is ecological and economic, focusing on landscape alterations and underlying economic processes. A fundamental assumption is that the economic organizational plane, identified by the use of water, land, and labor, is the primary filter through which the other aspects of culture draw definition and direction. Although this assumption may be less apposite in the complex industrial and capitalistic economies of historical and present-day nation-states, it is championed here for the formative period of the earliest experiments in statecraft.

Students of cultural complexity and state formation generally conceive culture as having either an internal or an external locus of control and power. The larger composite model developed here suggests that the issue is dependent on context, the rate of change being determined by the culture's regulatory principles and environment. I have given attention to the sometimes appropriate, sometimes not, division between urban and rural as a subset of these factors. Accretional labortasking systems (for example, Maya, and perhaps Sinhalese in certain periods) frequently do not make the rural-urban split, whereas technotasking economies often do.

Economic Practices

Much of this book presents a body of data examining the scale and complexity of the water problem, that is, the physical possibilities and constraints experienced by water users cross-culturally. I have described the variation and range of water management features and identified the physical—and, to a degree, social—contexts. Temporal control is maintained and the rate and process of change assessed by employing anthropological archaeology—the only discipline positioned to contextualize the longitudinal depth of the material record. I stress ecological (human-land) relationships because these data are readily available cross-culturally and cross-temporally. Also, they provide an initial perspective on the way a group organizes for resource use. Repeatedly, I argue that human ecology is best understood as the most immediately accessible aspect of the "generic" economy (cf. Polanyi 1957). Interpreting social complexity, however, requires the more difficult task of examining a group's underlying regulatory principles, entailing a study of the variable rates and processes of culture change.

Chapters 7 and 8 present a focused examination of four regions, divided by hemisphere (Old World and New World) and environmental zone (arid and humid). Highland Mexico (arid) is compared with the Maya Lowlands (humid), and southern

Pakistan and western India (arid) are juxtaposed with Sri Lanka (humid). In addition to these complex early states, I examine two secondary cases influenced by earlier and nearby primary arid-land states: the Hohokam of the U.S. Southwest and the Mycenaeans of mainland Greece. The Hohokam occupied an extremely harsh environment but successfully manipulated it and developed a complex social organization, although less sociopolitically stratified than the archaic states. Late Bronze Age (Mycenaean) Greece has received considerable excavation attention by a wide range of humanists, classicists, and anthropologists, but little attention has been devoted to water management until recently (Crouch 1993; T. Smith 1995).

A necessary prelude to these case studies, as well as to the study of the economic outlays of water management in general, was a close look at the techniques employed by early water managers. Chapters 4 and 5 introduce the variability apparent in hydraulic systems, emphasizing the broad sweep of adaptations made in urban and rural settings. Both simple and complex systems can exist together or apart. Sometimes simple systems combined or incrementally spread, resulting in "complex adaptive systems," as in Bali (Lansing and Kremer 1993). Other times, water management techniques were planned from the outset, or more commonly, new organizational parameters usurped simpler systems in an attempt to knit them into more coordinated, controllable systems that complemented state bureaucracy. This did not necessarily stimulate or initiate these bureaucracies in the Wittfogelian sense.

The six case studies showcase the similarities and differences among early complex societies, based on how they constituted and modified their landscapes and water management systems. The rate and process of organizational change vary considerably among them, and within each individual case. The organizational outlooks (regulatory principles) posited for historical and ethnographic Asia, Europe, and Africa do not provide an exact analogy for understanding early social complexity leading to statecraft. However, the identified facts of water and landscape use show a significant correlation to the organizational models.

Maya Lowlands

The best-documented ancient state to occupy a built environment altered by accretional modifications based on a labortasking organizational outlook is that of the Classic-period Maya. The seasonally dependent water system structured around reservoirs and swamp margins within a semitropical rain forest resulted in a still-water adaptation. Within about 1,500 years, the demographic situation in this karstic setting evolved from a sparse settlement mosaic to a compacted population on the Yucatán Peninsula estimated at ten million people (Rice and Culbert 1990).

Because of the environmental constraints of a semitropical setting, the Maya's dispersed urban structure reveals few examples of a highly centralized or exploitative political economy. The Maya did not concentrate resources in the same manner as some other, better-understood archaic states. Consequently, communities became more interdependent and relied more on their altered hinterland landscape.

Highland Mexico

The ancient civilizations of highland Mexico present a different set of environmental restrictions and societal regulatory principles than those revealed for the ancient Maya. In Classic-period Teotihuacan (AD 1–750) and Aztec-period Tenochtitlan (AD 1350–1519), huge urban concentrations dominated the landscape of highland Mexico. In both cases, precipitous growth followed an exploitative pace within a New World version of a technotasking economy. For Teotihuacan, I argue that the resources concentrated into the nucleated urban setting enabled a degree of order and an intensity of landscape manipulation never before approached in the New World. Novel ways of controlling spring activity and intensifying *chinampa* (raised and reclaimed swamp for agriculture) productivity promoted fitter varieties of certain food staples and larger, more predictable yields than found elsewhere. Order and control are the key descriptors for this unique early city. The increased workloads of those feeding the urban complex served to restructure the society. The efforts of a highly stratified labor pool were directed toward exploiting the landscape and concentrating resources within the city. Only a small population inhabited the sizable sustaining area composing the Basin of Mexico.

The organizational planes supporting Teotihuacan's meteoric ascendancy were probably as centralized and reflective of hegemonic control as was possible in an early archaic state. After two hundred years, however, personalized rule was suppressed. The extent of separation between planes, which characterized the Maya from the outset, began to reshape Teotihuacan's fundamental organization. Maintenance expenditures replaced the grand investment in pyramids and avenues, physically and probably socially. The hegemonic control at this juncture in Teotihuacan's history became a facade of power, symbolized by the still-famous Pyramids of the Sun and the Moon, constructed earlier. Throughout the highlands, the city remained a major broker. Even with a diminishing organizational hegemony, it sustained its primacy as *the* urban aggregate in Mesoamerica for another four hundred years.

Hohokam of the U.S. Southwest

The other New World case studied, the Hohokam, developed rapidly upon the coalescence of canal networks. A culture of much lesser scale than most of the other cases examined, the Hohokam manifested a superior technology of irrigation associated with a small population (relative to the Maya or Teotihuacan), indicating a technotasking economy. As in many other examples of technotasking, an exploitative pace of development is discernible. A building spike in canal networks, dispersed compact settlements, and ball courts as centralizing architecture and nodes for decision making show early correlations. A few hundred years later, irrigation systems stabilized and reinvested in maintenance work, communities aggregated into compact settlements, and platform mounds replaced ball courts, indicating changes in decision-making institutions.

Like the much more complicated organizational planes ordering groups in highland Mexico, the planes here initially aligned—stimulated by significant changes in the built environment, especially in water management systems—to produce a highly exploitable landscape. A new manner of organizing (in the Hohokam case, around the institution of the ball game) was the outcome. Growth subsequently slowed after a change in the social order, signaled by alterations in settlement design and the replacement of ball courts with platform mounds. Unlike Teotihuacan, the other New World technotasking case study, Hohokam society was too small to develop the kind of strong personal rule that was eventually suppressed at Teotihuacan. Nevertheless, an early Hohokam growth and landscape modification spike was eventually compromised, resulting in a slippage between the organizational planes composing Hohokam society (refer to figure 3.4).

North-Central Sri Lanka

The Old World examples involve levels of technological development dissimilar to those of the New World cases, immediately suggesting differences in organizational outlook. However, it is not technology that drives or dictates the pathways of the regulatory principles. Technology frequently mediates human ecological relationships, but it does not directly generate or determine a culture's underlying decision-making structures.

Semitropical north-central Sri Lanka is a case example for which a prehistoric labortasking economy is posited. The ancient Sinhalese constructed a landscape of reservoirs and a still-water adaptation to water management not unlike Maya water and land use. Sinhala was a secondary locus for statecraft established long after developments in India, with possible ancestral roots to the Harappans (suggested by linguistic associations). Nevertheless, Sinhala's early regulatory principles and adaptations to the environment—one tank, one village—suggest a less exploitative use of water and land than that posited for the semiarid Indus Valley occupants some two thousand years earlier.

The Sinhalese settlement pattern was dispersed, but the greater landscape was probably as densely occupied as the Maya rain forest at a comparable time. Furthermore, the two "nuclear areas" defined by Gunawardana (1971) on Ceylon resemble the two principal regional states of Classic-period Maya political geography, Tikal and Calakmul. These states controlled some aspects of the greater Maya political economy (Martin and Grube 1996). Sri Lanka and the Maya Lowlands reveal that hegemonic control over a dispersed settlement design and still-water land-use adaptation was never very likely. Nevertheless, occasional periods of organizational plane alignment did promote greater centralization and resource exploitation than at other moments in their history. In the Sinhalese case, the complicated investment in irrigation—at least within the nuclear areas—suggests a significant exploitative adaptation at particular times and places in Ceylon's history.

Chapter 5 discusses the role of ritual and the symbolic appropriation of everyday water and other common but critical resources. Both the Maya and the Sinhalese accentuated public theater and ritual performance by the elite. To an extent not demonstrable for the other great archaic state areas canvassed—highland Mexico (Teotihuacan) or the Indus Valley—Sinhala presented elaborate displays of art and architecture depicting individuals and gods conducting everyday affairs and extraordinary activities. Furthermore, in the less centralized Sinhalese and Maya states, water iconography suggests an appropriation of water symbolism by kings and the development of a state ideology that helped define and control a large but dispersed sustaining population (Scarborough 1998). This ideological organizational plane played a prominent role in the regulatory principles guiding both the Maya and the Sinhalese.

Harappans of the Indus Valley

Harappan regulatory principles had much in common with those guiding ancient Teotihuacan in central Mexico, even though the specific ecological relationships of their respective cultures are quite distinct. Both experienced explosive growth rates resulting in an extent of order and planning unique to their respective hemispheres. Harappan society was likely based on a technotasking organizational outlook predicated on an intensive exploitation of the Indus floodplain and an extremely dense set of urban nodes. Unfortunately, postabandonment deposits prevent a clear view of how the Indus was used, but bund-field agriculture like that employed along the heavily silted Nile is posited. The standardization of measures and the extent of resource control apparent in Harappan society support the notion of an archetypical hegemonic state. Also, analogous to early Teotihuacan, the Early Indus period seems to have had a more coercive set of leaders who stimulated the initial concentration of resources that heightened the greatness of the Indus cities. Nevertheless, other significant aspects of this early state run counter to easy definitions of centralization and power. As in the case of late Teotihuacan, there is no evidence of self-aggrandizing rulers or nobles; rather, a faceless elite directed the order. In contrast to Teotihuacan, though, Harappan monumental architecture is limited, preventing an assessment of the focused resource concentrations invested by that faceless elite. Public and private wealth displays were suppressed, but the exceedingly high physical-health indices for the entire population suggest an equitable distribution of resources uncommon for a state. For a stratified early state, ordered and controlled to an extent seldom replicated in the archaeological record, Harappan society reveals a different set of regulatory principles than are evident elsewhere.

Ritual and the symbolic import of water affected Harappan organization, as attested by the Great Bath and related civic features. Perhaps the ideological organizational plane had a similar effect in Harappan society as in the Lowland Maya case. Nevertheless, I would argue that the Indus represents an organizational pathway to complexity most closely analogous to that of Teotihuacan in highland Mexico.

Mycenaeans of Bronze Age Greece

The Mycenaeans' small-scale, statelike, complex society was based on an exploitative adaptation grounded in the warfare technology of the European technotasking economy. Like Sri Lanka, the Argolid was the seat of a secondary state affected by political and military turmoil. The diminutive scale of the citadel sites was partly a consequence of the availability of water and land, an initial environmental limitation identical to that faced by the Hohokam of the U.S. Southwest. Water availability revolved around spring access, but impluvium-like catchments within citadel walls are conjectured. Mycenaean citadel towns were located atop defensible hillocks containing correlating geological fault lines and spring sources. Because of the hostilities among communities, an aspect of the overall organizational outlook, the citadel towns had limited options when even a slight change in the environs diminished resource availability. I have posited that earth tremors caused a dropping water table and, ultimately, cultural abandonment.

Of all the cultures assessed, the Mycenaean was the most short-lived. Its regulatory principles were the least resilient of those examined for coping with a specialized environmental niche. Its case emphasizes the influence on culture that the natural ecology can and does wield. The degree of influence depends on the regulatory principles present. Late Bronze Age Greece illustrates the functional trap into which inflexible regulatory principles may fall.

Final Overview

Generally speaking, those groups with technotasking economies—ancient highland Mexicans, the Harappans, Hohokam society, and the Mycenaeans—distinguished clearly between a well-defined urban or centralizing core and the rural hinterlands. For the Mycenaeans and the Harappans, city walls helped define the separation, whereas Teotihuacan's abrupt density decrease and overall intimidating size provided very real boundaries between the urban zone and the countryside. The Hohokam present the least such dichotomy, although density decreases are apparent between their towns and the remainder of the irrigation community.

The Maya and the Sinhalese present a less apparent division between urban and rural. These cases show a continuum of settlement dependent on the dispersed natural distribution of critical resources in a semitropical setting. Reservoirs and other still-water systems allowed the artificial concentration of water and the widespread colonization of environmental settings away from permanent rivers, streams, and springs, which were the necessary water sources for the semiarid complex societies discussed. A semitropical setting tends to favor a labortasking economy, at least in the initial stages of sociopolitical complexity.

Multitasking as a process or an organizational outlook was not identifiable in the prehistoric cases presented in this book. Nevertheless, it is a fundamental process usually embedded in other, more visible or dominant organizational outlooks.

Multitasking rural populations operate expediently on their landscapes, evolving resilient sets of activities that yield a living whether conditions are good or bad. These systems were noted for Africa and portions of indigenous Latin America today. (In the latter area, multitasking is often the result when these populations are pushed or compressed into marginal settings, with neither adequate land nor adequate available labor.) In any case, multitasking represents a degree of independence operative in the hinterlands, away from the urban nodes that frequently concentrate a society's critical resources.

From my vantage, the separation between city (town) and countryside is most apparent when a society's dominant sector is organized predominantly around a technotasking economy. Precisely in such cases, multitasking develops most effectively. Barriers—physical or otherwise—placed between the urban nodes and the greater landscape, reducing interaction and communication, cultivate a tendency toward autonomy and isolation in both spheres. The kinds of divisions arise that R. McC. Adams (1978) has identified (see chapters 2 and 3).

Hinterland populations inevitably see the landscape differently than their urban brethren. However, rural groups practicing labortasking in early complex societies were less separated from their towns and cities, which were less likely to be circumscribed by urban walls. This is not to say that defensive moats and city walls were not elements of the engineered environment in both the Maya Lowlands and Ceylon. Nevertheless, these skill-oriented, labortasking economies were better coordinated and entwined with the physical and social environment than was the case in the technotasking examples presented. The dispersed settlement pattern of the semitropical settings in which early labortasking economies evolved entailed an ecological interdependency of resource use. As argued earlier, these environmental limitations stimulated an accretional rate of change on the landscape and a different kind or lesser degree of centralization and political economy, emphasizing heterarchical and segmental interrelationships (see chapter 2).

Although dependent on a culture's time and place in history, and on the positioning of its organization planes, multitasking tends to be less embedded in the inner workings of labortasking than of technotasking-predominant economies where these orientations co-occur. Labortasking economies are better integrated into the hinterlands of their less nucleated urban nodes and frequently rely heavily on the labor and resources of both spheres. Clearly, the more divisive separation made by technotasking economies, explicitly incorporating a certain extent of multitasking in the hinterlands, reflects Shaw's (1984) contrast between consumptive urban water systems and productive rural water systems (see chapter 6). This division is a recurrent Western model for taming an ostensibly limitless natural landscape. I suggest that this divisive orientation lacks the necessary flexibility for longevity.

The vast majority of anthropological research on water management has focused on agricultural systems affecting the immediate needs of a population, often a farming population influenced by an elite with varying degrees of authority (see chapter 6). Although agrarian systems are manipulated by powerful elites capable of enforcing sanctions, agricultural success or failure is frequently influenced by symbolic displays of control. Water management typically entails a series of decisions broadly rooted in a set of ritual practices. These rituals do not always relate functionally to the physical movement or diversion of water in an agrarian system. Nevertheless, the scheduling of necessary work activities (labortasking) or the acceptance of appropriate technologies (technotasking) is probably more important over the long haul than the ideological or symbolic justifications used by elites. All these factors combine in establishing the principles that structure a society's basic organization.

I have attempted to address the question of how we culturally allocate water and the labor force that redirects it. Discussing solutions to this question really means addressing more fundamental issues concerning the components of culture and their interdigitation: how humans modify water's availability and how its availability influences human decision making and organization. Water management is a set of technical adaptations to a landscape or environment that can be measured and evaluated empirically, lending scientific method and associated rigor to cross-cultural comparisons. Because water is the most frequently exploited resource and has very explicit physical properties that remain the same under all earthly conditions, it is an excellent unit of analysis. In short, the study of water management affords the best chance for a truly cross-cultural understanding of resource use and control and the key elements of power.

NOTES

Chapter 3

1. Fredrik Barth (1993:99–101) has noted the inevitable ambiguity in attempting to establish definitional equivalencies when comparing and contrasting social groups. He suggests that a set of well-defined research problems can prevent the enigma—at least partially—from spiraling out of control. I have tried to identify data sets, presented by others, that lend themselves to comparison and then have attempted to evaluate and interpret the apparent trends.

2. Chaos theory as developed by "hard" sciences appears to be less appreciated by those sciences today because of its inability to explain the unpredictable predictably. In its wake, researchers from the Santa Fe Institute are examining "complex adaptive systems" (CAS). Although complexity studies have replaced chaos theory in theoretical circles, they may prove no more profound.

> Various attempts have been made to provide an equally precise definition of complexity [as that given to the ill-defined notion of chaos]. The most widely touted definition involves "the edge of chaos." The basic idea is that nothing novel can emerge from systems with high degrees of order and stability, such as crystals. On the other hand, completely chaotic systems, such as turbulent fluids or heated gases, are too formless. Truly complex things— amoebae, bond traders and the like—appear at the border between rigid order and randomness. (Horgan 1995:104–09)

3. Of all the early water monographs, Gray's may have been the most explicit in its attempt to test Wittfogel's theory. He argued that the irrigation-dependent Sonjo of East Africa lacked despotic tendencies when compared to neighboring interlacustrine groups, the latter being more class structured (1963:166). Seldom cited by others, Gray suggests that Sonjo society would have strong deep genealogical roots by way of clan divisioning if it were not for the destabilizing ecology associated with irrigation. This forced recurrent adjustments in the definition and availability of land and water. He indicates that as population increases and resources are stressed, society will become more and more "segmental" or segmentary unless united by centralizing government.

> Corporate lineages and centralized government existing together produce instability; instability is incompatible with the hydraulic economy of the Sonjo; therefore, in order for successful adaptation to take place, the antagonistic element least adaptive to the ecological situation (the clan) had to give way to the element best adapted to this situation (central government). (Gray 1963:171)

4. Polders are reclaimed wetlands generally near the sea or the margins of an estuary. Through dike and weir construction, lands are drained and nutrients added to the soils (see chapter 6).

Chapter 4

1. Outside the Americas, Hawaii is noteworthy for reservoir management. The diminutive pond-fields of protohistoric Hawaii also acted as reservoirs and silt traps. Terraced hillsides irrigated from permanent sources allowed the intensification of taro agriculture by these sociopolitically complex islanders (Earle 1978; Kirch 1994; Tuggle 1979).

2. In an unbridled bashing of the hydraulic hypothesis as it has influenced interpretations of Angkorian Khmer society, Stott (1992) suggests that little formal irrigation actually depended on the *barays*. His argument rests on the abundant productivity of flood-recessional agricultural methods in this portion of Southeast Asia and on the relative ease with which reservoirs could have been constructed, given their shallow depths. Although I am in agreement with Stott's reaction to Wittfogel, I am less convinced that these huge tanks were not a major source of water put to agricultural ends.

3. It should be noted that Spriggs (1985) has suggested a similar deliberate "landscape enhancement" associated with Oceanic pond-field developments.

Chapter 7

1. Cowgill (1992:90–91) argues that the earliest village-level colonization of Teotihuacan was initiated by Cuanalan times (500–150 BC), drawn to the site as the nearest high ground in proximity to the swampy setting that rests in the subsequently drained western portion of the city.

> Nothing suggests ceremonial or civic structures of more than very modest size in any of the Cuanalan settlements near Teotihuacan, or that any unusual sacred, commercial, or military significance was attached to any of these sites. The most obvious explanation for the location of the relatively large Cuanalan settlement centered in S1W6 is that it is on the closest dry land to what is today a small zone (100 hectares or so) of highly productive *chinampa*-like (drained field) cultivation in land that would be swampy if it were not drained. This zone is watered by springs in squares S1W5 and S1W4 that provide a year-round flow for it and also for several thousand hectares of canal-watered land.

Chapter 8

1. Most scholars associate the initial colonization of Sri Lanka with Indo-Iranian (Aryan) types, perhaps the same Indo-Iranians responsible, in part, for the demise of the Harappans. The Mahavamsa chronicle, written in the sixth century AD, elucidates this early period (Gunawardana 1971).

2. Traditional interpretation suggests that Harappan populations were likely replaced by Indo-European speakers from the West as early as 1700 BC. These likely horsemen introduced new technologies and organizational outlooks that rapidly spread through the Indus and Gangetic plains. However, Renfrew (1987) suggests that Indo-Iranian languages (a subset of Indo-European) were introduced to the area much earlier and perhaps by a slow-moving wave of agriculturalists (cf. Kenoyer 1998:26).

3. Mughal (personal communication, 1997) suggests that oxbows and backwash settings within the floodplain's margins may have been intensively utilized. Perhaps bunded fields similar to those documented along the ancient Nile were employed (see chapter 4).

4. Substantial occupational evidence exists at Lerna from Neolithic to Late Bronze Age times on the west side of the plain, whereas less well-preserved but abundant

evidence underlying most Mycenaean sites exists for Early to Middle Bronze Age occupations in the eastern flank of the Argolid.

Chapter 9

1. Unfortunately, Childe's position was not championed widely after the economy concept transformed into an ecology concept as the principal concern in anthropology (both archaeology and ethnology).

REFERENCES

Adams, R. E. W.

1980   Swamps, Canals and the Locations of Ancient Maya Cities. *Antiquity* 54:206–14.

Adams, R. E. W. (editor)

1984   *Rio Azul Report No. 1.* Center for Archaeological Research, University of Texas at San Antonio, San Antonio.

Adams, R. E. W., W. E. Brown, and T. P. Culbert

1981   Radar Mapping, Archaeology and Ancient Maya Land Use. *Science* 213:1457–62.

Adams, R. McC.

1955   Developmental Stages in Ancient Mesopotamia. In *Irrigation Civilization,* edited by J. H. Steward, pp. 6–18. Pan American Union, Washington, DC.

1965   *Land behind Baghdad.* University of Chicago Press, Chicago.

1966   *The Evolution of Urban Society: Early Mesopotamia and Prehistoric Mexico.* Aldine, Chicago.

1974   Historic Patterns of Mesopotamian Irrigation Agriculture. In *Irrigation's Impact on Society,* edited by T. E. Downing and McGuire Gibson, pp.1–6. Anthropological Papers of the University of Arizona 25. University of Arizona Press, Tucson.

1978   Strategies of Maximization, Stability and Resilience in Mesopotamian Society, Settlement and Agriculture. *Proceedings of the American Philosophical Society* 122:329–35.

        Heartland of Cities. University of Chicago Press, Chicago.

        Property Rights and Functional Tenure in Mesopotamian Rural Communities. In *Societies and Languages of the Ancient Near East: Studies in Honor of I. M Diakonoff,* edited by M. T. Larsen and J. N. Postgate, pp. 1–14. Aris and Phillips, Warminster, England.

Adams, R. M., and H. J. Nissen

1972   *The Uruk Countryside.* University of Chicago Press, Chicago.

Allchin, B., and R. Allchin

1982   *The Rise of Civilization in India and Pakistan.* Cambridge University Press, Cambridge.

Anderson, P.

        The Asiatic Mode of Production. In *Lineages of the Absolute State,* pp. 462–549. Humanities Press, London.

Andronicos, M.

1976   *Delphi.* Ekdotike Athenon, Athens.

Angulo, J.

1987   El sistema *otli-apantli* dentro del área urbana. In *Teotihuacan, Nuevos Datos, Nuevas Síntesis, Nuevos Problemas,* edited by
            E. McClung de Tapia and E. Rattray, pp. 399–415. Universidad Nacional Autónoma de México, Mexico City.

            Water Control and Communal Labor during the Formative and Classic Periods Central Mexico (ca. 1000 BC–AD 650).
            In *Economic Aspects of Water Management in the Prehispanic New World* (Research in Economic Anthropology, Supplement
            7), edited by V. L. Scarborough and B. L. Isaac, pp.151–220. JAI Press, Greenwich, CT.

Annis, S.

1987   *God and Production in a Guatemalan Town.* University of Texas Press, Austin.

Armillas, P.

1971   Gardens on Swamps. *Science* 174: 653–61.

Ashmore, W.

1984   Classic Maya Wells at Quirigua, Guatemala: Household Facilities in a Water-Rich Setting. *American Antiquity*
            49:148–53.

Barber, R.

1988   *Blue Guide: Greece.* Norton, New York.

Barnes, M., and D. Fleming

1991   Filtration-Gallery Irrigation in the Spanish New World. *Latin American Antiquity* 2:48–68.

Barth, F.

1961   *Nomads of South Persia: The Biasseri Tribe of the Khamseh Confederacy.* Oslo University Press, Oslo.

1965   *Political Leadership among Swat Pathans.* Athalone Press, London.

1969   *Ethnic Groups and Boundaries.* Little, Brown and Company, Boston.

1973   A General Perspective on Nomad-Sedentary Relations in the Middle East. In *The Desert and the Sown: Nomads in the
            Wider Society,* edited by C. Nelson, pp. 11–23. Institute for International Studies Research Series 21. University of
            California, Berkeley.

1993   *Balinese Worlds.* University of Chicago Press, Chicago.

Bar-Yosef, O.

1986   The Walls of Jericho: An Alternative Interpretation. *Current Anthropology* 27:157–62.

Basham, A. L.

1968   *The Wonder That Was India.* 3rd ed. Taplinger, New York.

Bawden, G., and R. M. Reycraft, eds.

2000   *Natural Disaster and the Archaeology of Human Response.* Maxwell Museum of Anthropology and the University of New
            Mexico Press, Albuquerque.

Baxter, J. O.

1997   *Dividing New Mexico's Waters, 1700–1912.* University of New Mexico Press, Albuquerque.

Bayman, J. A., and S. K. Fish

1992   Reservoirs and Locational Shifts in Sonoran Desert Subsistence. In *Long-Term Subsistence Change in Prehistoric North
            America (Research in Economic Anthropology, Supplement 6),* edited by D. R. Croes, R. A. Hawkins, and B. L. Isaac,
            pp. 267–306. JAI Press, Greenwich, CT.

Beardsley, R. K., J. H. Hall, and R. E. Ward

1959   *Village Japan.* University of Chicago Press, Chicago.

Bell, C.

1992   *Ritual Theory, Ritual Practice.* Oxford University Press, New York.

Betancourt, P. P.

1976   The End of the Greek Bronze Age. *Antiquity* 50:40–47.

Blanton, R. E., S. A. Kowalewski, G. M. Feinman, and L. M. Feinsten

1993   *Ancient Mesoamerica: A Comparison of Change in Three Regions.* 2nd ed. Cambridge University Press, Cambridge.

Bloch, M.

1987   The Ritual of the Royal Bath in Madagascar: The Dissolution of Death, Birth and Fertility into Royalty. In *Ritual of Royalty: Power and Ceremonial in Traditional Societies,* edited by D. Cannadine and S. Price, pp. 271–97. Cambridge University Press, New York.

Bonfil Batalla, G.

1996   *México Profundo: Reclaiming a Civilization,* trans. P. A. Dennis. University of Texas Press, Austin.

Bonine, M. E.

1996   Qanats and Rural Societies: Sustainable Agriculture and Irrigation Cultures in Contemporary Iran. In *Canals and Communities,* edited by J. A. Mabry, pp. 183–209. University of Arizona Press, Tucson.

Boserup, E.

1965   *The Conditions of Agricultural Growth.* Aldine, Chicago.

Bowen, R. L., and F. P. Albright

     Archaeological Discoveries in South Arabia. Johns Hopkins Press, Baltimore.

Brady, J. E.

1997   Settlement Configuration and Cosmology: The Role of Caves at Dos Pilas. *American Anthropology* 99:602–18.

Braidwood, R. J.

1960   The Agricultural Revolution. *Scientific American* 203:130–41.

Braidwood R. J., and G. R. Willey, eds.

1962   *Courses toward Urban Life.* Viking Fund Publications in Anthropology, No. 32. Wenner-Gren Foundation for Anthropological Research, New York.

Brainerd, G. W.

1958   *The Archaeological Ceramics of Yucatan.* Anthropological Records, vol. 19. University of California, Berkeley.

Bray, F.

1984   Agriculture. In *Science and Civilisation in China,* vol. 4, pt. 2, edited by J. Needham, pp. 1–617. Cambridge University Press, Cambridge.

1986   *The Rice Economies: Technology and Development in Asian Societies.* Basil Blackwell, Oxford.

Briggs, L. P.

1951   *The Ancient Khmer Empire.* Transactions of the American Philosophical Society, vol. 41, pt. 1. American Philosophical Society, Philadelphia.

Brohier, R. L.

1935   *Ancient Irrigation Works in Ceylon,* vol. 2. Ministry of Mahaweli Development, Colombo.

Broneer, O.

1939   A Mycenaean Fountain on the Athenian Acropolis. *Hesperia* 8:317–430.

Bronson, B.

1978   Angkor, Anuradhapura, Prambanan, Tikal: Maya Subsistence in an Asian Perspective. In *Pre-Hispanic Maya Agriculture,* edited by P. D. Harrison and B. L. Turner II, pp. 255–300. University of New Mexico Press, Albuquerque.

Burger, R. L.

1984   *The Prehistoric Occupation of Chavín de Huántar, Peru.* University of California Publications in Anthropology 14. University of California Press, Berkeley.

Burn, A. R., and M. Burn

1980   *The Living Past of Greece.* Harper Collins, New York.

Butzer, K. W.

1976   *Early Hydraulic Civilization in Egypt: A Study in Cultural Ecology.* University of Chicago Press, Chicago.

Calnek, E. E.

1972   Settlement Pattern and Chinampa Agriculture at Tenochtitlan. *American Antiquity* 37:104–15.

1973   The Location of the Sixteenth-Century Map Called the Maguey Plan. *American Antiquity* 38:190–95.

Carr, R. F., and J. E. Hazard

1961   *Tikal Report No. 11: Map of the Ruins of Tikal, El Petén, Guatemala.* Museum Monographs, University Museum, University of Pennsylvania, Philadelphia.

Carter, V. G., and T. Dale

1974   *Topsoil and Cultivation.* University of Oklahoma, Norman.

Caskey, J. L.

1977   *Lerna in the Argolid.* University of Cincinnati, Cincinnati.

Chambers, R.

1980   Basic Concepts in the Organization of Irrigation. In *Irrigation and Agricultural Development in Asia,* edited by E. W. Coward, Jr., pp. 28–50. Cornell University Press, Ithaca.

Chang, K. C.

1986   *The Archaeology of Ancient China.* Yale University Press, New Haven.

Charlton, T. H., and D. L. Nichols

1997   Diachronic Studies of City-States: Permutations on a Theme—Central Mexico from 1700 BC to AD 1600. In *The Archaeology of City-States,* edited by D. L. Nichols and T. H. Charlton, pp. 169–207. Smithsonian Institution Press, Washington, DC.

Chi, Ch'ao-ting

1936   *Key Economic Areas in Chinese History, as Revealed in the Development of Public Works for Water Control.* Issued under the Auspices of the American Council, Institute of Pacific Relations, London.

Childe, V. G.

1950   The Urban Revolution. *Town Planning Review* 21:3–17.

1951   *Social Evolution.* Schuman, New York.

Clark, G. E.

1992   *Space, Time and Man: A Prehistorian's View.* Cambridge University Press, Cambridge.

Clark, J. E.

1986   From Mountains to Molehills: A Critical Review of Teotihuacan's Obsidian Industry. In *Economic Aspects of Prehispanic Highland Mexico (Research in Economic Anthropology, Supplement 2),* edited by B. L. Isaac, pp. 23–74. JAI Press, Greenwich, CT.

Codrington, H. W.

1939   *A Short History of Ceylon.* MacMillan and Co., Ltd., London.

Coe, M. D.

1964   The Chinampas of Mexico. *Scientific American* 211:90–98.

Coe, M. D., and R. A. Diehl

1980   *In the Land of the Olmec: The Archaeology of San Lorenzo Tenochtitlan,* vol. 1. University of Texas Press, Austin.

Coe, W. R.

1967   *Tikal: A Handbook of the Ancient Maya Ruins.* University Museum, University of Pennsylvania, Philadelphia.

1990   *Excavations in the North Acropolis, North Terraces and Great Plaza of Tikal. Tikal Report 14,* vol. 2. University Museum, University of Pennsylvania, Philadelphia.

Cohen, M. N.

1977   *The Food Crisis in Prehistory: Overpopulation and the Origins of Agriculture.* Yale University Press, New Haven.

Coleridge, S.

1999   The Rime of the Ancient Mariner. In *Now Read On: A Course in Multicultural Reading,* edited by J. McCrae and M. E. Vethamani, pp. 55–59. Routledge Press, London.

Coningham, R.

1999   *Anuradhapura: The British-Sri Lanka Excavations at Anuradhapura Salagha Watt 2, vol. 1: The Site.* Society for South Asia Studies Monograph no. 3, British Archaeological Reports S824. Archaeopress, Oxford.

Cooke, C. W.

1931   Why the Mayan Cities of the Petén District, Guatemala, Were Abandoned. *Journal of the Washington Academy of Science* 21:283–87.

Coward, E. W., Jr.

1979   Principles of Social Organization in an Indigenous Irrigation System. *Human Organization* 38:28–36.

Cowgill, G. L.

1992   Toward a Political History of Teotihuacan. In *Ideology and Precolumbian Civilization,* edited by A. A. Demarest and G. W. Conrad, pp. 87–114. School of American Research Press, Santa Fe.

1997   State and Society at Teotihuacan, Mexico. *Annual Reviews of Anthropology* 26:129–61.

Crawford, S.

1988   *Mayordomo: Chronicle of an Acequia in Northern New Mexico.* Doubleday, New York.

Cressey, G. B.

1958   Qanats, Karez and Foggaras. *Geographical Review* 48:27–44.

Cresson, F. M., Jr.

1938   Maya and Mexican Sweat Houses. *American Anthropologist* 40:88–104.

Cronon, W.

1983   *Changes in the Land.* Hill and Wang, New York.

Crouch, D. P.

1993   *Water Management in Ancient Greek Cities.* Oxford University Press, Oxford.

Crowfoot, J. W., and F. L. Griffith

1911   *The Island of Meroe.* Archaeological Survey of Egypt, Memoir 19. London.

Crown, P. L.

1987a   Water Storage in the Prehistoric Southwest. *Kiva* 52:209–28.

1987b   Classic Period Hohokam Settlement and Land Use in the Casa Grande Ruins Area, Arizona. *Journal of Field Archaeology* 14:147–62.

Crumley, C. L.

1987   A Dialectical Critique of Hierarchy. In *Power Relations and State Formation,* edited by T. C. Patterson and C. W. Gailey, pp. 155–59. American Anthropological Association, Washington, DC.

1995   Heterarchy and the Analysis of Complex Societies. In *Heterarchy and the Analysis of Complex Societies,* edited by R. M. Ehrenreich, C. L. Crumley, and J. E. Levy, pp. 1–6. Archaeological Papers of the American Anthropological Association 6. Washington, DC.

Crumley, C. L., ed.
1994   *Historical Ecology: Cultural Knowledge and Changing Landscapes.* School of American Research Press, Santa Fe.

Culbert, T. P.
1977   Maya Development and Collapse: An Economic Perspective. In *Social Process in Maya Prehistory,* edited by N. Hammond, pp. 510–31. Academic Press, London.

Culbert, T. P., L. J. Levi, and L. Cruz
1989   The Rio Azul Agronomy Program: 1986 Season. In *Rio Azul Reports 4: The 1986 Season,* edited by R. E. W. Adams, pp. 189–214. University of Texas at San Antonio, San Antonio.

Culbert, T. P., and D. S. Rice, eds.
1990   *Precolumbian Population History in the Maya Lowlands.* University of New Mexico Press, Albuquerque.

Dahlin, B. H.
1984   A Colossus in Guatemala: The Preclassic City of El Mirador. *Archaeology* 37:18–25.

Dales, G. F.
1965   New Investigations at Mohenjo-daro. *Archaeology* 18:145–50.

de Jong, J.
1987   Water and Land Management in the Netherlands: History, Present Day's Situation and Future. In *Water for the Future,* edited by W. O. Wunderlich and J. E. Prins, pp. 79–90. A. A. Balkema, Boston.

de los Reyes, R. P.
1980   *Forty-Seven Communal Gravity Systems: Organizational Profiles.* Institute of Philippine Culture, Ateneo de Manila University, Quezon City.

de Villiers, M.
2000   *Water: The Fate of Our Most Precious Resource.* Houghton Mifflin Co., Boston.

Dean, J. S., R. C. Euler, G. J. Gumerman, F. Plog, R. H. Herly, and T. N. V. Karlstrom
1985   Human Behavior, Demography, and Paleoenvironment on the Colorado Plateaus. *American Antiquity* 50:537–54.

Denevan, W. M.
1970   Aboriginal Drained-Field Cultivation in the Americas. *Science* 169:647–54.

2001   *Cultivated Landscapes of Native Amazonia and the Andes: Triumph over the Soil.* Oxford University Press, Oxford.

Di Peso, C. C., J. B. Rinaldo, and G. J. Fenner
1974   *Casas Grandes,* vols. 4 and 5. Northland Press, Flagstaff.

Diamond, J.
1999   *Guns, Germs, and Steel: The Fates of Human Societies.* Norton, New York.

Díaz del Castillo, B.
1956   *The Discovery and Conquest of Mexico 1517–1521,* trans. A. P. Maudslay. Farrar, Strauss, and Giroux, New York.

Donkin, R. A.
1979   *Agricultural Terracing in the Aboriginal New World.* Viking Fund Publications in Anthropology 56. University of Arizona Press, Tucson.

Doolittle, W. E.
1985   The Use of Check Dams for Protecting Downstream Agricultural Land in the Prehistoric Southwest: A Contextual Analysis. *Journal of Anthropological Research* 41:279–305.

1990a   *Canal Irrigation in Prehistoric Mexico.* University of Texas Press, Austin.

1990b   Terrace Origins: Hypothesis and Research Strategies. *Yearbook of the Conference of Latin American Geographers* 16:94–97.

Doumas, C.

1974   The Minoan Eruption of the Santorini Volcano. *Antiquity* 48:110–15.

Downing, T. E., and M. Gibson, eds.

1974   *Irrigation's Impact on Society.* Anthropological Papers of the University of Arizona 25. Tucson.

Drennan, R. D.

1984a   Long-Distance Movement of Goods in the Mesoamerican Formative and Classic. *American Antiquity* 49:27–43.

1984b   Long-Distance Transport Costs in Pre-Hispanic Mesoamerica. *American Anthropologist* 86:105–12.

Drennan, R. D., P. T. Fitzgibbon, and H. Dehn

1990   Imports and Exports in Classic Mesoamerican Political Economy. *Research in Economic Anthropology* 12:177–99.

Dunning, N., and T. Beach

1994   Soil Erosion, Slope Management and Ancient Terracing in the Maya Lowlands. *Latin American Antiquity* 5:51–69.

Dunning, N., S. Luzzadder-Beach, T. Beach, J. Jones, V. Scarborough, and T. P. Culbert

2002   Arising from the Bajos: Anthropogenic Change of Wetlands and the Rise of Maya Civilization. *Annals of the Association of American Geographers* 92:267–83.

Dunning, N., V. L. Scarborough, F. Valdez, Jr., S. Luzzadder-Beach, T. Beach, and J. G. Jones

1999   Temple Mountains, Sacred Lakes, and Fertile Fields: Ancient Maya Landscapes in Northwestern Belize. *Antiquity* 73:650–60.

Eadie, J. W., and J. P. Oleson

1986   The Water-Supply Systems of Nabataen and Roman Humayma. *Bulletin of the American School of Oriental Research* 262:49–76.

Earle, T. K.

1978   *Economic and Social Organization of a Complex Chiefdom: The Halelea District Kaua'i, Hawaii.* Museum of Anthropology, University of Michigan Anthropological Papers 63. Ann Arbor.

Edwards, A. B.

1888   *A Thousand Miles up the Nile.* Lovell, Coreyell, and Co., New York.

English, P. W.

1966   *City and Village in Iran: Settlement and Economy in the Kirman Basin.* University of Wisconsin Press, Madison.

Erickson, C. L.

1993   The Social Organization of Prehispanic Raised Field Agriculture in the Lake Titicaca Basin. In *Economic Aspects of Water Management in the Prehispanic New World (Research in Economic Anthropology, Supplement 7),* edited by V. L. Scarborough and B. L. Isaac, pp. 369–426. JAI Press, Greenwich, CT.

Evans, A.

1928   *The Palace of Minos at Knossos,* vol. 2, Pt. 2. Macmillan and Co., London.

1930   *The Palace of Minos at Knossos,* vol. 3. Macmillan and Co., London.

Evans, S.

2000   Aztec Royal Pleasure Parks: Conspicuous Consumption and Elite Status Rivalry. *Studies in the History of Gardens and Designed Landscapes* 20:206–28.

Evenari, M., and D. Koller

1956   Ancient Masters of the Desert. *Scientific American* 194:39–45.

Evenari, M., L. Shanan, and N. Tadmor
1971   *The Negev: The Challenge of a Desert.* Harvard University Press, Cambridge.

Fahlbusch, H.
1987   Municipal Water Supply in Antiquity. In *Water for the Future,* edited by W. O. Wunderlich and J. E. Prins, pp. 113–24. A. A. Balkena, Boston.

Fairley, J. P., Jr.
n.d.   Geologic Water Storage in Pre-Columbian Peru. *Latin American Antiquity.* In press.

Fairservis, W. A.
1971   *The Roots of Ancient India.* 2nd ed. University of Chicago, Chicago.

Fallers, L. A.
1964   Social Stratification and Economic Processes. In *Economic Transition in Africa,* edited by M. J. Herskovits and M. Harwitz, pp. 113–30. Northwestern University Press, Evanston.

Farrington, I. S.
1980   The Archaeology of Irrigation Canals, with Special Reference to Peru. *World Archaeology* 11:287–305.

1983   The Design and Function of the Intervalley Canal: Comments on a Paper by Ortloff, Moseley and Feldman. *American Antiquity* 43:360–75.

Fentress, M. A.
1978   Regional Interaction in Indus Valley Urbanization: The Key Factors of Resource Access and Exchange. In *American Studies in the Anthropology of India,* edited by S. Vatuk, pp. 389–424. Manohar, New Delhi.

Ferdon, E. N., Jr.
1959   Agricultural Potential and the Development of Cultures. *Southwestern Journal of Anthropology* 15:1–19.

Fernea, R. A.
1970   *Shaykh and Effendi: Changing Patterns of Authority among the El Shabana of Southern Iraq.* Harvard University Press, Cambridge.

Flannery, K. V.
1972   The Cultural Evolution of Civilizations. *Annual Review of Ecology and Systematics* 3:399–426.

Flannery, K. V., A. V. T. Kirkby, M. J. Kirkby, and A. Williams, Jr.
1967   Farming Systems and Political Growth in Ancient Oaxaca. *Science* 158:445–54.

Fletcher, R.
1986   Settlement Archaeology: World-Wide Comparisons. *World Archaeology* 18:59–83.

Folan, W. J.
1992   Calakmul, Campeche: A Centralized Urban Administrative Center in Northern Petén. *World Archaeology* 24:158–68.

Folan, W. J., J. Gunn, J. D. Eaton, and R. W. Patch
1983   Paleoclimatological Patterning in Southern Mesoamerica. *Journal of Field Archaeology* 10:453–68.

Folan, W. J., E. R. Kintz, and L. A. Fletcher
1983   *Cobá: A Classic Maya Metropolis.* Academic Press, New York.

Fowler, M. L.
1987   Early Water Management at Amalucan, State of Puebla, Mexico. *National Geographic Research* 3:52–68.

Fox, R. G.
1977   *Urban Anthropology: Cities in Their Cultural Setting.* Prentice-Hall, Englewood Cliffs, NJ.

Freidel, D. A., and V. L. Scarborough
1982   Substance, Trade and Development of the Coastal Maya. In *Maya Subsistence: Studies in Memory of Dennis E. Puleston,* edited by K. V. Flannery, pp. 131–51. Academic Press, New York.

French, K.
2002   Creating Space through Water Management at the Classic Maya Site of Palenque, Chiapas, Mexico. M.A. Thesis, Department of Anthropology, University of Cincinnati, Cincinnati.

Gallant, T. W.
1991   *Risk and Survival in Ancient Greece.* Stanford University Press, Stanford.

Garbrecht, G.
1987   Irrigation Throughout History: Problems and Solutions. In *Water for the Future,* edited by W. O. Wunderlich and J. E. Prins, pp. 3–18. A. A. Balkema, Boston.

Geertz, C.
1959   Form and Variation in Balinese Village Structure. *American Anthropologist* 61:991–1012.

1963   *Agricultural Involution.* University of California Press, Berkeley.

1973   The Wet and the Dry: Traditional Irrigation in Bali and Morocco. *Human Ecology* 1:23–29.

1980   *Negara: The Theatre State in Nineteenth-Century Bali.* Princeton University Press, Princeton.

Geertz, H., and C. Geertz
1975   *Kinship in Bali.* University of Chicago Press, Chicago.

Gibson, M.
1974   Violation of Fallow and Engineered Disaster in the Mesopotamian Civilization. In *Irrigation's Impact on Society*, edited by T. E. Downing and M. Gibson, pp. 7–20. Anthropological Papers of the University of Arizona, 25. University of Arizona Press, Tucson.

Gill, D.
1991   Subterranean Waterworks of Biblical Jerusalem: An Adaptation of a Karst System. *Science* 254:1467–70.

Gill, R. B.
2000   *The Great Maya Drought.* University of New Mexico Press, Albuquerque.

Gleissman, S. R., B. L. Turner II, F. J. Rosado May, and M. F. Amador
1983   Ancient Maya Raised Field Agriculture in the Maya Lowlands of Southeastern Mexico. In *Drained Field Agriculture in Central and South America,* edited by J. P. Darch, pp. 91–110. Proceedings of the 44th International Congress of Americanists. British Archaeological Research International Series 189. Oxford.

Glick, T. F.
1970   *Irrigation and Society in Medieval Valencia.* Harvard University Press, Cambridge.

Goody, J.
1976   *Production and Reproduction: A Comparative Study of the Domestic Domain.* Cambridge University Press, Cambridge.

Gould, S. J.
1994   The Persistently Flat Earth. *Natural History* 103(3):12–19.

Gowlett, J.
1993   *Ascent to Civilization.* Knopf, New York.

Graham, I.
1967   *Archaeological Explorations in El Petén, Guatemala.* Middle American Research Institute Publication 33. Tulane University, New Orleans.

Gray, R. F.

1963   *The Sonjo of Tanganyika: An Anthropological Study of an Irrigation-Based Society.* Oxford University Press, Cambridge.

Groslier, B-P.

1974   Agriculture et religion dans l'Empire Angkorien. Etudes Rurales 53–56; *Agriculture et Societes en Asie du Sud-est* 95–117.

1979   La cite hydraulique angkorienne: Exploitation ou surexploitation du sol. *Bulletin de l'Ecole Francaise d'Extreme-Orient* LXVI:161–202.

Guillet, D. W.

1987   Terracing and Irrigation in the Peruvian Highlands. *Current Anthropology* 28: 409–30.

1991   *Covering Ground: Communal Water Management and State in the Peruvian Highlands.* University of Michigan Press, Ann Arbor.

Gunawardana, R. A. L. H.

1971   Irrigation and Hydraulic Society in Early Medieval Ceylon. *Past and Present* 53:3–27.

1978   Hydraulic Engineering in Ancient Sri Lanka: The Cistern Sluice. In *Senarat Paranavitana Commemoration Volume,* edited by L. Prematilleke and K. Indrapala, pp. 61–74. E. J. Brill, Leiden.

1981   Social Function and Political Power: A Case Study of State Formation in Irrigation Society. In *The Study of the State,* edited by H. S. M. Claessen and P. Skalnik, pp.133–54. Mouton, The Hague.

Gunn, J. D., W. J. Folan, and H. R. Robichaux

1995   A Landscape Analysis of the Candelaria Watershed in Mexico: Insights into Paleoclimates Affecting Upland Horticulture in the Southern Yucatan Peninsula Semi-Karst. *Geoarchaeology* 10:3–42.

Hack, J. T.

1942   *The Changing Physical Environment of the Hopi Indians of Arizona.* Papers of the Peabody Museum of American Archaeology and Ethnology 35. Harvard University, Cambridge.

Halperin, R. H.

1994   *Cultural Economies: Past and Present.* University of Texas Press, Austin.

Hamdan, G.

1961   Evolution of Irrigation Agriculture in Egypt. *Arid Zone Research* 17:119–42.

Hammond, P. C.

1967   Desert Waterworks of the Ancient Nabataeans. *Natural History* 76:38–47.

Hanks, L. M.

1972   *Rice and Man: Agricultural Ecology in Southeast Asia.* Aldine-Atherton, Chicago.

Hard, R. J., and J. R. Roney

1998   A Massive Terraced Village Complex in Chihuahua, Mexico, 3000 Years Before Present. *Science* 279:1661–64.

Hard, R. J., J. E. Zapata, B. K. Moses, and J. R. Roney

1999   Terrace Construction in Northern Chihuahua, Mexico: 1150 BC and Modern Experiments. *Journal of Field Archaeology* 26:129–46.

Hardin, G.

1968   The Tragedy of the Commons. *Science* 162:1243–48.

Harlan, J. R.

1992   *Crops and Man.* 2nd ed. American Society of Agronomy, Inc., Madison, WI.

Harrison, P. D.

1977 The Rise of the Bajos and the Fall of the Maya. In *Social Process in Maya Prehistory: Studies in Memory of Sir Eric Thompson,* edited by N. Hammond, pp. 469–508. Academic Press, London.

1978 Bajos Revisited: Visual Evidence for One System of Agriculture. In *Pre-Hispanic Maya Agriculture,* edited by P. D. Harrison and B. L. Turner II, pp. 247–54. University of New Mexico Press, Albuquerque.

1982 Subsistence and Society in Eastern Yucatan. In *Maya Subsistence: Studies in Memory of Dennis E. Puleston,* edited by K. V. Flannery, pp. 119–28. Academic Press, New York.

1993 Aspects of Water Management in the Southern Maya Lowlands. In *Economic Aspects of Water Management in the Prehispanic New World (Research in Economic Anthropology, Supplement 7),* edited by V. L. Scarborough and B. L. Isaac, pp. 71–119. JAI Press, Greenwich, CT.

Harrison, P. D., and B. L. Turner II, eds.

1978 *Prehispanic Maya Agriculture.* University of New Mexico Press, Albuquerque.

1983 *Pulltrouser Swamp: Ancient Maya Habitat, Agriculture and Settlement in Northern Belize.* University of Texas Press, Austin.

Hatch Popenoe, Marion

1997 *Kaminaljuyu/San Jorge: Evidencia arqueológica de la actividad economica en el Valle de Guatemala 300 a.C. a 300 d.C.* Universidad del Valle de Guatemala, Guatemala City.

Healy, P. F., J. D. H. Lambert, J. T. Arnason, and R. J. Hebda

1984 Caracol, Belize: Evidence of Ancient Maya Agricultural Terraces. *Journal of Field Archaeology* 10:397–410.

Hedrick, R.

1997 The Waters of Babylonia: The Management of Water Resources in the Old Babylonian Period. Ph.D. diss., Hebrew Union College, Cincinnati.

Helbaek, H.

1969 Plant Collecting, Dry-Farming and Irrigation Agriculture in the Prehistoric Deh Luran. In *Prehistoric and Human Ecology of the Deh Luran Plain,* edited by F. Hole, K. V. Flannery, and J. A. Neely, pp. 383–426. Memoir 1, Museum of Anthropology, University of Michigan, Ann Arbor.

1972 Samarran Irrigation Agriculture at Choga Mami in Iraq. *Iraq* 34(1):35–48.

Helms, S. W.

1981 *Jawa: Lost City of the Black Desert.* Methuen, London

Herschel, C.

1899 *The Two Books on the Water Supply of the City of Rome of Sextus Julius Frontinus.* Dana Estes, Boston.

Hewitt, W. P., M. C. Winter, and D. Peterson

1987 Salt Production at Hierve el Agua, Oaxaca. *American Antiquity* 52:799–814.

Higham, C.

1989 *The Archaeology of Mainland Southeast Asia.* Cambridge University Press, Cambridge.

Hoddell, D. A., J. H. Curtis, and M. Brenner

1995 Possible Role of Climate in the Collapse of Classic Maya Civilization. *Nature* 375:391–94.

Horgan, J.

1995 From Complexity to Perplexity. *Scientific American* 272:74–79.

Houston, S. D.

1996 Symbolic Sweatbaths of the Maya: Architectural Meaning in the Cross Group at Palenque, Mexico. *Latin American Antiquity* 7:132–51.

Howard, J. B.

1993 A Paleohydraulic Approach to Examining Agricultural Intensification in Hohokam Irrigation Systems. In *Economic Aspects of Water Management in the Prehispanic New World (Research in Economic Anthropology, Supplement 7)*, edited by V. L. Scarborough and B. L. Isaac, pp. 263–314. JAI Press, Greenwich, CT.

Howard, J. B., and D. R. Wilcox

1988 The Place of Casa Buena and Locus 2 in the Evolution of Canal System 2. In *Excavations at Casa Buena: Changing Hohokam Land Use Along the Squaw Peak Parkway*, vol. 2, edited by J. Howard, pp. 903–39. Soil Systems Publications in Archaeology 11, Phoenix.

Hsu, Cho-Yun

1980 *Han Agriculture: The Formation of Early Chinese Agrarian Economy (206 BC.–AD 220)*. University of Washington Press, Seattle.

Hunt, E.

1972 Irrigation and the Socio-Political Organization of Cuicatec Cacicazgos. In *Chronology and Irrigation: The Prehistory of the Tehuacan Valley*, vol. 4, edited by F. Johnson, pp. 162–259. University of Texas Press, Austin.

Hunt, E., and R. C. Hunt

1974 Irrigation, Conflict and Politics: A Mexican Case. In *Irrigation's Impact on Society*, edited by T. E. Downing and M. Gibson, pp. 129–58. Anthropological Papers 25. University of Arizona, Tucson.

Hunt, R. C.

1988 Size and the Structure of Authority in Canal Irrigation Systems. *Journal of Anthropological Research* 44:335–55.

Hunt, R. C., and E. Hunt

1976 Canal Irrigation and Local Social Organization. *Current Anthropology* 17:389–411.

Ingold, T.

1993 The Temporality of the Landscape. *World Archaeology* 25:152–74.

Institute for Geology and Subsurface Research

1970 *Geological Maps of Greece.* The Institute for Geology and Subsurface Research, Athens.

Isaac, B. L.

1993 Asiatic Mode of Production, Hydraulic Hypothesis, and Oriental Despotism: Some Comments. In *Economic Aspects of Water Management in the Prehispanic New World (Research in Economic Anthropology, Supplement 7)*, edited by V. L. Scarborough and B. L. Isaac, pp. 429–71. JAI Press, Greenwich, CT.

1998 Why the Mende Became Tree-Croppers. *Research in Economic Anthropology* 19:267–88.

Isager, S., and J. E. Skydsgaard

1992 *Ancient Greek Agriculture.* Routledge, London.

Jacob, J. S.

1995 Archaeological Pedology in the Maya Lowlands. In *Pedological Perspectives in Archaeological Research*, edited by D. M. Kral, pp. 51–80. Soil Science Society of America Special Publication 44. Madison, WI.

Jacobsen, T., and R. McC. Adams

1958 Salt and Silt in Ancient Mesopotamian Agriculture. *Science* 128:1251–58.

Jansen, G. C. M.

1991 Voorzieningen van water, sanitair en afvalwaterafvoer in het Romeinse provinciestadje Herculaneum (Italië). *Overdruk uit H20, veirentwintigste jaargang*, no. 7:180–189.

Jansen, M.

1979 Architectural Problems of the Harappan Culture. In *South Asian Archaeology 1977*, edited by M. Taddei, pp. 405–32. Instituto Universitario Orientale, Naples.

1998   Water Supply and Sewage Disposal at Mohenjo-Daro. *World Archaeology* 21:177–92.

Johnson, B. L. C.
1979   *Pakistan.* Heinemann, London.

Kaplan, D.
1963   Men, Monuments and Political Systems. *Southwestern Journal of Anthropology* 19:397–410.

Keegan, W. F., and J. M. Diamond
1987   Colonization of Islands by Humans: A Biogeographical Perspective. In *Advances in Archaeological Method and Theory,* vol. 10, edited by M. B. Schiffer, pp. 49–92. Academic Press, New York.

Kelly, W. W.
1983   Concepts in the Anthropological Study of Irrigation. *American Anthropologist* 85:880–86.

Kennedy, D.
1995   Water Supply and Use in the Southern Hauran, Jordan. *Journal of Field Archaeology* 22:275–90.

Kennedy, K.
1982   Skulls, Aryans and Flow Drains: The Interface of Archaeology and Skeletal Biology in the Study of the Harappan Civilization. In *Harappan Civilization,* edited by G. Possehl, pp. 289–96. Aris and Phillips, Warminster, England.

Kenoyer, J. M.
1997   Early City-States in South Asia. In *The Archaeology of City-States,* edited by D. L. Nichols and T. H. Charlton, pp. 51–70. Smithsonian Institution Press, Washington, DC.

1998   *Ancient Cities of the Indus Valley Civilization.* Oxford University Press, New York.

Kenyon, K.
1981   *Excavations at Jericho, Vol. 3: The Architecture and Stratigraphy of the Tell,* edited by T. A. Holland, pp. 1–370. British School of Archaeology in Jerusalem, London.

Kessing, F. M.
1962   *The Ethnohistory of Northern Luzon.* Stanford University Press, Stanford.

Kienast, H. J.
1995   *Wasserleitung des Eupalinos auf Samos, Samos XIX.* Deutsches Archäologisches Institut, Bonn.

Kirby, A. V. T.
1973   *The Use of Land and Water Resources in the Past and Present Valley of Oaxaca, Mexico.* Museum of Anthropology Memoir 5. University of Michigan, Ann Arbor.

Kirch, P. V.
1994   *The Wet and the Dry: Irrigation and Agricultural Intensification in Polynesia.* University of Chicago Press, Chicago.

Kolata, A. L.
1991   The Technology and Organization of Agricultural Production in the Tiwanaku State. *Latin American Antiquity* 2:99–125.

Lambrick, H. T.
1964   *Sind: A General Introduction. History of Sind Series,* vol. 1. Sindhi Adabi Board, Hyderabad.

Lambrinoudakis, V. K.
1994   *Argolida: Archaeological Sites and Museums of the Argolid.* Editions Apollo, Athens.

Lansing, J. S.
1987   Balinese "Water Temples" and the Management of Irrigation. *American Anthropologist* 89:326–41.

1991   *Priests and Programmers: Technologies of Power in the Engineered Landscape of Bali.* Princeton University, Princeton.

Lansing, J. S., and J. N. Kremer

1993   Emergent Properties of Balinese Water Temples. *American Anthropologist* 95:97–114.

Lansing, J. S., J. N. Kremer, V. Gerhart, J. N. Kremer, P. Kremer, A. Arthawiguna, Sang Kaler Putu Surata, Suprapto, I. Bagus Suryawan, I. Gusti Arsana, J. Schoenfelder, V. L. Scarborough, and K. Mikita

2001   Volcanic Fertilization of Balinese Rice Paddies. *Ecological Economics* 38:383–90.

Leach, E. R.

1954   *Political Systems of Highland Burma.* Beacon Press, Boston.

1959   Hydraulic Society in Ceylon. *Past and Present* 15:2–26.

1961   *Pul Eliya: A Village in Ceylon.* Cambridge University Press, Cambridge.

Lees, S. H.

1973   *Sociopolitical Aspects of Canal Irrigation in the Valley of Oaxaca.* Memoir 6, Museum of Anthropology, University of Michigan, Ann Arbor.

1974   Hydraulic Development as a Process of Response. *Human Ecology* 2:159–75.

Liefrinck, F. A.

1969   Rice Cultivation in Northern Bali. In *Bali: Further Studies in Life, Thought and Ritual,* edited by J. L. Swellengrebel, pp. 3–73. M. Nijhoff, The Hague.

Linares, O. F.

1981   From Tidal Swamp to Inland Valley: On Social Organization of Wet Rice Cultivation among the Diola of Senegal. *Africa* 51:557–95.

Lumbreras, L. G.

1974   *The Peoples and Cultures of Ancient Peru.* Smithsonian Institution Press, Washington, DC.

Mabry, J. B., ed.

            Canal Communities: Small-Scale Irrigation Systems. University of Arizona Press, Tucson.

1998   *Archaeological Investigations of Early Village Sites in the Middle Santa Cruz Valley, Part II: Analysis and Synthesis.* Anthropological Papers 19. Center for Desert Archaeology, Tucson.

Marshall, S. J.

1960   *A Guide to Taxila.* 4th ed. Cambridge University Press, Cambridge.

Marx, K.

1959   Articles on India. In *Karl Marx and Friedrich Engels: Basic Writings of Politics and Philosophy,* edited by L. S. Feuer, pp. 474–81. Double Day/Anchor, Garden City, NY.

1967   *Capital, Vol. 1: A Critical Analysis of Capitalism.* International Publishers, New York.

Masse, B.

            Prehistoric Irrigation Systems in the Salt River Valley, Arizona. *Science* 214:408–15.

Matheny, R. T.

1976   Maya Lowland Hydraulic Systems. *Science* 193:639–46.

1978   Northern Maya Lowland Water Control Systems. In *Pre-Hispanic Maya Agriculture,* edited by P. D. Harrison and B. L. Turner II, pp. 185–210. University of New Mexico Press, Albuquerque.

Matheny, R. T., ed.

1980   *El Mirador, Petén, Guatemala: An Interim Report.* Papers of the New World Archaeological Foundation 45. Provo.

Matheny, R. T., D. L. Gurr, D. W. Forsyth, and F. R. Hauck

1983   *Investigations at Edzna, Campeche, Mexico, Vol. 1, Part 1: The Hydraulic System.* Papers of the New World Archaeological Foundation 46. Provo.

McAnany, P. A.

1990 Water Storage in the Puuc Region of the Northern Maya Lowlands: A Key to Population Estimates and Architectural Variability. In *Precolumbian Population History in the Maya Lowlands,* edited by T. P. Culbert and D. Rice, pp. 263–84. University of New Mexico Press, Albuquerque.

1995 *Living with the Ancestors.* University of Texas Press, Austin.

McIntosh, R. J., and S. K. McIntosh

1983 Current Direction in West African Prehistory. *Annual Review of Anthropology* 12:215–58.

Mercer, H. C.

1975 *The Hill-Caves of Yucatan.* University of Oklahoma Press, Norman.

Messenger, L. C., Jr.

1990 Ancient Winds of Change: Climatic Settings and Prehistoric Social Complexity in Mesoamerica. *Ancient Mesoamerica* 1:21–40.

Miller, A. G.

1973 *The Mural Painting of Teotihuacan.* Dumbarton Oaks, Washington, DC.

Miller, D.

1985 Ideology and the Harappan Civilization. *Journal of Anthropological Archaeology* 4:34–71.

Miller, S. G., ed.

1990 *Nemea: A Guide to the Site and Museum.* University of California Press, Los Angeles.

Millon, R.

1970 Teotihuacan: Completion of Map of Giant Ancient City in the Valley of Mexico. *Science* 170:1077–82.

1971 Variation in Social Responses to the Practice of Irrigation Agriculture. In *Civilization in Arid Lands,* edited by Richard Woodbury, pp. 56–88. University of Utah Anthropological Papers 62. Salt Lake City.

1973 The Teotihuacan Map. In *Urbanization at Teotihuacan, Mexico,* vol. 1, pt. 1, edited by R. Millon, pp. 1–154. University of Texas Press, Austin.

1992 Teotihuacan Studies: From 1950–1990 and Beyond. In *Art, Ideology and the City of Teotihuacan,* edited by J. C. Berlo, pp. 339–429. Dumbarton Oaks, Washington, DC.

Millon, R., C. Hall, and M. Díaz

1962 Conflict in the Modern Teotihuacan Irrigation System. *Comparative Studies in Society and History* 4:494–524.

Mindeleff, Victor

1891 *A Study of Pueblo Architecture: Tusayan and Cibola.* Smithsonian Institution, Bureau of American Ethnology Annual Report, vol. 8. Washington, DC.

Mitchell, W. P.

1973 The Hydraulic Hypothesis: A Reappraisal. *Current Anthropology* 14:532–34.

1976 Irrigation and Community in the Central Peruvian Highlands. *American Anthropologist* 78:25–44.

Monjarás-Ruiz, J.

1980 *La nobleza mexicana: Surgimiento y consolidación.* Editorial Edico, Mexico City.

Moore, J. D.

1988 Prehistoric Raised Field Agriculture in the Casma Valley, Peru. *Journal of Field Archaeology* 15:265–76.

Morris, I.

1997 An Archaeology of Equalities: The Greek City-States. In *The Archaeology of City-States,* edited by D. L. Nichols and T. H. Charlton, pp. 91–106. Smithsonian Institution Press, Washington, DC.

Morrison, K. D.

1993 Supplying the City: The Role of Reservoirs in an Indian Urban Landscape. *Asian Perspectives* 32:133–51.

Morrison, K. D., and M. T. Lycett

1994 Centralized Power, Centralized Authority? Ideological Claims and Archaeological Patterns. *Asian Perspectives* 32:327–50.

Moseley, M. E.

1974 Organizational Preadaptation to Irrigation: The Evolution of Early Water Management Systems in Coastal Peru. In *Irrigation's Impact on Society,* edited by T. E. Downing and M. Gibson, pp. 77–82. Anthropological Papers of the University of Arizona 25, Tucson.

1983 The Good Old Days Were Better: Agrarian Collapse and Tectonics. *American Anthropologist* 85:773–99.

Mughal, M. R.

1982 Recent Archaeological Research in the Cholistan Desert. In *Harappan Civilization,* edited by G. L. Possehl, pp. 85–95. Oxford and IBH and American Institute of Indian Studies, New Delhi.

1997 *Ancient Cholistan: Archaeology and Architecture.* Ferozons, Ltd., Rawalpindi.

Murphey, R.

1957 The Ruins of Ancient Ceylon. *Journal of Asian Studies* 16:181–200.

Mylonas, G. E.

1966 *Mycenae and the Mycenaean Age.* Princeton University Press, Princeton.

1994 *Mycenae: A Guide to Its Ruins and Its History.* Ekdotike Athenon, Athens.

Needham, J., and W. Ling

1965 *Science and Civilization in China, Vol. 4, Pt. 2: Mechanical Engineering.* Cambridge University Press, Cambridge.

Needham, J., Lu Gwei-Djen, and W. Ling

1971 *Science and Civilization in China, Vol. 4, Pt 3: Civil Engineering and Nautics.* Cambridge University Press, Cambridge.

Neely, J.

1995 Mogollon/Western Pueblo Soil and Water Control Systems of the Reserve Phase: New Data from West-Central New Mexico. In *Soils, Water, and Belief in Southwestern Prehistoric and Traditional Agriculture,* edited by H. W. Toll, pp. 239–62. New Mexico Archaeological Council, Special Publication 2. Albuquerque.

2001a A Contextual Study of the "Fossilized" Prehispanic Canal Systems of the Tehuacan Valley, Puebla, Mexico. *Antiquity* 75:505–06.

2001b Prehistoric Agricultural Fields and Water Management Technology of the Safford Valley, Southern Arizona. *Antiquity* 75:681–82.

Neely, J. A., S. C. Caran, and B. M. Winsborough

1990 Irrigated Agriculture at Hierve El Agua, Oaxaca, Mexico. In *Debating Oaxaca Archaeology,* edited by J. Marcus, pp. 115–90. Anthropological Papers 84. Museum of Anthropology, University of Michigan, Ann Arbor.

Neely, J. A., and H. T. Wright

1994 *Early Settlement and Irrigation on the Deh Luran Plain: Village and Early State Societies in Southwestern Iran.* Museum of Anthropology Technical Report 26. University of Michigan, Ann Arbor.

Netting, R. M

1974 The System Nobody Knows: Village Irrigation in the Swiss Alps. In *Irrigation's Impact on Society,* edited by T. E. Downing and M. Gibson, pp. 67–76. Anthropological Papers of the University of Arizona 25. Tucson.

1993 *The Smallholders, Householders: Farm Families and the Ecology of Intensive, Sustainable Agriculture.* Stanford University Press, Stanford.

Nicholas, L., and J. Neitzel

1984   Irrigation and Sociopolitical Organization in the Lower Salt River Valley: A Diachronic Analysis. In *Prehistoric Agricultural Strategies in the Southwest,* edited by S. K. Fish and P. R. Fish, pp. 161–78. Anthropological Research Paper 33. Arizona State University, Phoenix.

Nichols, D. L.

1982   A Middle Formative Irrigation System near Santa Clara Coatitlan in the Basin of Mexico. *American Antiquity* 47:133–44.

1987   Risk and Agricultural Intensification during the Formative Period in the Northern Basin of Mexico. *American Anthropologist* 89:596–616.

1988   Infrared Aerial Photography and Prehispanic Irrigation at Teotihuacan: The Tlajinga Canals. *Journal of Field Archaeology* 15:17–27.

Nichols, D. L., and C. D. Fredrick

1993   Irrigation Canals and Chinampas. In *Economic Aspects of Water Management in the Prehispanic New World (Research in Economic Anthropology, Supplement 7),* edited by V. L. Scarborough and B. L. Isaac, pp. 123–50. JAI Press, Greenwich, CT.

Nichols, D. L., M. W. Spence, and M. D. Borland

1991   Watering the Fields of Teotihuacan: Early Irrigation at the Ancient City. *Ancient Mesoamerica* 2:119–29.

Nichols, D. L., and T. H. Charlton, eds.

1997   *The Archaeology of City-States.* Smithsonian Institution Press, Washington, DC.

Nishioka, H.

1981   Sodai Sushu Ni Okeru Urato Kanri To Hakoda Kochiku [The Management of Creeks and Construction of Diked Fields in Suzhou in the Song Dynasty]. In *Chūgoku Suirishi Ronshū* [Collected Essays on the History of Water Control in China], edited by Chūgoku Suirishi Kenkyūkai, pp. 121–54. Kokusho Press, Tokyo.

Oates, D., and J. Oates

1976   *The Rise of Civilization.* Phaidon Press, Oxford.

Oates, J.

1972   Prehistoric Settlement Patterns in Mesopotamia. In *Man, Settlement and Urbanism,* edited by P. Ucko, R. Trigham, and G. W. Dimbleby, pp. 299–310. Duckworth, London.

1973   The Background and Development of Early Farming Communities in Mesopotamia and the Zagros. *Proceedings of the Prehistoric Society* 39:147–81.

O'Brien, M. J., R. D. Mason, D. E. Lenarch, and J. A. Neely

1982   *A Late Formative Irrigation Settlement below Monte Albán.* University of Texas Press, Austin.

Odum, E. P.

1971   *Fundamentals of Ecology.* 3rd ed. Saunders Company, Philadelphia.

O'Leary, B.

1989   *The Asiatic Mode of Production: Oriental Despotism, Historical Materialism and Indian History.* Basil Blackwell, Cambridge.

Oleson, J. P.

1988   Nabatean and Roman Water Use in Edom: The Humayma Hydraulic Survey, 1987. *Classical Views,* n.s., 7:117–29.

Ortloff, C. R.

1988   Canal Builders of Pre-Inca Peru. *Scientific American* 259(6):100–07.

1993   Chimu Hydraulic Technology and Statecraft on the North Coast of Peru, AD 1000–1470. In *Economic Aspects of Water Management in the Prehispanic New World (Research in Economic Anthropology, Supplement 7)*, edited by V. L. Scarborough and B. L. Isaac, pp. 327–68. JAI Press, Greenwich, CT.

Ortloff, C. R., R. A. Feldman, and M. E. Moseley
1985   Hydraulic Engineering and Historical Aspects of the Pre-Columbian Intravalley Canal Systems of the Moche Valley, Peru. *Journal of Field Archaeology* 12:77–98.

Ortloff, C. R., and A. Kolata
1989   Hydraulic Analysis of Tiawanaku Aqueduct Structures at Lukurmata and Pajchiri, Bolivia. *Journal of Archaeological Science* 16:513–35.

Ortloff, C. R., M. E. Moseley, and R. A. Feldman
1982   Hydraulic Engineering Aspects of the Chimu Chicama-Moche Intervalley Canal. *American Antiquity* 47:572–95.

Ozis, U.
1987   Historical Parallels in the Water Supply Development of Rome and Istanbul. In *Water for the Future*, edited by W. O. Wunderlich and J. E. Prins, pp. 35–44. A. A. Balkema, Boston.

Palerm, A.
1955   The Agricultural Basis of Urban Civilization in Mesoamerica. In *Irrigation Civilizations: A Comparative Study*, edited by J. H. Steward, pp. 28–42. Pan American Union, Washington, DC.

Palerm, A., and E. R. Wolf
1957   Ecological Potential and Cultural Development in Mesoamerica. *Pan American Union, Social Science Monograph* 3:1–38.

Panabokke, C. R.
1976   *Soils of Ceylon and Fertilizer Use.* Ceylon Association for the Advancement of Science, Colombo.

Park, T. K.
1992   Early Trends Toward Class Stratification: Chaos, Common Property and Flood Recession Agriculture. *American Anthropologist* 94:90–117.

Park, T. K., ed.
1993   *Risk and Tenure in Arid Lands: The Political Ecology of Development in the Senegal River Basin.* University of Arizona Press, Tucson.

Parpola, A.
1986   The Indus Script: A Challenging Puzzle. *World Archaeology* 17:399–419.

Parsons, J. J.
1969   Ridged Fields in the Rio Guayas Valley, Ecuador. *American Antiquity* 34:76–80.

Parsons, J. S., and W. A. Bowen
1966   Ancient Ridged Fields of the San Jorge River Floodplain, Colombia. *The Geographical Review* 56:317–43.

Parsons, J. J., and W. Denevan
1967   Pre-Columbian Ridged Fields. *Scientific American* 217:92–101.

Parsons, J. R.
1968   The Archaeological Significance of Mahamaes Cultivation on the Coast of Peru. *American Antiquity* 33:80–85.
1991   Political Implications of Prehispanic Chinampa Agriculture in the Valley of Mexico. In *Land and Politics in the Valley of Mexico*, edited by H. R. Harvey, pp. 17–41. University of New Mexico Press, Albuquerque.

Parsons, J. R., and N. P. Psuty
1975   Sunken Fields and Prehispanic Subsistence on the Peruvian Coast. *American Antiquity* 40:259–82.

Pasztory, E.

1988   A Reinterpretation of Teotihuacan and Its Mural Painting Tradition. In *Feathered Serpents and Flowering Trees: Reconstructing the Murals of Teotihuacan,* edited by K. Berrin, pp. 281–320. Fine Arts Museums of San Francisco, San Francisco.

Piggott, S.

1950   *Prehistoric India to 1000 BC.* Penguin Books, Baltimore.

Pohl, M. D., ed.

1990   *Ancient Maya Wetland Agriculture: Excavations on Albion Island, Northern Belize.* Westview Press, Boulder.

Pohl, M. D., K. D. Pope, J. G. Jones, J. S. Jacobs, D. R. Piperno, S. de Franco, D. L. Lentz, J. Gifford, M. Danforth, and J. K. Josserand.

1996   Early Agriculture in the Maya Lowlands. *Latin American Antiquity* 7:355–72.

Polanyi, K.

1957   The Economy as Instituted Process. In *Trade and Market in the Early Empires,* edited by K. Polanyi, C. M. Arensberg, and H. W. Pearson, pp. 243–69. Free Press, New York.

Pope, K. D., and B. H. Dahlin

1989   Ancient Maya Wetland Agriculture: New Insights from Ecological and Remote Sensing Research. *Journal of Field Archaeology* 16:87–106.

Possehl, G. L.

1967   The Mohenjo-daro Floods, A Reply. *American Anthropologist* 69:32–40.

1982   The Harappan Civilization: A Contemporary Perspective. In *Harappan Civilization,* edited by G. L. Possehl, pp. 15–28. Oxford and IBH Publishing Company, New Delhi.

1990   Revolution in the Urban Revolution: The Emergence of Indus Urbanization. *Annual Review in Anthropology* 19:261–82.

1997   The Transformation of the Indus Civilization. *Journal of World Prehistory* 11:425–71.

2000   The Drying up of the Sarasvati: Environmental Disruption in South Asian Prehistory. In *Environmental Disaster and the Archaeology of Human Response,* edited by G. Bawden and R. Reycraft, pp. 63–74. Maxwell Museum of Anthropology and the University of New Mexico Press, Albuquerque.

Possehl, G. L., and M. H. Raval

1989   *Harappan Civilization and Rojdi.* E. J. Brill, New York.

Potter, D. F.

1977   *Maya Architecture of the Central Yucatan Peninsula, Mexico.* Middle American Research Institute, Publication 44. Tulane University, New Orleans.

Pozorski, T., and S. Pozorski

1982   Reassessing the Chicama-Moche Intervalley Canal: Comments on "Hydraulic Aspects of the Chimu Chicama-Moche Intervalley Canal." *American Antiquity* 47:851–68.

Prasad, T., B. S. Kumar, and S. Kumar

1987   Water Resources Development in India—Its Central Role in the Past and Crucial Significance for the Future. In *Water for the Future,* edited by W. O. Wunderlich and J. E. Prins, pp. 19–34. A. A. Balkema, Boston.

Price, B. J.

1971   Prehispanic Irrigation Agriculture in Nuclear America. *Latin American Research Review* 6:3–60.

1982   Cultural Materialism: A Theoretical Review. *American Antiquity* 47:709–41.

Puleston, D. E.

1973   Ancient Maya Settlement and Environment at Tikal, Guatemala: Implications for Subsistence Models. Ph.D. diss., University of Pennsylvania, Philadelphia.

Puleston, D. E., and D. W. Callender Jr.
1967   Defensive Earthworks at Tikal. *Expedition* 9:40–48.

Puleston, D., and O. S. Puleston
1971   An Ecological Approach to the Origins of Maya Civilization. *Archaeology* 24:330–37.

Raab, L. M.
1975   A Prehistoric Water Reservoir from Santa Rosa Wash, Southern Arizona. *Kiva* 40:295–307.

Raikes, R. L.
1964   The End of the Ancient Cities of the Indus. *American Anthropologist* 66:284–99.

1965   The Mohenjo-daro Floods. *Antiquity* 39:196–203.

1984   *Water, Weather and Prehistory.* 2nd ed. Humanities Press, New York.

Rao, S. R.
1979   *Lothal: A Harappan Port Town (1955–62),* vol. 1. Archaeological Survey of India, Memoir 78. New Delhi.

Redman, C. L.
1978   *The Rise of Civilization.* W. H. Freeman, San Francisco.

Rehman, A.
1981   *Islamic Architecture of Pakistan: An Introduction.* Khyber Printers, Peshawar.

Renfrew, C.
1978   Trajectory Discontinuity and Morphogenesis: The Implications of Catastrophe Theory for Archaeology. *American Antiquity* 43:203–22.

1987   *Archaeology and Language: The Puzzle of Indo-European Origins.* Cambridge University Press, New York.

Reynolds, V., and R. Tanner
1995   *The Social Ecology of Religion.* Oxford University Press, New York.

Rice, D. S., and T. P. Culbert
1990   Historical Contexts for Population Reconstruction in the Maya Lowlands. In *Precolumbian Population History in the Maya Lowlands,* edited by T. P. Culbert and D. S. Rice, pp.1–36. University of New Mexico Press, Albuquerque.

Richards, P.
1983   Ecological Change and the Politics of African Land Use. *The African Studies Review* 26:1–72.

Rodriguez, S.
2002   Procession and Sacred Landscape in New Mexico. *New Mexico Historical Review* 77:1–26.

Rohn, A. H.
1963   Prehistoric Soil and Water Conservation on Chapin Mesa, Southwestern Colorado. *American Antiquity* 28:441–55.

Ronan, C. A., and J. Needham
1995   *The Shorter Science and Civilization in China,* vol. 5. Cambridge University Press, Cambridge.

Roosevelt, A.
1991   *Moundbuilders of the Amazon: Geophysical Archaeology on Marajo Island, Brazil.* Academic Press, San Diego.

Rothman, M. S., ed.
2001   *Uruk Mesopotamia and Its Neighbors.* School of American Research Press, Santa Fe.

Ruppert, K.
1952   *Chichén Itzá: Architectural Notes and Plans.* Carnegie Institution of Washington, Publication 595. Washington, DC.

Sahlins, M. D.
1972   *Stone Age Economics.* Aldine-Atherton, Chicago.

Sanders, W. T., J. R. Parsons, and R. S. Santley

1979   *The Basin of Mexico: Ecological Processes in the Evolution of a Civilization.* Academic Press, New York.

Sanders, W. T., and B. J. Price

1968   *Mesoamerica: The Evolution of a Civilization.* Random House, New York.

Sanders, W. T., and R. S. Santley

1977   A Prehispanic Irrigation System near Santa Clara Xalostoc in the Basin of Mexico. *American Antiquity* 42:582–87.

1983   A Tale of Three Cities: Energetics and Urbanism in Prehispanic Mexico. In *Prehistoric Settlement Patterns,* edited by E. V. Vogt and R. Leventhal, pp. 243–92. University of New Mexico Press, Albuquerque.

Sanders, W. T., and D. Webster

1988   The Mesoamerican Urban Tradition. *American Anthropologist* 90:521–46.

Santley, R. S.

1983   Obsidian Trade and Teotihuacan Influence in Mesoamerica. In *Highland-Lowland Interaction in Mesoamerica: Interdisciplinary Approaches,* edited by A. G. Miller, pp. 69–124. Dumbarton Oaks, Washington, DC.

1984   Obsidian Exchange, Economic Stratification and the Evolution of Complex Society in the Basin of Mexico. In *Trade and Exchange in Early Mesoamerica,* edited by K. G. Hirth, pp. 43–86. University of New Mexico Press, Albuquerque.

1986   Prehispanic Roadways, Transport Network Geometry, and Aztec Politics—Economic Organization in the Basin of Mexico. In *Economic Aspects of Prehispanic Highland Mexico (Research in Economic Anthropology, Supplement 2),* edited by B. L. Isaac, pp. 223–44. JAI Press, Greenwich, CT.

Sarcina, A.

1979   A Statistical Assessment of House Patterns at Mohenjo-daro. *Mesopotamia* 13–14:155–99.

Satterthwaite, L., Jr.

1936   An Unusual Type of Building in the Maya Old Empire. *Maya Research* 3(1):62–73.

Scarborough, V. L.

1983a   A Preclassic Water System. *American Antiquity* 48:720–44.

1983b   Raised Field Detection at Cerros, Northern Belize. In *Drained Field Agriculture in Central and South America,* edited by J. P. Darch, pp. 123–36. Proceedings of the 44th International Congress of Americanists, British Archaeological Research International Series 189. Oxford.

1988a   A Water Storage Adaptation in the American Southwest. *Journal of Anthropological Research* 44:21–40.

1988b   Pakistani Water: 4,500 Years of Manipulation. *Focus* 38(1):12–17.

1991a   Water Management Adaptations in Non-Industrial Complex Societies: An Archaeological Perspective. In *Archaeological Method and Theory,* vol. 3, edited by M. B. Schiffer, pp. 101–54. University of Arizona Press, Tucson.

1991b   *Archaeology at Cerros, Belize, Central America, Vol. 3: The Settlement System in a Late Preclassic Maya Community.* Southern Methodist University Press, Dallas.

1993a   Water Management in the Southern Maya Lowlands: An Accretive Model for the Engineered Landscape. In *Economic Aspects of Water Management in the Prehispanic New World (Research in Economic Anthropology, Supplement 7),* edited by V. L. Scarborough and B. L. Isaac, pp. 17–69. JAI Press, Greenwich, CT.

1993b   Introduction. In *Economic Aspects of Water Management in the Prehispanic New World (Research in Economic Anthropology, Supplement 7),* edited by V. L. Scarborough and B. L. Isaac, pp. 1–14. JAI Press, Greenwich, CT.

1994a   Maya Water Management. In *Research and Exploration* 10:184–99.

1994b   Water Management Studies at Midea and Adjacent Areas, Greece. Technical report submitted to G. Walberg and the Department of Classics, University of Cincinnati, Cincinnati.

1998   The Ecology and Ritual: Water Management and the Maya. *Latin American Antiquity* 9:135–59.

192 ≈≈≈   Flow of Power

2000   Resilience, Resource Use, and Socioeconomic Organization: A Mesoamerican Pathway. In *Natural Disaster and the*
            Archaeology of Human Response, edited by G. Bawden and R. Reycraft, pp. 195–212. Maxwell Museum of Anthropology
            and the University of New Mexico Press, Albuquerque.

Scarborough, V. L., M. E. Becher, J. L. Baker, G. Harris, and F. Valdez Jr.
1995   Water and Land at the Ancient Maya Community of La Milpa. *Latin American Antiquity* 6:98–119.

Scarborough, V. L., and G. G. Gallopin
1991   A Water Storage Adaptation in the Maya Lowlands. *Science* 251:658–62.

Scarborough, V. L., and R. Robertson
1986   Civic and Residential Settlement at a Late Preclassic Maya Center. *Journal of Field Archaeology* 13:155–75.

Scarborough, V. L., J. W. Schoenfelder, and J. S. Lansing
1999   Early Statecraft on Bali: The Water Temple Complex and the Decentralization of the Political Economy. *Research in*
            Economic Anthropology 20:299–330.

2000   Ancient Water Management and Landscape Transformations at Sebatu, Bali. *Bulletin of the Indo-Pacific Prehistory*
            Association 20:79–92. Canberra, Australia.

Scarborough, V. L., and F. Valdez Jr.
n.d.   The Engineered Environment and Political Economy of the Three Rivers Region. In *Heterarchy, Political Economy and*
            the Ancient Maya: The Three Rivers Region of the East-Central Yucatan Peninsula, edited by V. L. Scarborough, F. Valdez,
            and N. Dunning. University of Arizona Press, Tucson. In press.

Scarborough, V. L., and B. L. Isaac, eds.
1993   *Economic Aspects of Water Management in the Prehispanic New World (Research in Economic Anthropology, Supplement 7).*
            JAI Press, Greenwich, CT.

Scarborough, V. L., and D. R. Wilcox, eds.
1991   *The Mesoamerican Ballgame.* University of Arizona Press, Tucson.

Scarre, C., ed.
1999   *The Seventy Wonders of the Ancient World.* Thames and Hudson, London.

Schneider, H. K.
1974   *Economic Man.* Free Press, New York.

Schreiber, K., and J. Lancho Rojas
1995   The Puquios of Nasca. *Latin American Antiquity* 6:229–54.

Sears, W. H.
1982   *Fort Center: An Archaeological Site in the Lake Okeechobee Basin.* University of Florida Press, Gainesville.

Sebastian, L.
1992   *The Chaco Anasazi: Sociopolitical Evolution in the Prehistoric Southwest.* Cambridge University Press, Cambridge.

Shaffer, J. G.
1982   Harappan Culture: A Reconsideration. In *Harappan Civilization,* edited by G. Possehl, pp. 41–50. Oxford and IBH
            Publishing Company, New Delhi.

Sharrock, F. W., D. S. Dibble, and K. M. Anderson
1961   The Creeping Dune Irrigation Site in Glen Canyon, Utah. *American Antiquity* 27:188–202.

Shaw, B. D.
1984   Water and Society in the Ancient Maghrib: Technology, Prosperity and Development. *Antiquites Africaines* 20:121–73.

Sherbondy, J.
1982   The Canal Systems of Hanan Cuzco. Ph.D. diss., University of Illinois, Urbana.

Shinnie, P. L.
1967   *Meroe: A Civilization of the Sudan.* Praeger, New York.

Sidky, H.
1996   *Irrigation and State Formation: The Anthropology of a Hydraulic Kingdom.* University Press of America, New York.

Siemens, A. H.
1978   Karst and the Pre-Hispanic Maya in the Southern Lowlands. In *Pre-Hispanic Maya Agriculture,* edited by P. D. Harrison and B. L. Turner II, pp. 117–44. University of New Mexico Press, Albuquerque.

1982   Prehistoric Agricultural Use of the Wetlands of Northern Belize. In *Maya Subsistence: Studies in Memory of Dennis E. Puleston,* edited by K. V. Flannery, pp. 205–22. Academic Press, New York.

Siemens, A. H., R. J. Hebda, M. Navarrete Hernández, D. R. Piperno, J. K. Stein, and M. G. Zota Baez
1988   Evidence for a Cultivar and a Chronology from Patterned Wetlands in Central Veracruz, Mexico. *Science* 242:105–07.

Siemens, A. H., and D. E. Puleston
1972   Ridged Fields and Associated Features in Southern Campeche. *American Antiquity* 37:228–39.

Singer, C., E. J. Holmyard, and A. R. Hall, eds.
1954   *A History of Technology,* vol. 2. Clarendon Press, Oxford.

Small, D.
1997   City-State Dynamics through a Greek Lens. In *The Archaeology of the City-States,* edited by D. L. Nichols and T. H. Charlton, pp. 107–18. Smithsonian Institution, Washington, DC.

Smith, B. D.
1978   *Mississippian Settlement Patterns.* Academic Press, New York.

Smith, C. T., W. M. Denevan, and P. Hamilton
1968   Ancient Ridged Fields in the Region of Lake Titicaca. *Geographical Journal* 134:353–67.

Smith, R. T.
1979   The Development and Role of Sunken Field Agriculture on the Peruvian Coast. *Geographical Journal* 145:387–400.

Smith, T.
1995   Water Management in the Late Bronze Age Argolid, Greece. Ph.D. diss., Classics Department, University of Cincinnati, Cincinnati.

Solis, R. S., J. Haas, and W. Creamer
2001   Dating Caral, a Preceramic Site in the Supe Valley on the Central Coast of Peru. *Science* 292:723–26.

Southall, A.
1956   *Alur Society: A Study in Processes and Types of Domination.* Heffer, Cambridge.

1988   The Segmentary State in Africa and Asia. *Comparative Studies in Society and History* 30:52–82.

Spencer, C. S., E. M. Redmond, and M. Rinaldi
1994   Drained Fields at La Tigra, Venezuela Llanos: A Regional Perspective. *Latin American Antiquity* 5:119–43.

Spriggs, M. J. T.
1985   Prehistoric Man-Induced Landscape Enhancement in the Pacific: Examples and Implications. In *Prehistoric Intensive Agriculture in the Tropics,* edited by I. S. Farrington, pp. 409–34. BAR International Series 232, Pt. 2. Oxford.

Stargardt, J.
1983   *Satingpra I: The Environmental and Economic Archaeology of South Thailand.* Studies in Southeast Asian Archaeology I: ISEAS, British Archaeological Research International Series 158. Oxford.

Stark, B. L.

1999   Formal Architectural Complexes in South-Central Veracruz, Mexico: A Capital Zone? *Journal of Field Archaeology* 26:197–225.

Steensburg, A.

1976   Comments on Canal Irrigation and Local Social Organization, by R. C. Hunt and E. Hunt. *Current Anthropology* 17:403–04.

Stephens, J. L.

1843   *Incidents of Travel in Yucatan.* 2 vols. Harper and Brothers, New York.

Steward, J. H.

1933   Ethnography of the Owens Valley Paiute. *University of California Publications in American Archaeology and Ethnology* 33:233–350.

1955a   *Theory of Culture Change.* University of Illinois Press, Urbana.

1955b   Some Implications of the Symposium. In *Irrigation Civilization,* edited by J. H. Steward, pp. 58–78. Pan American Union, Washington, DC.

Steward, J. H., ed.

1955   *Irrigation Civilizations: A Comparative Study.* Pan American Union. Washington, DC.

Steward, J. H., and L. C. Faron

1959   *Native Peoples of South America.* McGraw-Hill, New York.

Stone, E.

1997   City-States and Their Centers: The Mesopotamian Example. In *The Archaeology of City-States,* edited by D. L. Nichols and T. H. Charlton, pp. 15–26. Smithsonian Institution Press, Washington, DC.

Stott, P.

1992   Angkor: Shifting the Hydraulic Paradigm. In *The Gift of Water: Water Management, Cosmology and the State in South East Asia,* edited by J. Rigg, pp. 47–58. School of Oriental and African Studies, London.

Taylor, G. C.

         Water, History and the Indus River. *Natural History* 74:40–49.

Thompson, J. E.

1959   The Role of Caves in Maya Culture. *Mitteilungen aus dem Museum fur Völkunde im Hamburg* 25:122–29.

Travitian, C., L. Tiniakos, G. Papageorgopoulos, and C. Spanos

1994   Drought Water Quality Relation of a Coastal Karstic Spring. In *Water Down Under 1994: Vol. 2, Part A,* pp. 229–32. Institution of Engineers, Australia. Adelaide.

Trigger, B. G.

1989   *A History of Archaeological Thought.* Cambridge University Press, New York.

1990   Monumental Architecture: A Thermodynamic Explanation of Symbolic Behavior. *World Archaeology* 22:119–32.

Tuggle, H. D.

1979   Hawaii. In *The Prehistory of Polynesia,* edited by J. D. Jennings, pp. 167–99. Harvard University Press, Cambridge.

Turner, B. L., II

1974   Prehistoric Intensive Agriculture in the Maya Lowlands. *Science* 185:118–24.

Turner, B. L., II, and P. D. Harrison

1981   Prehistoric Raised Field Agriculture in the Maya Lowlands. *Science* 213:399–405.

Valeri, V.

1991   Afterword. In *Priests and Programmers,* edited by J. Stephen Lansing, pp. 134–44. Princeton University Press, Princeton.

Vandermeer, J. H.

1971   Water Thievery in a Rice Irrigation System in Taiwan. *Annals of the Association of American Geographers* 61:156–79.

Vann, L.

1987   Tanks and Canals: Irrigation Systems in Ancient Sri Lanka. In *Water for the Future: Water Resources Developments in Perspective,* edited by W. O. Wunderlicht and J. E. Prins, pp. 163–76. A. A. Balkema, Boston.

Veblen, T.

1934   *The Theory of the Leisure Class.* Modern Library, New York.

Vivian, R. G.

1974   Conservation and Diversion: Water Control Systems in the Anasazi Southwest. In *Irrigation's Impact on Society,* edited by T. E. Downing and M. Gibson, pp. 95–112. Anthropological Papers of the University of Arizona 25. Tucson.

1990   *The Chacoan Prehistory of the San Juan Basin.* Academic Press, New York.

Vogt, E.

1968   Some Aspects of Zinacantan Settlement Patterns and Ceremonial Organization. In *Settlement Archaeology,* edited by K. C. Chang, pp. 154–73. National Press Books, Palo Alto.

1969   *Zinacantan: A Maya Community in the Highlands of Chiapas.* Belknap Press, Harvard University, Cambridge.

Wace, A.

1949   *Mycenae: An Archaeological History and Guide.* University Press, Princeton.

Watson, J. L.

1975   *Emigration and the Chinese Lineage: The Mans in Hong Kong and London.* University of California Press, Berkeley.

Weaver, M. P.

1981   *The Aztecs, Maya and Their Predecessors.* 2nd ed. Academic Press, New York.

Webster, D.

1976   *Defensive Earthworks at Becan, Campeche, Mexico: Implications for Maya Warfare.* Middle American Research Institute, Publication 41. Tulane University, New Orleans.

Weigand, P. C.

1993   Large-Scale Hydraulic Works in Prehistoric Western Mesoamerica. In *Economic Aspects of Water Management in the Prehispanic New World (Research in Economic Anthropology, Supplement 7),* edited by V. L. Scarborough and B. L. Isaac, pp. 223–62. JAI Press, Greenwich, CT.

Well, B., C. Runnels, and E. Zangger

1993   In the Shadow of Mycenae. *Archaeology* 46:54–58, 63.

West, M. L.

1979   Early Watertable Farming on the North Coast of Peru. *American Antiquity* 44:138–44.

Wheatley, P.

1965   Agricultural Terracing. *Pacific Viewpoint* 6:123–44.

Wheeler, M.

1968   *The Indus Civilization.* 3rd ed. Cambridge University Press, Cambridge.

White, G. F., D. J. Bradley, and A. U. White

1972   *Drawers of Water: Domestic Water Use in East Africa.* University of Chicago Press, Chicago.

Wilber, D. N.

1979   *Persian Gardens and Garden Pavilions.* 2nd ed. Dumbarton Oaks, Washington, DC.

Wilcox, D.

1979   The Hohokam Regional System. In *Archaeological Tests of Sites in the Gila Butte-Santan Region, South-Central Arizona,* edited by G. Rice, pp. 77–116. Anthropological Research Papers 18. Arizona State University, Tempe.

1991   The Mesoamerican Ballgame in the American Southwest. In *The Mesoamerican Ballgame,* edited by V. L. Scarborough and D. Wilcox, pp. 101–28. University of Arizona Press, Tucson.

Willey, G. R.

1953   *Prehistoric Settlement Patterns in the Viru Valley, Peru.* Bureau of American Anthropology Bulletin 155. Smithsonian Institution, Washington, DC.

Willey, G. R., ed.

1974   *Archaeological Researches in Retrospect.* Winthrop, Cambridge.

Williams, L. S.

1990   Agricultural Terrace Evolution in Latin America. *Yearbook of Conference of Latin Americanist Geographers* 16:82–93.

Wilson, D.

1985   *Moated Sites.* Shire Publication, Aylesbury, England.

Wittfogel, K. A.

1957   Oriental Despotism: A Comparative Study of Total Power. Yale University Press, New Haven.

Wolf, E.

1957   Closed Corporate Peasant Communities in Mesoamerica and Central Java. *Southwestern Journal of Anthropology* 13:1–18.

1966   *Peasants.* Prentice Hall, Englewood Cliffs, NJ.

1982   *Europe and the People without History.* University of California Press, Berkeley.

Wolf, E. R., and A. Palerm

1955   Irrigation in the Old Acolhua Domain, Mexico. *Southwestern Journal of Anthropology* 11:265–81.

Woodbury, R. B.

1961   A Reappraisal of Hohokam Irrigation. *American Anthropologist* 63:550–60.

Woodbury R. B., and J. A. Neely

1972   Water Control Systems of the Tehuacan Valley. In *Chronology and Irrigation: The Prehistory of the Tehuacan Valley,* vol. 4, edited by F. Johnson, pp. 81–153. University of Texas Press, Austin.

Worster, D.

1985   *Rivers of Empire: Water, Aridity and the Growth of the American West.* Pantheon Books, New York.

1990   The Ecology of Order and Chaos. *Environmental History Review* 14:1–18.

Yangzi Regional Planning Commission

1979   *A Brief History of Water Control in the Yangzi.* Irrigation and Hydroelectricity Press, Beijing.

Yoffee, N., and G. Cowgill, eds.

1998   *The Collapse of Ancient States and Civilizations.* University of Arizona Press, Tuscon.

Zangger, E.

1991   Prehistoric Coastal Environment in Greece: The Vanished Landscapes of Dimini Bay and Lake Lerna. *Journal of Field Archaeology* 18:1–15.

1994   Landscape Changes around Tiryns during the Bronze Age. *American Journal of Archaeology* 98:189–212.

INDEX